LUIGI PIRANDELLO

Three Plays

The Rules of the Game
Six Characters in Search of an Author
Henry IV

Translated by
Robert Rietty
and Noel Cregeen,
John Linstrum,
Julian Mitchell

With an introduction by
John Linstrum

METHUEN DRAMA

Methuen's World Dramatists Series

This collection first published in Great Britain in 1985 in paperback by
Methuen London Ltd

Reprinted 1988 by Methuen Drama, Michelin House, 81 Fulham Road,
London SW3 6RB

The Rules of the Game first published in this translation by Penguin
Books in 1959.
Thoroughly revised for this edition, 1985.
Copyright © 1959, 1985 by Familiari Pirandello, Roma.
Originally published in Italian as *Il gioco delle parti*.

Six Characters in Search of an Author first published in this translation by
Eyre Methuen in 1979. Revised and reprinted by Methuen London in 1982.
Copyright © 1979 by Familiari Pirandello, Roma.
Originally published in Italian in 1921 as *Sei personaggi in cerca d'autore*.

Henry IV first published in this translation by Eyre Methuen in 1979.
Copyright © 1979 by Familiari Pirandello, Roma.
Originally published in Italian in 1922 as *Enrico IV*.

Introduction copyright © 1985 John Linstrum

Set IBM Journal by   Tek-Art, Croydon, Surrey
Printed and bound in Great Britain
by Cox & Wyman Ltd, Reading, Berks

Pirandello, Luigi
    Three plays. — (The Master playwrights)
    I. Title   II. Pirandello, Luigi. [Il gioco
    delle parti. *English*] . The rules of the game
    III. Pirandello, Luigi. [Sei personaggi in
    cerca d'autore. *English*] . Six characters in
    search of an author IV.   Pirandello, Luigi
    [Enrico IV. *English*] Henry IV.   V. Series
    852'.912   PQ4835.17

    ISBN 0—413—57560—8

Contents

Editor's Note

I would like to thank Jennifer Lorch of the University of Warwick and Antonio Alessio of McMaster University, Canada, for permission to use their published work. I have also made use of quotations from the following sources: Susan Basnett-Maguire, *Pirandello*, Methuen, 1981; G. Giudice's biography, *Pirandello*, translated by Alistair Hamilton, Oxford University Press, 1975; Walter Starkie, *Pirandello*, University of California Press, 1963; and Domenica Vittorini, *The Drama of Luigi Pirandello*, Russell and Russell (New York), 1935, 1962. The sources are indicated in the Introduction by use of the author's name.

Readers might like to know that there is a British Pirandello Society which publishes a Yearbook of new articles and information about Pirandello. The Society has an annual one-day conference and details can be obtained from Susan Basnett at the Graduate School of Comparative Literature, University of Warwick.

LUIGI PIRANDELLO

Three Plays

The Rules of the Game, Six Characters in Search of an Author, Henry IV

Pirandello is ranked with Brecht and Beckett as one of the foremost innovators in the theatre of this century. The three plays in this volume, his masterpieces, are products of the burst of dramatic creative activity which followed his reluctant decision in 1918 to commit his wife to an asylum for the insane. This personal tragedy provided him with many of his themes, which are well represented in these plays. There is the absurdity of human life and its social conventions in *The Rules of the Game* (1918); in *Henry IV* (1922), the uncertain boundary between sanity and insanity, with its story of a modern man apparently stuck forever in the role of a medieval Holy Roman Emperor; and in *Six Characters* (1921), his best-known play, there is a fascinating variation on the theme of Life versus Art.

Preceded by an introduction to Pirandello's life and work by John Linstrum, all three plays appear in recent, eminently stageable translations. Commissioned by the National Theatre, the translation of *Henry IV* is by playwright Julian Mitchell, author of *Another Country*. John Linstrum's translation of *Six Characters* was successfully premiered at the Greenwich Theatre in 1979. And Robert Rietty's translation of *The Rules of the Game*, though first staged in the fifties, has been revised for successive productions, most recently with Leonard Rossiter at the Theatre Royal, Haymarket in 1982.

Luigi Pirandello was born in Sicily in 1867 and died in Rome in 1936, where he had first settled as a professional writer in 1893. The following year he married a woman whose mental health collapsed in 1904 leading finally to her commitment to an asylum in 1919. He was already well-known as a novelist and critic before achieving international recognition as a playwright with Right You Are! (If You Think So) *in 1917,* The Rules of the Game *(1918),* Six Characters in Search of an Author *(1921),* Henry IV *(1922),* The Man with the Flower in His Mouth *(1923),* As You Desire Me *(1930) and* Each in His Own Way *(1924) and* Tonight We Improvise *(1929), the last two forming a trilogy with* Six Characters. *Of his 43 plays, over half are adaptations from his own short stories written during the most difficult period of his life (1900–1918). He established and directed his own theatre in Rome, the Teatro D'Arte (1925–1928), and in 1934 he was awarded the Nobel Prize for Literature.*

The front cover shows Conversation among the Ruins *by Giorgio de Chirico, 1927 (courtesy of the National Gallery of Art, Washington; Chester Dale Collection 1962). The photograph of Pirandello on the back cover is courtesy of Popperfoto.*

Introduction

The progress of arts and sciences is punctuated by important publications, discoveries and performances after which nothing can ever be the same. In 1921 the first production of *Six Characters in Search of an Author* caused a riot in Rome at the Teatro Valle, with Pirandello and his daughter forced to run the gauntlet of a crowd shouting wild abuse at the stage door after the performance. In 1923 Pitoëff's production in Paris caused another sensation, although milder and confined at first to the smaller circle of theatrical and literary enthusiasts: however, the tone was generally approving and appreciative. From that moment on, Pirandello's reputation and success grew steadily.

I am the Son of Chaos

Pirandello was born in Sicily in 1867 in a district called Cavusu (Chaos) close to Girgenti, now known as Agrigento. The house was on the coast looking towards North Africa and has become the Centre for Pirandello Studies: the rooms on the first floor are set out as a small museum of publications and photographs, documents and paintings, memorabilia of public and private life. The house, gardens and the path down to the pine tree on the cliff are well-cared for and quite unlike the earliest photographs which show the building as rather exposed and neglected. Behind the house on the slopes of the hill three or four miles away rise the buildings of modern Agrigento lifting themselves cleanly out of the lower and older parts of the city. It was not so a hundred years ago when it was described as a 'mass of huts and hovels' whose streets 'were infected by evil smells'. Garibaldi's revolution had been only seven years before, when Stefano Pirandello, Luigi's father, had fought in the streets of Palermo. Stefano was big and arrogant and in 1867, the year of Luigi's birth, he fought again, this time in the streets of Girgenti, against a Mafioso who was trying to extort protection money. Stefano was wounded badly but survived: his opponent was, rather surprisingly, gaoled for seven years. Stefano Pirandello was the manager and owner of one of the sulphur mines at Porto Empedocle, and Luigi Pirandello, who worked there for a short time, witnessed in his youth lives and conditions of such industrial slavery as Zola wrote about in *Germinal*.

This was his Sicilian background and inheritance: an island of astonishing natural beauty and human degradation, inhabited by people of passion with a highly developed sense of formality. The social mores were extreme in their rigidity: hypocrisy, repression and exploitation all went hand in hand with a powerful church regime, a strict morality and a feudal society.

Pirandello was fortunate to escape from this atmosphere, to go to the Universities of Palermo, Rome and Bonn where he was admitted to the degree of Doctor of Philosophy in 1891. His doctoral thesis was on *The Phonetic Development of the Agrigento Dialect*, and almost immediately after completing his studies in Bonn he moved to Rome intent on pursuing a career as a writer.

In 1894 he married Maria Antonietta Portulano, who was also from Agrigento; this was arranged by the two families and seems to have been successful until 1903 when his father was suddenly made bankrupt. The sulphur mines had been flooded and Stefano had made some unwise speculations: Antonietta's dowry was invested in the same mines so that the young Pirandello family, living in Rome, were without the regular allowance from Stefano or the income from the dowry investment. By now they had three children and Pirandello had already been teaching for some time: he had to find a way of producing even more for his family, so he began teaching private pupils as well as fulfilling his full-time lectureship. Unhappily, the family financial disaster unbalanced Antonietta and she became unreasonably jealous of both Pirandello's work and his pupils at the Istituto Superiore di Magisterio Femminile. From this time on the marriage became a tormented relationship. The figure of the suffering and jealous wife often occurs in his work: sometimes she appears as nothing more than a destructive oppression, driving the husband to anger as in *The Man with the Flower in His Mouth*.

'She watches me from a distance. And believe me, I'd like to go over there and kick her but it wouldn't be any use. She's like one of those stray dogs, obstinate. The more you kick them the closer they stick to you. And you can't imagine what that woman is suffering on my account . . . she makes me so angry you wouldn't believe it. Sometimes I jump out at her from behind to frighten her off . . . Sometimes, you know, a savage desire to strangle her comes into my fingers. But nothing ever happens.'

At other times it is invested with a great sympathy, yet a sympathy tinged with exasperation. Soon after his wife was removed to a mental home in 1919 he wrote in *Six Characters*:

'I couldn't bear the sight of this woman near me. Not so much because of the annoyance she caused me, you see, or even the feeling of being stifled, being suffocated that I got from her, as for the sorrow, the painful sorrow that I felt for her . . . After she'd gone away my house seemed empty. She'd been like a weight on my spirit but she filled the house with her presence. Alone in the house I wandered around like a lost soul.'

Antonietta's derangement had shown itself in spasms, and this continuous uncertainty about her state of mind must have caused far more tension in the family than if she had been constantly needing care. She was convinced that her husband was unfaithful, and she created her own image that was far from the reality. Pirandello was condemned to live with the constant picture of this other man presented to himself, yet he and his family remained close and devoted. The years between 1914 and 1918 were terrible for them all: Pirandello was oppressed by his wife's illness, one son was a prisoner of war in Austria, the other was ill in the Italian army and his daughter, Lietta, was the constant object of his wife's vicious accusations. Pirandello himself was having to teach to earn money and had little enough time to write or do more than survive the pressures of family and financial worries.

Immediately after *Six Characters* was performed in 1921 he began writing his next play, *Henry IV*. The keynote of the play is the counterpointing of sanity and madness and how the appearance of mental disturbance alters people's behaviour and perception. During the same period of personal distress,

1918–1919 he wrote *The Rules of the Game*, in which we find Leone Gala and his wife Silia separated: their only contact is a formal visiting procedure, reminiscent of the courting ritual of Pirandello's own early meetings with Antonietta.

Eventually in 1919 Antonietta was committed to the mental home in which she remained until her death in 1959. At first Pirandello seemed to live in the hope that she would return to him at some time, restored and happy, but finally in 1924 he seems to have given up this hope. The date coincides with a new phase in his life, one of travel and living with few possessions, mostly in hotels and temporary apartments.

Pirandello and the Actors

It was not until he was in his middle forties that Pirandello began seriously writing for the theatre. There had been a frustrating period during the 1880s when he wrote several plays which are now known only by their titles, but from 1916 until his death in 1936 he wrote around forty plays. He had made a dramatic adaptation of two of his short stories in 1911, but in 1917 he began a remarkable surge of creative energy with six plays before *The Rules of the Game* in 1919, five more before *Six Characters in Search of an Author* in 1921 and with *Henry IV* following immediately after that. Between 1922 and his death in 1936 he wrote another twenty-six plays, although none enjoyed the international success of *Six Characters* and *Henry IV*.

Once this outburst of drama had begun, he rarely returned to the novel or the short story and seemed to neglect verse altogether. It is not surprising that the drama absorbed all his energies, because in 1924 he helped to form and then soon began to direct a theatrical company called The Arts Theatre of Rome; with this company he toured all over Europe and America, directing and writing all the time. He recruited actors who seemed to him to be especially sympathetic to his work and methods; they formed a close-knit group. The Arts Theatre existed from 1924 until 1928. It toured Italy, of course, and performed in London, Paris, Basle, Hamburg, Frankfurt, Berlin, Prague, Vienna, Budapest as well as in Argentina and Brazil, but by 1928 the company was heavily in debt, despite Government subsidies, and was dissolved.

Pirandello was attempting to blend the compelling improvisational skill of the best Italian performers with the thoroughness of the new Russian approach that Stanislavsky had evolved for the Moscow Art Theatre and which was being followed by other European directors. Their programme included plays other than those by Pirandello, but like other great theatrical figures, Stanislavsky and Brecht, for instance, his intent was to urge his performers to the limits of their art, to demand of them a commitment and dedication that would make them exceptional interpreters of the plays they were presenting.

> 'When I direct, the actors must study their parts and learn them
> by heart. They must study carefully, at home, on their own, in
> silence and meditation. And when they come on stage, they
> must not be actors any longer, they must be the characters in
> the play they are acting. That way they will have a reality in
> their own right that is absolute not relative: it won't be the
> false truth of the stage but the positive undeniable truth of
> life.' (Niccodemi quoted in Basnett-Maguire)

The Italian theatre that Pirandello's audience was accustomed to was not commonly so dedicated and professional in its approach, not so concerned with truth as this. It was a theatre where rehearsals were casual and the ultimate success of a performance would depend on individual brilliance and not on a general high standard. Performers like Duse and Salvini were clearly outstanding but their own special talents were idiosyncratic and not suitable within Pirandello's company. Although Duse was apparently very interested in *The Life I Gave You* and it was agreed that she should perform in it, she never did.

He recruited one very promising performer from Milan, Marta Abba, and she became his leading actress and his close companion. In his own strange way Pirandello seems to have been in love with her, almost to the end of his life. Ruggero Ruggeri, who performed *Henry IV* at its first performances and who was close to Pirandello for many years as a fellow artist and as a friend, refers to Pirandello's own illuminative powers as a performer. He said that if he were ever uncertain what sort of expression to use during a rehearsal he only had to look at

Pirandello and copy his face. Dario Niccodemi tells us that when Pirandello was reading a script to the company:

> 'It was irresistible! Without ever looking up from the script, his hands gripping the table . . . his eyes glistening with a truly superhuman intoxication his burning brow furrowed as if by lightning, pouring with sweat, dealing violent punches on the page as if to emphasise certain words to make them sink into the minds of the others. He seemed to be alone with the passion of his characters, with their will dominating his own.'
> (Basnett-Maguire)

Such violence, such Sicilian passion are constant elements in a dramatist whose work has often been characterised as cerebral: but it is this intensity, this passion, this burning energy that has always made Pirandello an exciting challenge to actors and directors, not only to those of his own time, like Ruggeri, but to actors ever since. The things that concern Pirandello are also the essential materials of the actor's craft: role-play, the fragmentation of character, the uncertainty about the frontiers of truth and make-believe and where Life and Art separate. Actors and directors appreciate him as a writer dealing with the ideas they know about from their own experience in the exercise of their skills, and their own imaginative patterns are in sympathy with those of Pirandello — that is, if they are performers who enjoy the stimulating intellectual challenge that Pirandello holds out to them. He needs actors capable of the intensity and energy that he demonstrated himself and directors who can lead us with a similar energy and delight as the arguments and the drama twist and turn.

Puppets

The dramatic background of *commedia dell'arte* combined with Sicilian puppets could hardly have been a better foundation for Pirandello's creation of dramatic paradoxes. The puppet's face is unchanging no matter what the story demands: there is a feeling of the contrary in the visual presentation. The *commedia dell'arte* often demanded mercurial changes of attitude, apparent contradictions: the traditional scenarii contain tears and laughter together. They also contain masked and unmasked faces.

If we refer to specific points in the three plays in this volume we shall find in *Six Characters* a description of The Characters' first appearance.

> *The* CHARACTERS *should not appear as ghosts, but as created realities, timeless creations of the imagination, and so more real and consistent than the changeable realities of the* ACTORS. *The masks are designed to give the impression of figures constructed by art, each one fixed forever in its own fundamental emotion; that is, Remorse for the* FATHER, *Revenge for the* STEPDAUGHTER, *Scorn for the* SON, *Sorrow for the* MOTHER. *Her mask should have wax tears in the corners of the eyes and down the cheeks like the sculptured or painted weeping Madonnas in a church. Her dress should be of a plain material, in stiff folds, looking almost as if it were carved and not of an ordinary material you can buy in a shop and have made up by a dressmaker.*

And at the end of the play:

> *Slowly the* SON *comes on from the right, followed by the* MOTHER *with her arms raised towards him. Then from the left, the* FATHER *enters. They come together in the middle of the stage and stand there as if transfixed.*

In *Henry IV* the physical presentation of Henry recalls the Sicilian puppets. On his first entrance the stage directions read:

> *He is close to fifty, extremely pale, and already grey at the back of his head, though at the temples and forehead he seems fair, the result of an almost childishly obvious use of dye. He wears equally very obvious doll-like make-up on his cheekbones, over his tragic pallor . . . His eyes are fixed in a frightening agonised stare.*

On stage there are two life-size portraits, and in Act III Frida and Di Nolli are dressed as the figures in the portraits and stand there in the place of the painting:

> *In the gloom the rear wall can only just be made out. The canvasses with the two portraits have been removed, and in their place, within the frames which remain surrounding the hollows of the niches, placed in the exact poses of the portraits, are* FRIDA, *dressed as the 'Marchioness of Tuscany', as in Act Two and* CARLO DI NOLLI *as 'Henry IV'.*

And a few lines later:

> *She sticks her head out of the niche a little and looks towards the other niche, though still trying to keep up the role she's been allotted.*

In *The Rules of the Game* we do not find puppets or masks, although Leone's face is one of the best masks of all, betraying nothing of his feelings: but there is a twist of the plot worthy of a *commedia* device with its sudden contradiction, a twist that is both an intellectual somersault and a *commedia lazzo*. Leone Gala is wakened early to fight a duel in defence of his wife's honour. Guido Venanzi is his wife's lover and also his second in the duel.

GUIDO. You have to fight.

LEONE. I have to fight, too, have I?

BARELLI. 'Too'? What do you mean?

LEONE. Oh, no, my friends. You're mistaken!

GUIDO. Do you want to withdraw?

BARELLI. Don't you want to fight, now?

LEONE. I? Withdraw? But you know perfectly well that I always firmly maintain my position . . . You and my wife upset my whole day yesterday, Venanzi, trying to make me do what I admitted all the time was my duty.

GUIDO. But . . . but . . .

BARELLI. You're going to fight!

LEONE. That's not my duty.

BARELLI. Whose is it then?

LEONE (*pointing to* GUIDO). His.

BARELLI. Guido's?

LEONE. Yes, his.

By a clever side-stepping movement, Leone has left Guido responsible as his second, for upholding the honour of Silia, the wife of Leone and subject of the duel. It was Guido and Silia who planned the duel so that Leone would be removed from their path: now it is Guido who falls into his own trap, a truly *commedia dell'arte* device of substitution.

Pirandello's Fellow Writers

The end of the nineteenth century and the beginning of the

twentieth was the time for Pirandello's ideas to crystallize and we must look for the background to this in the shaking of traditional fundamental religious beliefs begun by Darwin, the attempts to describe the springs of human mental activity by Freud, the Nietzschean description of man's role, the imaginative realism of Ibsen, the tortured creatures of Strindberg, the realism of Zola, the poetic countercharge of the *fin de siècle* to realism. Pirandello's academic background in the eighties and his café society literary circles of the nineties in Rome made him very familiar with the intellectual and artistic development of Europe. One must add to that, however, the peculiar strength of his Sicilian background. Giovanni Verga and Luigi Capuana, both Sicilians, had renamed the European realism movement and now called it *verism* or *verismo*, and in this linguistic distinction lay an awareness of the separation they identified not only between Sicily and Europe but between Sicily and Italy. The dialect that Pirandello studied for his doctorate was of prime importance for Sicilians, and Nino Martaglio had even set up a repertory company in 1903 to perform plays in Sicilian. Several of Pirandello's own plays were first written in Sicilian and not standard Italian.

But despite his Sicilian roots Pirandello lived mostly in Rome and there the poetic counter-revolution to Realism or Verism was best seen in Gabriele D'Annunzio, the romantic leader whose verse plays were successful with the opera-loving Italian audience and at the same time anathema to Pirandello and his literary friends. D'Annunzio, with his extravagant romanticism, seemed to Pirandello to be 'extraordinarily ridiculous'.

More to Pirandello's taste was Rosso di san Secondo, another Sicilian, whose play, *Marionettes, What Passion!* was written in 1918 just before *The Rules of the Game*. However, the most notable play of this period before Pirandello's success was Luigi Chiarelli's *The Mask and the Face*, written in 1913 but not performed until 1916. This is the best expression of a group of writers writing for what is known as the *teatro del grottesco* and is a clear prelude to Pirandello's mature work. It has the paradoxes, the theatrical antitheses that Pirandello himself used so skilfully: for instance, at one moment in *The Mask and the*

Face a character quietly and secretly watches from a window as her own funeral procession goes past.

A title like *teatro del grottesco* can rarely be more than a convenient label: it can even be misleading. But the tone is accurately expressed in the word 'grotesque'. Pirandello's own wry, ironic sense of the 'contrariness' of things and events is the *grotteschi* dramatists' view stretched to a greater length: it includes the notion of comedy and tragedy co-existing, vision and reality melting into each other, the reflection in the mirror being confused with the original thing itself, the mask and the face sometimes being indistinguishable.

The theatre in Italy between 1900 and 1914 is well described by Chiarelli:

'Italian theatre slumbered. It was impossible to go to the theatre without meeting languid loquacious grand-daughters of Marguerite Gautier or some tardy follower of Oswald or Cyrano. The public dropped sentimental tears and left the playhouse weighed down in spirit,' (Giudice)

The vigour of Chiarelli's own work, of Rosso di San Secondo's, of Pirandello's in 1917, 1918 and 1919 — *Liola, Cap and Bells, Right You Are (If You Think So)* and *The Rules of the Game* in particular — was an antidote to the fag-end of romanticism and the pale imitation of French drama. But it was not until the 1921 performance in Rome of *Six Characters* caused an uproar that Pirandello began to assume his true role as a dramatic force in Europe. Even then it needed the Pitoëff production in Paris in 1923 and the tours of the Arts Theatre between 1924 and 1928 to consolidate not merely a success but a dramatic revolution. No single writer can be seen as the sole begetter of a revolution: Pirandello was not alone. He was preceded and accompanied by others, many of whom have already been mentioned here. But it is in *his* work that the most remarkable dramatic changes are seen: it is in *his* plays that idea and dramatic action make the most perfect liaison.

The Feeling of the Opposite
There is a paragraph in the essay on 'Humour' that Pirandello wrote in 1908 that is frequently quoted because it describes

succinctly what would otherwise take far longer.

> 'I see an old woman with her hair dyed and greasy with oil: she is made up garishly and is dressed like a young girl. I begin to laugh. I perceive that she is the exact opposite of what a respectable old lady should be . . . The sense of the comic consists of this *perception of the opposite*. But if, at this point, I reflect and consider that she may not enjoy dressing up like an exotic parrot, that she is distressed by it and does it only because she deceives herself, pitifully, into believing that she can retain the love of her younger husband by making herself up like this . . . then I can no longer laugh at her . . . from the initial *perception of the opposite*, *reflection* has led me to a *feeling of the opposite*. This is the difference between the comic and humour.'

And again:

> 'We are dealing with a comic representation, but from it we derive a feeling which either prevents us from laughing or disturbs our laughter making it bitter . . .
> The humorist will dismantle the character with its different conflicting elements and enjoy revealing the incongruities.'

This is the heart of the Pirandellian world — the awareness of different levels of thought and feeling in what might superficially seem obvious. An awareness of these is not only Pirandello's of course: it is in Ibsen in *Peer Gynt*, in Chekhov, in Synge's *Playboy of the Western World*, in O'Casey's *Juno and the Paycock*, in Wycherley's *The Country Wife*. It is the constant basis of a great deal of drama. What one must investigate is how it contributes to Pirandello's experience of the theatre and what use Pirandello makes of it.

Intellect into Passion

> 'People say that my drama is obscure and they call it cerebral drama. The new drama possesses a character distinct from the old: whereas the latter had as its basis passion, the former is the expression of intellect. One of the novelties that I have given to modern drama consists in converting the intellect into passion.' (Pirandello in 1924 quoted by Starkie)

Pirandello dramatised ideas: one might even say, as the critic

Robert Brustein did, that in *Six Characters* Pirandello dramatised 'the very act of creation'. He uses a whole play, *Henry IV*, to express the nature of the contradiction between appearance and reality, as well as exploring madness and personality. In *Six Characters* the emphases are different and the exploration is of personality and its complexity as well as of appearance and reality. The obsessions of Pirandello are easily identifiable: the human personality, appearance and reality, the mirror as a means of self-revelation, truth and what we think is the truth, Life and Art, Life and Form. The development of ideas about these themes could indeed seem cerebral: the arguments are often tortuous, the expression sometimes equally tortuous: it would be possible to transpose the arguments into an exclusively intellectual discussion if it were not for the affective note, the passion that is always there. There is an energy, an urgency that creates dramatic tension, forcing us to attend. The style of language, often fragmented, demands that we listen.

The plays are restless, they disturb, they erupt into violence. If there is not an obvious restlessness and potential violence, as there constantly is in the characters of King Henry and The Stepdaughter, then there is a simmering and seething, as in Leone Gala, in the eyes behind the mask that is offered to the world. The true stamp of Pirandello is a wry bitterness and a cry of exasperation, pessimism and emotional violence: at the core of his work there is a constant agonised searching for the truth in both character and motive, and an agony of self-doubt as the characters strip away illusions.

The Rules of the Game
'Suppose the egg turns out to be a bullet'

The Rules of the Game is a good title — it has a rhythm, balance and simplicity that make it admirable. It also demonstrates one of the problems in translation, because it is not what 'Il gioco delle parti' means. The exact translation should be 'The game of roles': yet simple as this is, it is difficult to translate. Other titles have been used — 'The game as he played it', 'Each in his own role' — but these are both clumsy. However, we should remember that Leone Gala, the central character in the play, often refers to 'the game' and its rules: the original title stressed another element which is itself part of 'the game' — that is, the roles that each of us plays in relation to others.

> 'But you must play your part, just as I am playing mine. It's all in the game. Even Silia has grasped that! Each of us must play his part through to the end — In this game one wears a mask according to the role and one obeys the rules which are themselves created by the roles assumed.'

The idea of role-playing is often used by Pirandello. In *Six Characters* for instance, the Father says:

> 'I only act, as everyone does, the part in life that he's chosen for himself, or that others have chosen for him.'

The puppet theme is also related to role-playing, since the puppet's role is wished upon it by the puppet-master: in the relationship of Leone, Silia and Guido, Leone is the master and the other two the puppets. In the first scene of the play there are many references to Leone's domination of Silia even when he is not there: the power he exercises over her, even though their marriage is only a form, is too strong for Guido Venanzi to overcome. Indeed, Venanzi himself is eventually controlled by Leone, even to the point of death. Dr. Spiga plays another role, that of 'the doctor at the duel' and is more concerned about what he should wear to play the role, what costume he should adopt. Philip, the cook, has a role that Leone thrusts upon him, that of a philosopher corrupted by Bergson, and this philosophical role is reinforced by Leone's nicknaming him Socrates. Philip is quite unmoved by the role he is supposed to assume: he is more concerned about cooking and food. That is his real role — a cook.

The play itself is more naturalistic than the later plays about theatre or the nightmarish world of *Henry IV*. It has a nearer relationship to Chiarelli's *The Mask and the Face* and is nearer to it in time. Yet Chiarelli's is a wryly amusing piece, not the bitter calculated play of revenge that is *The Rules of the Game*. Nor does Chiarelli's play depend so strongly on the dramatic inheritance of *commedia dell'arte*. *The Rules of the Game* constantly reminds us of its dramatic origin. Leone's face is, like himself, totally under control. His mind is clear and precise, and his face, like a *commedia* mask, never betrays his inner feelings.

He is an implacable opponent in the Renaissance tradition who enjoys 'the intellectual game that clears away all the sentimental sediment from your mind'. At the end of the play, when he has succeeded in arranging Venanzi's death and when Silia has hysterically rushed out into the garden, Leone is alone on the stage.

> LEONE *remains motionless, absorbed in deep, serious thought. A long pause.* PHILIP *enters with a breakfast tray and puts it down on the table.*
> PHILIP (*calling in a hollow voice*). Hey!

> LEONE *barely turns his head.* PHILIP *indicates the breakfast with a vague gesture.*

> Breakfast time!

> LEONE, *as though he has not heard, does not move.*

He has played the intellectual game to the end: Venanzi is now dead. Leone has punished both his wife and her lover and it appears that the honour that some might say he has lost is of little consequence to him. 'When one has emptied oneself of every passion . . . , ' and yet, one suspects that behind the mask there is a movement of the face. Triumph? Regret? There must be something; there cannot be nothing. Leone does not move, and appears not to have heard. Food no longer attracts. A moment earlier Dr. Spiga, who played the self-important role of the doctor earlier in the act, had dashed into the room 'pale and dishevelled in a grotesque discomposure': he had seized the surgical instruments in a bundle and rushed out 'without saying a word'. This grotesque note is the key to the play: Leone's is a grotesque composure as opposed to Spiga's discomposure. The puppet-master has destroyed those puppets who rose up against him: the cuckolded husband has destroyed his wife's lover, Pantaloon has destroyed Harlequin and left Columbine distraught, while the Doctor is confused and the insolent servant is uninvolved.

I have already referred to the *lazzo* of the *commedia*, the device by which Leone steps to one side and the custard-pie (or the bullet) hits the person behind, the one who thought

himself safe and free to watch unscathed. It is no accident that
Pirandello uses the image of the egg several times in the play: the
egg is for juggling, for the magician to palm, for the clown to have
dropped into his trousers or broken over his head. It is a perfect
shape, but when the shape is destroyed by cracking, the inside
will run in an uncontrollable way, quite contrary to the
impression that the outside gave. The 'mask' of the egg is plain,
smooth, logical, devoid of feeling: the 'face' inside the mask is
composed of different and contrasting elements, with an embryo
of life that would be capable of feeling. If you are Leone and
clever, you can catch a thrown egg, prick the end, and suck out
the inside, play with the shell as a toy and then crush it when you
are bored. This is Venanzi's fate and even Silia's. In the context
of this play of masters and servants, doctors and lovers, an egg is
the ideal comic image recalling the easily available stage
properties of the *commedia* and yet reminding us of a
mathematical, logical perfection.

An interpretation of this play as an elaborated *commedia*
scenario can only be a partial view: no *commedia* was ever so
shot through with the examination of thought processes, with
conversations that explore reason and emotion, with a
character's self-examination and self-revelation. That was not
the stuff of *commedia*: but it is the stuff of Pirandello.

The character of Leone is a fascinating challenge for the actor.
It is not sufficient to play his intelligent facade, emptied of
feeling: the turbulent emotions that are under the impassive mask
must break to the surface occasionally. He must let us see, in part
at least, how he is weaving a net to trap Venanzi and Silia, a net
made, moreover, of material that they have provided. Yet we
must not be shown this planning crudely: his every speech must
have an ambiguity, an irony that will permit a glimpse of the
thoughts behind the bland exterior. The Italian audience in 1918
at the Teatro Quirino in Rome received the play with great
doubt. Pirandello wrote to his son Stefano:

'*The Rules of the Game* was met with hostility, owing to the
incomprehension of the audience after the first act. It picked
up in the second act and at the third it aroused considerable
discussion . . . The morning and evening papers have, on the

whole, been favourable to me.' (Giudice)
But the play came off very quickly.

Ruggero Ruggeri played Leone. Pirandello wrote: 'Ruggero is in love with the part and thinks *The Rules of the Game* my best play.'

In Britain the play has been a little more fortunate and favoured than we might expect — the central ideas seem more accessible than those in *Six Characters* and *Henry IV*. In 1953 the Third Programme broadcast a translation by Noel Gregeen, adapted by Robert Rietty, and in 1955 Donald Pleasence appeared as Leone in Robert Rietty's own translation at the Arts Theatre in London. Paul Scofield played Leone in a National Theatre production at the New Theatre in June 1971, with Joan Plowright and Tom Baker: Anthony Page directed. The translation was again by Robert Rietty, assisted by David Hare. Scofield himself was well received although *The Times* was less enthusiastic about the rest of the cast, referring to the 1966 World Theatre Season when an Italian company had 'revealed that Pirandello was a specialist in icily sardonic comedy with a murderously perfect technique'.

The most recent professional performance at the time of writing was by the late Leonard Rossiter in a production by Anthony Quayle. It opened in Guildford and moved to the Theatre Royal, Haymarket, in London in July 1982. Some critics were unmoved as is the general rule in Britain for any play of Pirandello's: others were more enthusiastic. The play was, apparently, Rossiter's own choice and he was wonderfully capable of conveying the sardonic humour of Leone, tilting the play to biting comedy at many of the more ambiguous moments, as he played the puppet-master. For some critics he lacked the polish of an Italian gentleman: but his rather crumpled appearance, in comparison with the elegence of Silia and Venanzi, could be seen as a positive virtue — he was seemingly less concerned with outward appearances, professing himself a man of intellect: yet it might have been more satisfying perhaps, to have had a Leone who could wear his clothes as well as his intellect with more panache.

Six Characters in Search of An Author
'A play doesn't create people, people create a play'
The text of *Six Characters* as we read it here and as it is always
performed is not the same text that Dario Niccodemi's company
used in Rome at the Teatro Valle in 1921 nor even the script of
a few months later in Milan at the Teatro Manzoni. In 1923
Georges Pitoëff presented the play at the Théâtre des
Champs-Elysées and there were some remarkable alterations to
the original, so that in 1924 Pirandello incorporated many of
Pitoëff's changes in a new text and added some further
alterations of his own. The differences between the texts of 1921
and 1924 are of great interest.

From Paris Pitoëff had kept Pirandello informed about his
ideas in directing the play and these had caused some
disagreement between them. Pirandello was horrified because
Pitoëff planned to send the Characters on using a scenic-lift at
the back of the bare and open stage. He was so concerned by this
that he left Rome for Paris to remonstrate with Pitoëff. In the
event, he was convinced that it was an excellent idea, although we
find that in the later edition of the play he did not use it again.
Instead he wrote a new entrance for the Characters.

The STAGE DOORKEEPER, *in a braided cap, has come into
the auditorium, and he comes all the way down the aisle to the
stage to tell the* PRODUCER *the* SIX CHARACTERS *have
come, who, having come in after him, look about them a little
puzzled and dismayed.*

And a few lines later he described the Father as *'coming forward,
followed by the others, to the foot of one of the sets of steps'.*
This seems to have been an idea of Pirandello's, and differs from
both Pitoëff in Paris in 1923 and Max Reinhardt in Berlin in
1922, who had preserved the original entrance from the back of
the stage. Pirandello was involved in the designing of the
Odescalchi Theatre at the time of establishing the Arts Theatre
in 1924, and he insisted that the stage level should be lower than
the conventional height, reducing the gap between the audience
and the actors. Having used two sets of stairs to link the
auditorium and the stage, he also used them to allow the
Producer to move into the audience space and create a firmer

dramatic statement. With this arrangement of steps between the
two essential spaces, the Characters can move from our world,
that of the audience, Life, into the world of Art, that of the
Actors: but so can the Producer. We see him do this.

He goes down the steps into the auditorium and stands there
as if to get an idea of what the scene will look like from the
audience's viewpoint.

We are drawn more firmly into the world of theatre. The
Producer's objective view of the events on the stage is the same as
ours: his statements about dramatic form and continuity are ones
that a conventional audience could accept. This identification of
audience, conventional and predictable, with the Producer, who
is equally conventional, will help immeasurably in the eventual
disruption and shock that the play is aiming at. Pirandello even
supports this notion in a snatch of conversation between the
Actors.

LEADING ACTOR (*to other* ACTORS). Look at this. What
    a show!
LEADING ACTRESS. And we're the audience.
YOUNG ACTOR. For a change.

Not only are they the audience for this event as we all are, sitting
in the theatre, but also the audience for the astonishing
appearance of Madame Pace. She does not come from the
auditorium, however, where the Characters came from, but from
behind the proscenium arch, on the stage itself, the Actor's
own area which is now being invaded by these people from
beyond the proscenium arch.

Of course this bridging of the gap between auditorium and
stage is not new. Beaumont and Fletcher had used it, for instance
in *The Knight of the Burning Pestle* as long ago as 1611 and for a
not dissimilar purpose. In Pirandello, however, the recognition of
the territorial significance of stage and auditorium is critical in
recognising the central argument of the play about Art and Life.
To support the argument he also sub-divided the stage into areas
for the Actors and for the Characters.

The 1925 edition included the ending that Pitoëff used in
Paris. The first productions closed with the Producer sending the
Actors away, the Characters having left by the door at the back

of the stage through which they had entered. However, Pitoëff's production ended as the text now ends, with the Characters returning to the open stage without the children, before the Stepdaughter, laughing raucously, leaves through the auditorium. The final text shows a very clear increase in dramatic tension, a greater appreciation of the visual needs of drama and a more subtle awareness of the movement patterns within the play.

'The shadows were swarming with us'

As early as 1904 Pirandello wrote, 'If material cares and social commitments did not distract me, I think I would remain from morning to night here in my study at the beck and call of the characters of my stories who are struggling within me. Each wants to come to life before the others'. Then again in 1911, 'I have two or three new visitors a week. And sometimes the crowd is such that I have to listen to more than one of them at the same time. And sometimes my mind is so split and so dazed that it shouts in exasperation . . . the characters must go straight back to limbo, the three of them'. (Giudice)

It was eventually not three but six who invaded his imagination. This family group imagined in an author's creative mind but not yet given expression in either a play or a story, burst their way into the reality of a theatre company at rehearsal: their passion about the situation they wish to have dramatised is explosive. Their story is full of bitterness and distress, accusation and counter-accusation. What seems truth to one is falsehood to another: what seems cruelty to one is pity to another: what seems neglect is care. The Actors and the Producer try to compose the family's story into a coherent piece of theatre, and yet, in the characteristic paradox of Pirandello, what was Life, dynamic and mutable shown by the Actors at the beginning, has become flat, immutable, static and unimaginative. What was Art, shown by the Characters has become dynamic and has moved into Life with a nightmarish power. The Father's last line is: 'What do you mean, make believe? It's real, ladies and gentlemen! It's reality.'

The play is a number of interdependent circles: the outer circle is composed of us, the audience, watching a recognisable group of

people on the stage, whom we know to be professional actors.
But in a second circle, they are representing the Actors and the
Characters. In the third circle the Characters act out their own
story, and in the last circle the Actors represent the Characters in
another rehearsal of the scenes from the Characters' past, a past
that only existed in the world of Art, the world created by
Pirandello for them. This is the Pirandellian paradox at its best.
In the second circle he constantly explores the variations of
appearance and reality, the perpetual shifts in personality, and he
shows how a single situation has as many truths as there are
people involved in it. As the Father says:

'This is the real drama for me; the belief that we all, you see,
think of ourselves as one single person: but it's not true: each
of us is several different people and all these people live inside
us. With one person we seem like this and with another we
seem very different. But we always have the illusion of being
the same person for everybody and of always being the same
person in everything we do. But it's not true! It's not true!'

It is not only personality that is variable, but the very words
we use to convey our ideas are as imprecise as our personalities.
The Father explains how impossible it is to communicate
perfectly a sense of truth from one person to another.

'But isn't that the cause of all the trouble? Words! We all have
a world of things inside ourselves and each of us has his own
private world. How can we understand each other if the words
I use have the sense and the value that I expect them to have,
but whoever is listening to me inevitably thinks that those
same words have a different sense and value, because of the
private world he has inside himself too. We think we
understand each other; but we never do.'

In the third circle there is a brilliant demonstration of a
theatrical examination of Art and Life: this is in Act Two when
the Characters play out for the Actors the meeting of the Father
and the Stepdaughter in Madame Pace's shop. It is headed The
Scene and is on page 109 in this edition. The Characters recreate
an event that has never been real, that only existed imaginatively
and yet their recreation is as vivid as if it were totally true and
happening at that very moment. Here is a real reflection of an

imaginary event and it has such reality that the Producer's interruption is a shock:

'Hold it! Hold it! Don't put that last line down, leave it out. It's going well, it's going well.

The Leading Actor and the Father are the mask and the face of the same person: the Leading Lady and the Stepdaughter are another mask and face, and when the Actors attempt to recreate the scene in the dress-shop they totally fail. They pose, they grimace, they strike attitudes and have no truth: all they can do is to represent inadequately. The Actors do not search for truth, and Pirandello uses their assumption of a trite theatrical mask to rip away theatrical pretence and show the emptiness behind. After watching the Father play out the event that has mortified him, that reveals himself to himself in the most piercing and humiliating way, the Leading Actor describes him as 'an old man who has come to a knocking-shop'. The theatre that this Leading Actor works in has no concern for truth. All he can see and reflect is 'The lively, knowing air of an ageing roué'.

The eternal moment

MOTHER. . . to keep perpetually before me, always real, the
     anguish and the torment I've suffered on her account.
FATHER. . . to keep me too in that moment, trapped for all
     eternity, chained and suspended in that one fleeting,
     shameful moment of my life.

This is the moment when the Father, the Mother and the Stepdaughter meet in the room behind Madame Pace's shop, the moment when the mirror flings the reflection back in the face that is looking at it: the moment of crisis. Pirandello himself wrote:

'When a man lives he lives and does not see himself. Well, put a mirror before him and make him see himself in the act of living, under the sway of his passions: either he remains astonished and dumbfounded at his own appearance, or else he turns away his eyes so as not to see himself, or else in his disgust he spits at his image, or again clenches his fist to break it: and if he has been weeping, he can weep no more: if he has been laughing he can laugh no more, and so on. In a word, there is a crisis, and that crisis is my theatre.' (Starkie)

Six Characters is a powerful play although it has lost some of its capacity to shock over the years: the details of the family life of the Characters with its disruption, adultery, prostitution, illegitimacy and potential incest are no longer as disturbing as originally they were. Even so, the tension inside the Characters themselves and between them as they explain their relationship is still a vibrant dynamic force that compels attention. One essential contrast in the play, that between the Actors and the Characters, remains difficult to demonstrate, despite Pirandello's extending of the opening scene in the 1924 text, allowing the Actors and the Producer a longer time to establish themselves than he originally gave them in 1921. The members of the company need to be clear enough to act as contrasts with the Characters and yet their contribution to the play after the first few pages is almost negligible, except for the scene in Act Two where the Leading Actor and Actress play out the scene in Madame Pace's shop. It is a paradox, although hardly a characteristically Pirandellian one, that the failure to offer the Actors enough to create a sufficiently strong impact is the major weakness of the play in performance.

The play is rarely presented professionally in Britain. In the last twenty-five years there have been only two productions in London. In June 1963 Ralph Richardson played the Father and Barbara Jefford the Stepdaughter at the Mayfair Theatre in a translation by an American playwright, Paul Avila Mayer, that had been seen earlier in New York. Two months later Stephen Murray took over the part of the Father. At the Greenwich Theatre in 1979, which used the translation in this volume, the production was sufficiently successful for the run to be extended: this suggests that the play still makes a powerful appeal to an audience, still has something pertinent to say. It is, however, as are even the few of Pirandello's plays that are performed in Britain, better known about than encountered, more often read than seen.

Henry IV
'Am I or aren't I?'

If *Six Characters* is 'theatrical' in the sense that the play happens

in a theatre stripped of artifice until the Producer imposes
scenery upon it, makes truth assume an artifice, puts a mask on
its face, then *Henry IV* is decorated total theatre. The throne
room and the castle are theatrical representations of an
architectural reality which has itself become a total theatre where
'nothing is but what is not'. Because the central figure is thought
to believe himself to be King Henry IV, the others who serve him
must be able to improvise their roles on the basis of correct
historical information. They can step through the looking-glass,
as Alice did, and join in the world on the other side, the world
where the King lives. The King has no name — only Henry IV.
That is his only reality. So we are presented at the outset with a
visual paradox — a theatrical setting of a created castle built to
support the delusion of a man who believes himself to be
someone other than the person he really is. It has, we find later,
electric lights built into the ceiling, although, when Henry is
there in this looking-glass land, the only light is from oil-lamps.
Anyone who wishes to step through the looking-glass must play a
role, assume a costume, a mask.

> 'We've a whole wardrobe through there, all authentic costumes
> perfectly made to period designs.'

Anyone wearing one of these is, then, approaching the same
imaginative position that Henry occupies — hesitating between
one world and the other, permitting questions to be asked of the
sense of reality. There are over a score of visual references in the
play to role-playing and to the historical dress that Matilda, Frida,
Belcredi and the others wear. The Pirandellian 'mask and face' of
Six Characters has been translated into a fuller set of images, of
costume. The mirror images are improved, or at any rate
increased, by the huge portraits which show two characters,
Henry and Matilda, fixed for eternity in a moment when
appearance became reality and Henry changed from *pretending* to
be the King in the pageant to believing himself to *be* the King.
In Act Three the young people, Frida and Di Nolli, stand in the
niches wearing the two costumes of the portraits, and we move
another step as the painted illusion assumes a third dimension.

There is an abundance of energy in Pirandello's work and
especially in *Henry IV*. Even the more philosophical and difficult

passages are infused with a burning vitality: one is reminded of Dario Niccodemi's description of Pirandello reading a script to his cast. The sense of theatricality is also very positive and we are offered more visual colour, more involvement with a simple direct narrative than in *Six Characters*. We are also offered a more intense dramatic use of a 'mad' character, through whom Pirandello can explore again the aspects of a personality.

Henry is the central figure, and the most important thing about him is his madness, his delusion. It is also the most real, the most powerful: it is more real than the castle itself, his courtiers or his visitors, because it springs from the imagination. 'Reality resides not in the material used, but in the life that the magic power of imagination can awaken in it.' It is human logic, human reason that is the evil that represses the free flow of the imagination, the 'flux of life'. By this token we must question very seriously the proposition that a man is 'mad' because he seems to believe that he is a person other than we think him to be. Notice that Henry never declares that he is 'sane': he does use the words 'mad' and 'sane' in relation to himself, but once he has revealed to Landolfo and the others that he is no longer 'mad' he never actually claims sanity. Pirandello, through Henry, uses this moment of dramatic character revelation to examine the concept of reality, of sanity and insanity, of absolute truth or indeed absolute anything.

'Look me carefully in the eye . . . I'm not saying it's true, don't worry! Nothing is true! But look me in the eye! . . . You know what it means to be with a madman? To be with someone who shakes the foundations, the logic of the whole structure of everything you've built in and around yourselves.'

This is a play that offers reminders both of *Hamlet* with its assumed madness, frustrated love, sudden death and role-playing and of *King Lear* with its motif: 'When the mind's free, the body's delicate'.

An apparent prison for Henry in the castle is no prison when the mind is free, released by the 'magic power of imagination': yet the body, the corporeal reality, is vulnerable, and the result, as Henry's worlds clash, is disastrous. The wilful retention of the appearance of madness has led to a very different return to the 'sane' world from the one he would have made if he had unequivocally declared himself cured eight years before. Belcredi feels that they have been imposed upon, and Henry triumphs in the power he has been able to exercise,

> '. . . to make everyone who came to see me continue. . . but, by God, with me in charge this time. . . To make it no longer fancy dress, but a permanent reality, the reality of true madness: here. . .'

A few moments after this Henry is no longer in charge: he has killed Belcredi and is now in charge of his own crime, immured by the need to preserve the appearance of madness to avoid legal retribution.

This play, above any other of Pirandello's, is full of *coups de théâtre* when intellect and passion are inextricably bound up together. Act Two draws to an end with a riveting theatrical image. Henry speaks to his 'counsellors', who now know that he has pretended to madness for some time, and he presses them to represent themselves as different from their previous idea of reality and join him in his. With a painter's eye, Henry arranges them, constructs his own scene: he sits the puppets in their places and then surveys them.

> HENRY IV. There. A little light. Sit yourselves down, round the table. Not like that! Nice relaxed attitudes. (*To* ARIALDO.) You like this. . . (*Arranging him, then to* BERTOLDO.) And you like this. . . (*Arranging him.*) Like that, that's it. . . (*Goes and sits himself.*) And me here. . . (*Turning his head towards one of the windows,*) We should be able to order a nice decorative ray of moonlight. . . But look, what a wonderful nocturnal picture. . . the Emperor, with his trusty counsellors. . . don't you like it?
>
> LANDOLFO (*quietly to* ARIALDO, *as if not to break the spell*). Do you realise, if we'd known it wasn't true. . .
>
> HENRY IV. What wasn't true?

Once again, Landolfo and the others are baffled and uncertain about everything. The Act finishes a few lines later with Henry returning to his kingly self as he says: "Exactly! For real! Because that's the only way reality is not a joke!" And he resumes in complete seriousness, the dictating of his memoirs to a servant,

Giovanni, who is role-playing an amanuensis of the King. The visual and the aural drama embody the idea: the intellect and passion are inseparable.

The play culminates in that dense moment when the multifaceted ideas and emotions clash just before the end of Act Three. Henry speaks to Frida, referring to his mother as she was twenty years before, to the image that has been thrust upon her and the image that an accident thrust upon him. He passes to and fro through the looking-glass as appearance and reality, time past and time present, madness and sanity all distort and we veer chaotically with Henry between his opposed worlds. Henry points at Di Nolli, dressed as the King in the portrait.

I know very well that he can't be me, because *I* am Henry IV. .. I've been him here for twenty years. . . stuck in this eternity of fancy dress! (*Indicating* MATILDA.) She's. . . someone I can't recognise. . . (*Indicating* FRIDA.). . . for me she's always like this. . . What a terrible miracle! The dream that has come to life in you. . . They've made you flesh and blood. . . you're mine. . .mine! You're mine by right!

He puts his arms round her, laughing like a madman, while the others all shriek in terror; but when they rush up to pull FRIDA *from him, he becomes menacing and shouts to his four young men:*

Keep them back! Keep them back! I order you to keep them back!

The four youths, stunned, but acting as though under a spell, automatically try to restrain DI NOLLI, *the* DOCTOR *and* BELCREDI.

BELCREDI (*freeing himself at once and throwing himself on* HENRY iV). Let her go! Let her go! You're not mad!
HENRY IV (*quick as lightning, drawing the sword from* LANDOLFO'S *side, who is standing beside him*). Not mad? Take that, then!

And he wounds him in the stomach. There is a shriek of horror. Everyone rushes to prop up BELCREDI.

The speed of thought and event is like a brightly coloured merry-go-round out of control. The bizarre costumes and make-up, the flashing sword catching the light, the confusion and then the stillness and silence of the last line of the play as the now horrified puppet, 'eyes wide, appalled at the force of his own acting', says

> 'Yes. . . no choice now. . . Here together. . . here together. . . and for always!'

Henry IV was first presented on stage in February 1922 in Milan with Ruggero Ruggeri in the title role. Most of the critics admired it and some were enthusiastic. 'Henry IV. . . Pirandello's masterpiece. . . above all because of the breadth of vision.' Pirandello wrote to his daughter, Lietta, who was then in South America with her husband:

> '*Henry IV* has been a real triumph. Ruggeri acted magnificently and all the daily papers have devoted two columns to the event.' (Giudice)

The play went to Turin and there it had eighteen curtain calls on the opening night.

In Britain the first performance was by Ernest Milton in 1924 at the Everyman Theatre in London, in a translation by Edward Storer. In 1950 Frederick May, who led a great revival of interest in Pirandello in Britain and to whom so many students of Pirandello are forever in debt, translated many of the plays, including *Henry IV* and there was a minor professional production in London directed by the young Peter Hall at the Arts Theatre in 1953. Albert Finney appeared in it at the Citizens' Theatre, Glasgow in 1963 and Alan Badel performed it on television in 1967 but it was not until 1974 that the play was given a major London production. Rex Harrison appeared in the role at Her Majesty's Theatre in an unpublished translation and had a very subdued response from both critics and audience. The history of British neglect of this momentous play continued when the National Theatre commissioned Julian Mitchell to make the translation published in this edition but have so far failed to stage it or any other version. Indeed, despite its winning the 1980 John Florio translation prize, it remains unperformed.

The Hearse, the Horse, the Driver

In 1935 Pirandello wrote a very moving letter to Domenico Vittorini, who was preparing a book about him. It is worth quoting not merely for its sentiment but because it contains a note that contradicts the common charge of pessimism that is levelled at him.

> 'The world of international literary criticism has been crowded for a long time with numerous Pirandellos — lame, deformed, all head and no heart. . . I am very grateful to you, my dear Vittorini. . . I find in you one who. . . grants me as much heart as I need to love and pity this poor humanity of ours. . . I have tried to tell something to other men, without any ambition, except perhaps that of avenging myself for having been born. And yet life, in spite of all that it has made me suffer, is so beautiful! (Vittorini)

He died a year later with a play, *The Mountain Giants*, unfinished. He insisted on a funeral of such simplicity that many who would have wished to pay tribute to him must have been disappointed. But the burial was carried out as he had instructed.

> 'My death must be passed over in silence.
> No announcements or invitations to the funeral.
> Do not dress my corpse. Let me be wrapped naked in a winding sheet.
> A pauper's hearse. Bare. No one to accompany me, neither friends nor relations. The hearse, the horse, the driver — that is all.'

He died in Rome at his flat in the Via Antonio Bosio. The funeral took place as he had wished, but after the war the ashes were taken to Agrigento. They were eventually buried under the pine tree at the end of the garden of the house where he was born, now officially known as the Casa Natale (the birthplace) and headquarters of the Centre for Pirandello Studies.

France gave Pirandello the Légion d'Honneur in 1923, and he was awarded the Nobel Prize for Literature in 1934. The Americans received him with a great excitement in the 1923/24 tour, with Henry Ford considering his plays a good investment. The Communist Party in Russia gave an official blessing to his works in 1934 and approved of a publication of the majority of his plays. The popularity of Pirandello in Italy waned in the last seven or eight years of his life, although naturally his Nobel Prize produced a patriotic pleasure. His association with the Fascist party under Mussolini earned him many opponents at the time. He was a member of the party from 1922 onwards, but often quarrelled with it and was frequently ambiguous in his correspondence and pronouncements. His connection possibly came from a philosophical conflict rather than from a committed political allegiance.

There is still only a very small quantity of Pirandello's work available in English. His reputation and probably his influence rests upon a handful of plays — out of the full forty-three that he wrote — together with a slightly larger handful of short stories. Despite this, the effect of his work on subsequent writers is generally acknowledged: no book on the drama of the twentieth century could possibly ignore him and no course of lectures on the theatre could omit him. One enthusiastic critic refers to him as 'the most seminal dramatist of our time' and credits him with anticipating Ionesco, Albee, O'Neill, Pinter, Wilder, Giraudoux, Genet, Camus, Sartre, Beckett, Anouilh. Claims of this sort sound rather hysterical and one suspects that his true importance lies not so much in the direct influence on other writers but on the liberation of the theatre that he undoubtedly brought about.

Pirandello himself was probably quite right in asserting that his greatest contribution to the drama was in the blending of intellect and passion. He used the dramatic form to question the very form of drama itself, to question whether drama could truly pose questions that would disturb or enlighten us. Ionesco echoed this when he said that 'Pirandello is the manifestation of the unalterable archetype of the idea of the theatre which we have in us'.

Luigi Pirandello 1869–1936

1867	Born at Cavusu near Girgenti (Agrigento) in Sicily.
1884	The family went to live in Palermo where Luigi was at school. First publication of a short story in June.
1886 -7	He became a student reading law at the University of Palermo, and was engaged to his cousin Linuccia.
1887	He left Palermo to go to the University of Rome and gave up law to read literature. He had now written at least one five-act play, and a collection of poetry. The plays do not seem to have survived.
1889	Publication of a collection of poems. The same year he left Rome, having quarrelled with the University authorities and decided to go to the University of Bonn.
1891	Obtained his Doctorate in Philosophy at Bonn on 'The Dialect of Agrigento'. He wrote to his father breaking off the engagement with Linuccia. He published another volume of poetry.
1893	He wrote a novel called *The Outcast*, which was eventually published in 1908.
1894	Married Antonietta Portulano. Published four books of verse as well as some short stories, the first of fifteen volumes between 1894 and 1919.
1895	Birth of a son, Stefano.
1897	Birth of a daughter, Lietta.
1899	Birth of a son, Fausto.
1899	Pirandello became Professor of Italian at the Istituto Superiore di Magistero Femminile.
1903	Father went bankrupt, and Maria Antonietta had a breakdown. He began to teach private pupils because of financial problems.
1904	Publication of *Mattia Pascal*, a novel that was an immediate success in Italy: it was filmed by L'Herbier in 1925.
1908	Published *Humour*, a lengthy study of the nature of

humour and comedy. He later revised this (1920) for a second edition.

1911 -12   Published two short plays, *Sicilian Limes* and *The Doctor's Duty*. The first was later produced by Nino Martoglio in Rome. He also published the last volume of poetry that he was to write.

1915   Death of Pirandello's mother. His father was invited to live in Rome with Pirandello, despite the fact that they had not spoken to each other since his father had been found to have a mistress, many years before.

1917   Wrote *Liola* in Sicilian.

1918   Wrote *Right You Are (If You Think So)*, *Cap and Bells* and *The Pleasures of Honesty*.

1919   Wrote *The Rules of the Game*. His wife was finally committed to a mental home. He published short stories for the last time. From now his attention was almost exclusively focused on drama.

1921   Of four plays he published in this year, one was *Six Characters in Search of an Author*. Performed in Rome and later in Milan. At about this time he ceased teaching in Rome.

1922   Published *Henry IV* and two other plays, including *Man, Beast and Virtue*. Major foreign performances of *Six Characters* took place in London, New York, Paris, Vienna and Berlin. He joined the Fascist party.

1923   Published *Naked*! Awarded the Légion d'Honneur.

1924   Published *The Life I Gave You*. He formed the Arts Theatre and met Marta Abba for the first time.

1924 -28   Various tours of the Arts Theatre in Europe and South America.

1928   He began to live outside Italy for much of the time.

1929   Published *Lazarus* — the premiere was at the Huddersfield Theatre Royal. Elected to the Reale Accademia d'Italia.

1930   Lived in Berlin. Wrote *Tonight We Improvise*.
In London *The Man with the Flower in his Mouth* was the first play ever to be presented on television. It was an attempt to persuade the Broadcasting Control Board that television drama had a serious future.

1934   Awarded the Nobel Prize (the other candidates were
       G.K. Chesterton and Paul Valéry). He then went to Prague
       to the first night of his latest play, *No One Knows How*,
       which he regarded very highly. This year of a renaissance
       in his public reputation was crowned with a success when
       Pitoëff performed *Tonight We Improvise* for the first time
       in France (January 17).

1936   He had attacks of angina pectoris and finally died in
       December in Rome in Via Antonio Bosio. There were one
       or two publications after his death, the most important of
       which was *The Mountain Giants*, a play he had not
       finished but which he had been writing for a number
       of years.

The Pirandello Family

Parents

STEFANO (1835 - 1923). Luigi's father was descended from a
   Genoese family and was the eighteenth child in a family of
   twenty-three. He fought for Garibaldi's army in 1860 and
   followed him for the next two years. He married in 1863.

CATERINA (1835 - 1915). Luigi's mother came from a very
   formal Sicilian family politically devoted to the
   independence of Sicily. Luigi was her second child of six.

Wife

ANTONIETTA PORTULANO (1872 - 1959). Luigi's wife and
   the daughter of his father's business partner. She had a
   mental break-down in 1903 and was cared for by Luigi and
   the children until she was moved to a mental home in 1919.

Children

STEFANO (1895 - 1972). As a writer he changed his name to
   Stefano Landi to avoid trading on his father's name.

LIETTA (1897 - 1971). Her father's constant companion for some
   time before her marriage to Manuel Aguirre of Chile.

FAUSTO (1899 - 1975). He became a renowned painter. His
   father had been a painter all his life, carrying his materials with
   him wherever he went. He followed the career of his son with
   great love and interest, writing to him about painting.

THE RULES OF THE GAME

*Translated by Robert Rietty
and Noel Cregeen*

This play was first presented in England in an earlier version of this translation at the Arts Theatre, London, 13 January 1955, with the following cast:

LEONE GALA	Donald Pleasence
SILIA GALA, LEONE's wife	Melissa Stribling
GUIDO VENANZI, SILIA's lover	Robert Cartland
DOCTOR SPIGA	Dudley Jones
BARELLI	Peter Whitbread
PHILIP, nicknamed 'Socrates',	
LEONE's servant	Gilbert Davis
MARQUIS MIGLIORITI	Eric Hillyard
CLARA, SILIA's maid	Silia Sherry
1st DRUNK	Timothy Bateson
2nd DRUNK	Stewart Weller
1st TENANT	Frank Royd
2nd TENANT	Lucille Lee
3rd TENANT	Joan Harrison

Directed by John Fernald

Scene: any town in Italy
Time: 1919

(*Note:* the text has three drunks, but they can be reduced to two and the lines distributed accordingly.)

Act One

The smartly furnished drawing-room of SILIA GALA's *flat.*

At the back, a large double sliding door, painted white, with red glass panes in the upper panels, divides this room from the dining-room.

The front door and a window are on the left.

In the right-hand wall there is a fireplace, and on the mantelpiece an ormolu clock. Near the fireplace, another door leads to a third room.

When the curtain rises, both sections of the glass door are slid right back into the wall.

The time is about 10.15 PM.

GUIDO VENANZI, *in evening dress, is standing by the dining-room table, on which a number of liqueur bottles can be seen in a silver stand.*

SILIA GALA, *in a light dressing-gown, is in the drawingroom, huddled up day-dreaming in an armchair.*

GUIDO. Chartreuse?

> *He waits for an answer.* SILIA *ignores him.*

Anisette?

> *Same result.*

Cognac? Well? Shall I choose?

> *He pours out a glass of anisette, and takes it to* SILIA.

Here, try this.

> SILIA *still takes no notice, and remains motionless for a few seconds. Then, shuddering with annoyance at finding him near her with the glass in his hand, she utters an exclamation of irritation.* GUIDO, *annoyed, drinks the glass in one gulp.*

GUIDO (bowing). Thanks for the trouble! I didn't really want it.

> SILIA *resumes her original attitude.* GUIDO *puts down the glass, sits down, and turns to look at her.*

You might at least tell me what's the matter with you.

SILIA. If you imagine I'm here . . .

GUIDO. Oh, so you're not here? You're somewhere else, I suppose?

SILIA (*furiously*). Yes, I am somewhere else! Miles away.

GUIDO (*quietly, after a pause, as though to himself*). Then I'm alone, eh? In that case, I may as well see if there's anything worth stealing here.

> *He gets up and pretends to search about the room.*

Let me see . . . a few paintings. N . . . no, too modern! Silver . . . hardly worth bothering about!

> *He approaches* SILIA *as though he does not see her. When quite close to her he stops with an expression of mock surprise.*

Hullo! What's this? Your body left behind in the chair? I shall certainly take that! (*He tries to embrace her.*)

SILIA (*jumping to her feet and pushing him away*). Don't be so stupid! I've told you not to do that!

GUIDO. Pity! You're back again already! Your husband is right when he says our only real trips abroad are the ones we make in our imagination.

SILIA. That must be the fourth or fifth time you've mentioned *him* tonight.

GUIDO. It seems to be the only way of getting you to talk to me.

SILIA. No, Guido, it only makes you more of a bore.

GUIDO. Thanks!

SILIA (*after a long pause, with a sigh, distantly*). I saw it all so clearly!

GUIDO. What did you see?

SILIA. I must have read about it, I suppose. But everything was so clear and vivid. A woman, sitting there, smiling to herself as she worked.

GUIDO. What was she doing?

SILIA I don't know — I couldn't see her hands. But it was something women do while their men are away fishing. I think it's in Iceland. Yes, that's where it is.

GUIDO. You were dreaming you were in . . . Iceland?

SILIA. Yes, I was daydreaming. But that's the way I always travel. (*Pause*.) It's got to stop! It's got to stop! (*Aggressively:*) This can't go on any longer.

GUIDO. Meaning me?

SILIA. No. Me.

GUIDO. But don't you see that anything that concerns you concerns me too?

SILIA (*annoyed*). Oh, God! You always see everything on such a tiny scale. You're shut up in a smug little cut and dried world of your own, where nothing is allowed to exist that doesn't concern you personally. I bet geography still means nothing more to you than a textbook, and a map on a schoolroom wall!

GUIDO (*puzzled*). Geography?

SILIA. Yes. Didn't your teacher set you lists of names to be learnt by heart for homework?

GUIDO. Lord, yes! What a bore!

SILIA. But rivers, mountains, countries, islands, continents — they really *do* exist, you know.

GUIDO (*sarcastically*). Really? Thanks for telling me!

SILIA. And there are people living there — and all the time we're cooped up in this room.

GUIDO (*as though light had suddenly dawned on him*). Ah, I see. You're hinting that I ought to take you abroad.

SILIA. There you go again! I make a perfectly general statement, and you immediately think it must have some bearing on our situation. I'm not hinting at anything. I'm merely trying to broaden your outlook. I can't bear this life any longer. I'm stifled!

GUIDO. But what sort of life *do* you want?

SILIA. I don't know. Any life that's different from this! God, if I could only see the faintest glimmer of hope for the future! I tell you I'd be perfectly happy just basking in that ray of hope — without running to flatten my nose against the window-pane to see what there is in store for me outside.

GUIDO. You're talking as if you were in prison!

SILIA. I am in prison!

GUIDO. Oh? And who's keeping you there?

SILIA. You, and everyone else! Even my own body, because I can never forget that it's a woman's. How can I, when you men are always staring at my figure? I never think about my body until I catch men's eyes ogling. Often I burst out laughing. 'Well,' I say to myself, 'there's no getting away from it — I *am* a woman!'

GUIDO. I don't think you've any reason to complain about that.

SILIA. Because I'm attractive? (*Pause.*) But can't you see that all *this* is mainly due to my being continually reminded I'm a woman, and forced to be one when I don't want to be?

GUIDO (*slowly, detached*). Like tonight, for example.

SILIA. Being a woman has never given *me* any pleasure.

GUIDO. Not even the pleasure of making a man miserable?

SILIA. Yes, *that* perhaps. Often.

GUIDO (*as before*). Tonight, for example.

Pause. SILIA *sits, absorbed.*

SILIA (*fretfully*). But one's own life! . . . The life we don't share with anybody — not even ourselves . . .

GUIDO. What *are* you talking about?

SILIA. Have you never stood gazing at your reflection in a mirror, without thinking about yourself? Suddenly you feel that your face belongs to someone else, a stranger, and you study it intently. Then you see a stray lock of hair or some-thing — automatically you push it back into place, and immediately the spell is broken, everything is spoilt.

GUIDO. And so . . . ?

SILIA. Other people's eyes are like a mirror. So are our own,

when we are using them to look at ourselves to find out the
way we ought to live; the way we are bound to live, in fact.
Oh, I can't explain!

    Pause.

GUIDO (*approaching*). Shall I tell you frankly why you're
    getting so worked up?
SILIA (*promptly*). Because you're here — standing in front of me!
GUIDO (*taking it to heart*). Oh! In that case would you like me to
    go?
SILIA. Yes, you had better.
GUIDO. But why, Silia?

    SILIA *shrugs her shoulders.*

    Why do you treat me so badly?
SILIA. I'm not treating you badly. I don't want people to see you
    here too often, that's all.
GUIDO. Too often! Why, I hardly ever come here. It must be
    more than a week since I was here last. Obviously, time passes
    too quickly for you.
SILIA. Quickly? Every day seems an eternity!
GUIDO (*close*). Then why do you still pretend that I count for
    nothing in your life? Silia . . . (*he tries to embrace her.*)
SILIA (*irritated*). Oh, Guido, for heaven's sake!
GUIDO. I've waited for you day after day. You hardly let me see
    you any more . . .
SILIA. But can't you see the state I'm in?
GUIDO. That's simply because you don't know what you want.
    You go and invoke some vague hope or other that will open
    a chink for you into the future.
SILIA. According to you, I suppose I ought to go forward to
    meet the future with a ruler in my hand to measure all my
    desires. 'So much I may allow myself to want, and no more.'
    Like doling out sweets to a child!
GUIDO. I expect you think I'm being pedantic!
SILIA. Yes, I do. All that you've been saying bores me stiff!
GUIDO. Thanks!
SILIA. You want to make me believe that I have had everything

I could wish for, and that I'm getting 'worked-up' like this now — as you put it — because I'm snatching at something out of reach, at the impossible. Isn't that it? (*Mimicking him:*) 'It's not reasonable!' Oh, I know that! But what would you have me do? I *do* want the impossible!

GUIDO. What, for instance?

SILIA. Can you tell me what I've had out of life to make me happy?

GUIDO. Happiness is all a question of degree. One person is satisfied with little; another has everything, and is never satisfied.

SILIA. Do you imagine I have everything?

GUIDO. No, but you're never content with things as they are. What on earth *are* you hankering after?

SILIA (*as though to herself*). I want to be rich . . . my own mistress . . . free! (*Suddenly flaring up:*) Haven't you understood yet that all this has been *his* revenge?

GUIDO. It's your own fault! You don't know how to use the freedom he's given you.

SILIA. Freedom to let myself be made love to by you or any other man; freedom to stay here or go anywhere I please . . . Oh, yes! I'm free! Free as air . . . But what if I'm never myself?

GUIDO. What do you mean, never yourself?

SILIA. Do you really think I'm free to be myself and do just as I like, as though no one else were there to prevent me?

GUIDO. Well, who is preventing you?

SILIA. *He* is! Throwing this precious freedom at me like an old shoe, and going off to live by himself — after spending three years proving to me that this wonderful freedom has no real existence. No matter what use I try to make of it, I shall always be his slave! Even a slave of that chair of his! Look at it: standing in front of me determined to be one of *his* chairs, not something belonging to *me*, and made for *me* to sit in!

GUIDO. This is an obsession!

SILIA. That man haunts me!

GUIDO. But you hardly ever see him!

SILIA. But he's there, he exists, and I shall always be haunted by him as long as I know he exists. Dear God, I wish he were dead!

GUIDO. Well, he practically is dead as far as you're concerned.

He's stopped paying you those absurd visits in the evenings, hasn't he?

SILIA. Yes . . . Now he comes as far as the front door and sends the maid up to ask if I have any message for him.

GUIDO. Well, is that so terrible?

SILIA. Of course! Because he *ought* to come up to the flat and stay for half an hour every evening. That's what we agreed he was to do.

GUIDO. Really, Silia! You just said you were haunted by him, and now . . .

SILIA. Don't you see it's the fact of his being alive, his mere existence that haunts me? It's not his body at all. On the contrary; it would be much better if I did see him. And it's just because he knows that, he doesn't let me see him any more. If he did come in and sit down in that chair over there, he'd seem like any other man, neither uglier nor better-looking. I'd see those eyes of his that I never liked — God, they're horrible. Sharp as needles and vacant at the same time. I'd hear that voice of his that gets on my nerves. I'd have something tangible to grapple with — and I'd even get some satisfaction out of giving him the bother of coming upstairs for nothing!

GUIDO. I don't believe it.

SILIA. What don't you believe?

GUIDO. That anything could possibly bother him!

SILIA. Yes, that's the trouble! He's like a ghost, quite detached from life, existing only to haunt other people's lives. I sit for hours on end absolutely crushed by the thought. There he is, alone in his own apartment, dressed up as a cook — dressed up as a cook, I ask you! — looking down on everybody from above, watching and understanding every move you make, everything you do, knowing all your thoughts, and making you foresee exactly what you're going to do next — and, of course, when you know what it is, you no longer want to do it! That man has paralysed me! I've only one idea continually gnawing at my brain: how to get rid of him, how to free myself from him.

The telephone rings offstage.

GUIDO. Really, Silia, aren't you being rather melodramatic!

SILIA. It's the truth.

> *There is a knock at the door on the left.*

Come in.

CLARA (*opens the door*). Excuse me, Signora, the master has rung up from downstairs.

SILIA. Ah, so he's here!

CLARA. He wants to know if there's any message.

SILIA. Yes, there is. Tell him to come up, Clara.

GUIDO. But, Silia . . .

SILIA. Tell him to come up.

CLARA. Very good, Signora. (*She goes*).

GUIDO. But why, Silia? Why tonight when I'm here?

SILIA. For the very reason that you are here!

GUIDO. No, Silia — don't do it.

SILIA. Yes, I shall — to punish you for coming. What's more I'll leave you here to deal with him. I'm going to bed.

> *She goes towards the door on the right.*

GUIDO (*running after her and holding her back*). No, don't Silia! Are you mad? What will he say?

SILIA. What do you expect him to say?

GUIDO. Silia . . . listen . . . it's late . . .

SILIA. So much the better.

GUIDO. No, no, Silia. That would be going too far. It's madness.

SILIA (*freeing herself from him*). I don't wish to see him.

GUIDO. Neither do I.

SILIA. You're going to entertain him.

GUIDO. Oh, no, I'm not. He won't find me here either.

> SILIA *goes into her room.* GUIDO *immediately runs into the dining room, shutting the glass door.*

> *There is a knock at the front door.*

LEONE (*off*). May I come in?

> *He opens the door and puts his head round.*

May I? . . . (*he breaks off, seeing no one there*) well . . . well . . .

> *He looks round the room, then takes his watch out of his pocket, goes to the mantelpiece, opens the face of the clock and moves the hand so that it strikes twice, then puts his watch back in his pocket and settles down calmly to await the passing of the agreed half hour.*

> *After a short pause a confused whispering is heard from the dining room. It is* SILIA *trying to urge* GUIDO *into the drawing room.* LEONE *remains motionless. Presently, one section of the glass door opens and* GUIDO *enters, leaving the door open.*

GUIDO (*ill at ease*). Oh . . . hullo, Leone. I dropped in for a spot of chartreuse.

LEONE. At half past ten?

GUIDO. Yes . . . As a matter of fact . . . I was just going.

LEONE. I didn't mean that. Was it green chartreuse or yellow?

GUIDO. Oh, I . . . I don't remember. Green, I think.

LEONE. At about two o'clock you'll have the most horrible nightmare, and wake up with your tongue feeling like a loofah.

GUIDO (*shuddering*). Oh, don't say that!

LEONE. Yes, you will — result of drinking liqueurs on an empty stomach. Where's Silia?

GUIDO (*embarrassed*). Well, er . . . She was in there, with me.

LEONE. Where is she now?

GUIDO. I don't know. She . . . she sent me in here when she heard you had come. I expect she'll be . . . joining you soon.

LEONE. Is there something she wants to say to me?

GUIDO. N-no . . . I . . . don't think so.

LEONE. Then why did she make me come up?

GUIDO. Well, I was just saying good-bye, when the maid came in and told her you'd rung up from the hall . . .

LEONE. As I do every evening.

GUIDO. Yes, but . . . apparently she wanted you to come up.

LEONE. Did she say so?

GUIDO. Oh, yes, she said so.

LEONE. Is she angry?

GUIDO. A bit, yes, because . . . I believe that . . . Well, I think
you two agreed, didn't you? . . . For the sake of appearances . . .

LEONE. You can leave out the appearances!

GUIDO. I mean, to avoid scandal . . .

LEONE. Scandal?

GUIDO. . . . Without going to court.

LEONE. Waste of time!

GUIDO. Well, without openly quarrelling then — you separated.

LEONE. But who on earth would ever quarrel with me? I always
give way to everybody.

GUIDO. True. In fact, that's one of your most enviable qualities.
But — if I may say so — you go rather too far.

LEONE. You think so?

GUIDO. Yes, because, you see, so often you . . . (*He looks at him
and breaks off.*)

LEONE. Well?

GUIDO. You upset people.

LEONE (*amused*). No! Really? How?

GUIDO. Because . . . you always follow their suggestions. You
always do what other people want. I bet that when your wife
said to you 'Let's have a judicial separation', you answered . . .

LEONE. 'Very well, let's have a judicial separation.'

GUIDO. There you are, you see! And then when she changed
her mind because she didn't want any bother with lawyers and
suggested you separate merely by mutual agreement . . .

LEONE. I replied, 'All right, if that's the way you want it, we'll
separate by mutual agreement.' I even went away and left her
the apartment. I told her she could alter anything she liked,
redecorate the place, refurnish it to her own taste . . . The only
thing I insisted on was that she keep my clock — which she
always forgets to wind, bless her — and my favourite armchair,
so I can feel a little bit at home on these half hour visits. What
more could she want?

GUIDO. That's all very well, but if she came to you and said,
'We can't go on quarrelling like this' . . .

LEONE. . . . I should have said 'Well then, my dear, we'll not
quarrel any more. We'll forget there was ever a difference
between us, and start our life together afresh.'

GUIDO. But don't you see that all this is bound to upset people? One gets in the way of behaving as though you didn't exist, and then . . . How can I explain it? However one tries to ignore your existence, sooner or later, one gets to a point where one can't go any further. It's a deadend, and one stands there bewildered, because . . . Well, it's no use, you *do* exist!

LEONE. Undoubtedly. (*He smiles.*) I exist. (*In a rather sharper tone:*) Ought I *not* to exist?

GUIDO. No, good God, I didn't mean that.

LEONE. But you're right, my dear chap! I ought not to exist. I assure you I do my utmost to exist as little as possible — for my own sake as well as others! But what can you do? The fault lies with the fact: *I am alive.* And when a fact has happened, it stands there, like a prison, shutting you in. I married Silia, or to be more precise, I let her marry me. *Voilà*: another fact! Almost immediately after our wedding, she began to fume and fret, and twist and turn, in her frantic efforts to escape, and I . . . I tell you Guido, it caused me a great deal of unhappiness. In the end we hit upon this solution. I left her everything here, taking away with me only my books and my pots and pans, which, as you know, are quite indispensable to me. But I realise it's useless, because — in name, anyway — the 'part' assigned to me by a fact which cannot be destroyed, remains. I am her husband. That, too, perhaps ought occasionally to be borne in mind!

He pauses. GUIDO *looks a little uncomfortable.*

(*Suddenly:*) You know what blind people are like, don't you, Venanzi?

GUIDO. Blind people?

LEONE. They are never 'alongside' things, if you follow me.

GUIDO. I don't.

LEONE. If you see a blind man groping for something, and you try to help him by saying 'there it is, just beside you,' what does he do? He immediately turns and faces you. It's the same with that dear woman. She's never by your side — always facing you, opposed to you.

He pauses, glancing towards the glass door.

It looks as if my wife isn't coming in.

He takes his watch out of his pocket, sees that the half-hour is not yet up and puts it back.

LEONE. You don't know what it was she wanted to say to me?

GUIDO. I . . . don't think there was anything . . . really.

LEONE. In that case, all she wanted was *this*.
    (*He makes a gesture signifying 'you and me.'*)

GUIDO (*puzzled*). I don't follow.

LEONE. This situation, my dear chap. She wanted to have the satisfaction of forcing us two to meet like this, face to face.

GUIDO. Perhaps she thinks that I . . .

LEONE. . . . have already gone? No, she would have come in.

GUIDO ((*getting ready to go*). Oh, well, in that case . . .

LEONE (*quickly, detaining him*). Oh, no, please don't go. I shall be leaving in a few minutes. (*He rises.*) Ah, Venanzi, it's a sad thing when one has learnt every move in the game.

GUIDO. What game?

LEONE. Why . . . this one. The whole game — of life.

GUIDO. Have you learnt it?

LEONE. Yes, a long time ago. And the way to come through it unscathed.

GUIDO. I wish you'd teach me how to do that.

LEONE. Oh, my dear Venanzi, it wouldn't be of any use to you! To get through safe and sound you must know how to defend yourself. But it's a kind of defence that you, probably, wouldn't be able to understand. How shall I describe it? A desperate one.

GUIDO. How do you mean, desperate? Rash? Reckless?

LEONE. Oh no, not that at all. I mean desperate in its literal sense. Absolutely hopeless — but without the faintest shadow of bitterness, for all that.

GUIDO. Well, what is this defence?

LEONE. It's the firmest and most unshakeable of all defences. You see, when there's no more hope left, you're not tempted to make even the slightest concession, either to others or to yourself.

GUIDO. It doesn't sound like a defence to me — but, if it is, what are you defending?

LEONE (*looks at him severely and darkly for a moment: then, controlling himself, he sinks back into an impenetrable serenity.*)
The Nothing that lies inside yourself. That is, if you succeed, as I have done, in achieving this nothingness within you. What do you imagine you should defend? Defend yourself, I tell you, against the injuries life inevitably inflicts upon us all; I have injured myself, through Silia, for so many years. I am injuring her now, even though I isolate her from myself completely. You are injuring me . . .

GUIDO. I?

LEONE. Of course — inevitably! (*Looking into his eyes:*) Surely you don't imagine you are *not* doing me any injury.

GUIDO. Well . . . (*He pales.*) I'm not aware . . .

LEONE (*encouragingly*). Oh, unconsciously, my dear Venanzi, quite unconsciously. When you sit down to eat a roast chicken or a tender veal cutlet, do you ever consider who provides your meal? Are you consciously aware that the morsel impaled on your fork was once a living, breathing, feeling creature? No, you never think about it. Make no mistake, we all injure each other — and each man injures himself too, naturally! That's life! There's only one thing to do — empty yourself.

GUIDO. Oh, fine! And what's left then?

LEONE. The satisfaction, not of living for yourself any more, but of watching others live — and even of watching yourself, from outside, living that little part of life you are still bound to live.

GUIDO. Only too little, alas!

LEONE. Yes, but you get a marvellous compensation — the thrill of the intellectual game that clears away all the sentimental sediment from your mind, and fixes in calm, precise orbits all that moves tumultuously within you. But the enjoyment of this clear, calm vacuum that you create within you may be dangerous, because, among other things, you run the risk of going up among the clouds like a balloon, unless you put inside yourself the necessary measure of ballast.

GUIDO. Oh, I see! By eating well?

LEONE (*ignoring the interjection*). To re-establish your equilibrium, so that you will always stay upright. You know those celluloid toys? — those funny little hollow figures you give to children to play with? You can knock them over any way you like, and they always spring up again. That's because of their lead counter-weight. I assure you we're very much the same as they are. Only you have to learn how to make yourself hollow, and — more important — how to provide yourself with a counterweight.

GUIDO. I don't follow you.

LEONE. I feared you wouldn't.

GUIDO (*hastily*). I'm not really unintelligent, you know, but . . .

LEONE. An anchor then? Does that make sense to you? A ship riding at anchor in a storm? Find yourself an anchor, then, my dear Venanzi — some hobby, some absorbing mental occupation, some fanciful conceit — then you'll be safe.

GUIDO. Oh, no, no! Thanks very much! That sort of thing is not for me. It sounds much too difficult.

LEONE. It's not easy, I grant you, because you can't buy these anchors ready made. You have to make them for yourself — and not just one, either. You need many anchors, one to suit each emergency, every incident in life. And, too, they must be stout and strong, to stand the strain of any violent incident that may burst upon you without warning.

GUIDO. Yes, but surely there are certain unforeseen incidents, sometimes really shattering ones, that even you can't . . .

LEONE. That's just where my cooking comes in. It's wonderful what storms you can weather if you're a good cook.

GUIDO. What kind of storms? Domestic, do you mean?

LEONE. Any storm. Any emergency. After all, it is never the emergency itself which you have to fear, but its effect upon you.

GUIDO. But that in itself can be quite terrible.

LEONE. But more or less terrible according to the person who experiences it. That's why I say you must defend yourself against yourself — against the feelings immediately aroused in you by anything that happens to you. Your own feelings — they are the weapons which an incident uses in its attack upon you.

GUIDO. But I can't defend myself against my own feelings.

LEONE. Oh, you can. Counter-attack, my dear fellow. You must grapple with the incident without hesitation, before it gets a chance to engage your feelings, and get out of it anything that may be of advantage to you. The residue will be powerless to injure you, you can laugh at it, play with it, make it the fanciful conceit I mentioned just now.

GUIDO (*more and more bewildered*). I'm afraid I still don't quite . . .

LEONE. Look, Venanzi. Imagine for a moment that you notice an egg suddenly hurtling through the air straight towards you . . .

GUIDO. . . . an egg?

LEONE. Yes, an egg. A fresh one. It doesn't matter who has thrown it, or where it comes from; that's beside the point.

GUIDO. But suppose it turns out to be a bullet and not an egg?

LEONE (*smiling*). Then it's too late to think about emptying yourself. The bullet will do the job for you, and that's the end of the matter.

GUIDO. All right — let's stick to your egg; although what a fresh egg has to do with the matter, I'm blessed if I can see.

LEONE. To give you a fresh image of events and ideas. Well, now, if you're not prepared to catch the egg, what happens? Either you stand still and the egg hits you and smashes, or you duck and it misses you and smashes on the ground. In either case the result is a wasted egg. But if you are prepared, you catch it, and then — why there's no end to what you can do with it, if you're a good cook. You can boil it, or poach it, or fry it, or make an omelette of it. Or you can simply pierce it at each end and suck out the yoke. What's left in your hand then?

GUIDO. The empty shell.

LEONE. Exactly. That empty shell is your fanciful conceit. You can amuse yourself with it by sticking it on a pin and making it spin; or you can toss it from one hand to the other like a ping-pong ball. When you're tired of playing with it, what do you do? You crush it in your hand and throw it away.

At this point SILIA, *in the dining room, suddenly laughs loudly.*

SILIA (*hiding behind the closed section of the glass door*). But I'm not an empty eggshell in your hand.

LEONE (*turning quickly and going to the door*). No, dear. And you no longer come through the air towards *me* for *me* to catch.

> *He has hardly finished saying this when* SILIA, *without showing herself, shuts the other half-door in his face.* LEONE *stands there for a moment, nodding. Then he comes forward again and turns to* GUIDO.

That's a great misfortune for me, my dear Venanzi. She was a wonderful school of experience. I've come to miss her. She is full of unhappiness because she's full of life. Not one life only, many. But there isn't one of them that will ever give her an anchor. There's no salvation for her. (*Pointedly:*) And so there's no peace . . . either for her, or with her.

> GUIDO, *absorbed in thought, unconsciously nods too, with a sad expression on his face.*

You agree?

GUIDO (*thoughtfully*). Yes . . . it's perfectly true.

LEONE. You're probably unaware of all the riches there are in her . . . qualities of mind and spirit you would never believe to be hers — because you know only one facet of her character, from which you have built up your idea of what is for you, and always will be, the real and only Silia. You wouldn't think it possible, for example, for Silia to go about her housework some morning carefree, relaxed, happily singing or humming to herself. But she does, you know. I used to hear her sometimes, going from room to room singing in a sweet little quavering voice, like a child's. A different woman, I'm not saying that just for the sake of saying it. Really a different woman — without knowing it! For a few moments when she is out of herself, she is just a child, singing. And if you could see how she sits sometimes, absorbed, gazing into space; a distant, living glow reflected in her eyes, and unconsciously smoothing her hair with idly straying fingers. Who is she then? Not the Silia you know — another Silia, a Silia that can't live because

she is unknown to herself, since no one has ever said to her
'I love you when you are like that; that's the way I want you
always to be.'

If you told her that, she'd ask you, 'How do you want me
to be?' You would reply 'As you were just now.' Then she
would turn to you, 'What was I like,' she would say, 'what was
I doing?' 'You were singing.' 'I was singing?' 'Yes, and you
were smoothing your hair like this.' She would not know it.

She would tell you it wasn't true. She positively would
not recognise herself in your picture of her as you had just
seen her — if you *could* see her like that, for you always
see only one side of her! How sad it is, Guido! Here's a sweet,
gracious potentiality of a life she might have — and she hasn't
got it!

A sad pause. In the silence, the ormolu clock strikes eleven.

Ah, eleven o'clock. Say good-night to her from me.

SILIA (*quickly opening the glass door*). Wait — wait a moment.

LEONE. Oh, no. Time's up.

SILIA. I wanted to give you this.

She puts an egg shell into his hand, laughing.

LEONE. Oh, but *I* haven't sucked it! Here . . .

He goes quickly to GUIDO *and gives him the egg shell.*

Let's give it to Guido!

GUIDO *automatically takes the egg shell and stands stupidly
with it in his hand, while* LEONE, *laughing loudly, goes off
through the door on the left.*

SILIA. I'd give anything for someone to kill him!

GUIDO. I'd love to chuck this egg at his head.

He runs towards the window on the left.

SILIA (*laughing*). Here, give it to me! I'll throw it at him from
the window.

GUIDO *gives her the egg shell, or rather, lets her take it from him.*

GUIDO. Will you be able to hit him?
SILIA. Yes, as he comes out of the front door.

> *She leans out of the window, looking down, ready to throw the egg shell.*

GUIDO (*behind her*). Careful.

> SILIA *throws the shell, then suddenly draws back with an exclamation of dismay.*

What have you done?
SILIA. Oh, Lord!
GUIDO. Did you hit someone else?
SILIA. Yes. The wind made it swerve.
GUIDO. Naturally! It was empty. Trust a woman not to allow for the wind!
SILIA. They are coming up.
GUIDO. Who's coming up?
SILIA. There were four men talking by the door. They were coming in just as he went out. Perhaps they are tenants.
GUIDO. Well, what does it matter, anyway?

> *He takes advantage of her consternation and kisses her.*

SILIA. It looks as though it landed on one of them.
GUIDO. But an empty egg shell couldn't possibly hurt him! Forget about it! (*Recalling* Leone's *words, but passionately and without caricature*:) You know, darling, you are just like a child.
SILIA. What *are* you saying?
GUIDO. You are like a child tonight, and I love you when you're like that. That's the way I want you always to be.
SILIA (*laughs*). You're repeating what *he* said.
GUIDO (*not put off by her laughter, but is still passionate, his desire increasing*). Yes, I know I am, but it's true, it's true! Can't you see you're just a wayward child?
SILIA. A child? (*Raising her hands to his face, as though to scratch him*:) More likely a tigress!
GUIDO (*without letting her go*). For him, perhaps, but not for

me. I love you so. To me you're a child.

SILIA (*half laughing*). All right, then, you kill him for me!

GUIDO. Oh, darling, do be serious.

SILIA. Well, if I'm a child I can ask you to do that for me, can't I?

GUIDO (*playing up*). Because he's your 'bogeyman'?

SILIA. Yes, he's the 'bogeyman' who makes me so frightened. Will you kill him for me?

GUIDO. Yes, yes, I'll kill him . . . but not now, later. Now I want to . . .

 He clasps her more closely.

SILIA (*struggling*). No, no! Guido, please . . .

GUIDO. Oh, Silia, you must know how much I love you; how I long for you!

SILIA (*as before, but languidly*). No. I tell you.

GUIDO (*trying to lead her towards the door on the right*). Yes, yes! Come, Silia.

SILIA. No. Please! Leave me!

GUIDO. How can I leave you now, darling?

SILIA. No, Guido, no! Not in the flat! I shouldn't like the maid to . . .

 There is a knock on the door, left.

There, you see?

GUIDO. Don't let her in. I'll wait for you in your room.

 He goes towards the door on the right.

But don't be long.

 He leaves, shutting the door. SILIA *goes to the other door, but before she reaches it,* CLARA *is heard shouting outside.*

CLARA. Take your hands off me. Go away! She doesn't live here!

 The door bursts open and MARQUIS MIGLIORITI *enters with three other 'young-men-about-town', all in evening*

*dress. They are very drunk, very high spirited, and very
determined to enter.*

MIGLIORITI. Out of the way, you old owl. What do you mean
by saying she doesn't live here, when she's here all the time.

1st DRUNK. Lovely Pepita! The gay senorita!

2nd DRUNK. Viva Espana. Viva Espana.

3rd DRUNK (*not so stupidly drunk as the others*). I say, fellows.
Just look at this flat! *C'est tout a fait charmant!*

SILIA (*to* CLARA) What's the meaning of this? Who are they?
How did they get in?

CLARA. They forced their way in, Signora. They're drunk.

MIGLIORITI (*to* CLARA). Some force, eh! You old owl!

1st DRUNK. Some drunks!

2nd DRUNK. Georgeously drunk drunks!

MIGLIORITI (*to* SILIA). But you invited me, Senorita! You
dropped an egg shell on me from the window!

2nd DRUNK. D'you know what we are? We are four gentlemen!

1st DRUNK. Caballeros!

3rd DRUNK (*pointing to the dining room and then going into it*)
I wonder if a client gets a drink here? (*He notices the
decanters on the table.*) Ah, we're in luck! *C'est tout a fait
delicieux!*

SILIA (*noting the implications of the word 'client'*). Good Lord!
What do they want?

CLARA (*to* MIGLIORITI). How dare you! This is a respectable
house!

MIGLIORITI. But of course, we know that. (*to* SILIA:)
Charming Pepita!

SILIA. Pepita!?

CLARA. Yes, Signorina . . . that woman next door. I kept telling
them this wasn't her flat.

> SILIA *bursts out laughing. Then a sinister light comes into
> her eyes, as though a diabolical idea has come into her
> head.*

SILIA: Why yes, of course, gentlemen, I am Pepita.

2nd DRUNK. Viva Espana. Viva Pepita!

SILIA (*to all three*). Do sit down, won't you? Or perhaps you'd
 rather join your friend in there for a drink?

MIGLIORITI (*attempting to kiss her*). No, I . . . well, really . . .
 I'd rather . . .

SILIA (*evades him*). Rather what?

MIGLIORITI. I'd rather drink *you* first!

SILIA. Wait! Wait a moment!

2nd DRUNK (*imitating MIGLIORITI'S actions*). Me too, Pepita!

SILIA (*warding him off*). You too? All right . . . steady now.

2nd DRUNK. What we want is an ab-sho-lutely Spanish night!

1st DRUNK. Personally, I don't actually propose to do anything,
 but . . .

SILIA. Yes, all right . . . all right . . . steady now. Now come and
 sit down over here, boys.

> *She frees herself and pushes them towards chairs, making
> them sit down.*

That's right . . . fine! That's it.

> *They mutter among themselves.* SILIA *runs to* CLARA *and
> whispers,*

SILIA. Go upstairs and fetch some of the neighbours. Downstairs
 too. Hurry!

> CLARA *nods and runs off.*
> GUIDO *starts to open the bedroom door.*

SILIA (*to* MIGLIORITI *and the others*). Excuse me a minute . . .

> *She goes to the door on the right and locks it to prevent*
> GUIDO *from coming in.*

MIGLIORITI (*rising unsteadily*). Oh, if you've got a gentleman
 in there already, carry on you know, don't mind us!

2nd DRUNK. No, don't mind us, carry on — carry on — we don't
 mind waiting.

1st DRUNK. Personally, I don't actually propose to do anything
 but . . . (*He tries to get up.*)

SILIA (*to* MIGLIORITI *and the* 1st DRUNK). Don't get up!
 Stay where you are. (*To all three:*) Listen — you gentlemen are

quite . . . I mean, you know what you are doing, don't you?

ALL. Of course! Absolutely. Of course we do. Why shouldn't we? Know what we're doing, indeed!

SILIA. And you don't for a moment suspect that you are in a respectable house, do you?

3rd DRUNK (*staggering in from the dining room with a glass in his hand*). Oh, *oui . . . mais . . . n'exagere pas, mon petit chou! Nous voulons nous amuser un peu . . . Voila tout,* my little cabbage!

SILIA. But your little cabbage is at home only to friends. Now, if you want to be friends . . .

2nd DRUNK. *Mais certainement*!

1st DRUNK. Intimate friends! (*He tries to rise and bow, then subsides, muttering* 'Dear little Pepita! Lovely little Pepita! *etc.*)

SILIA. Then please tell me your names.

2nd DRUNK. My name is Coco.

SILIA. No . . . not like that . . .

2nd DRUNK. Honestly, my name is Coco.

1st DRUNK. And mine is Meme.

SILIA. No, no! I mean, will you give me your visiting cards?

2nd DRUNK. Oh no, no, no! Thank you very much, sweetheart.

1st DRUNK. I haven't got one . . . I've lost my wallet . . . (*To* MIGLIORITI:) Be a good chap, and give her one for me.

SILIA (*sweetly — to* MIGLIORITI) Yes, you're the nicest. You'll give me yours, won't you?

MIGLIORITI (*taking out his wallet*). Certainly. I have no objection.

2nd DRUNK. He can give you cards for all of us . . . *Voila*!

MIGLIORITI. Here you are, Pepita.

SILIA. Oh thank you. Good. (*She reads it.*) So you are Marquis Miglioriti?

1st DRUNK (*laughing*). That's right - he's a Marquis . . . But only a little one!

SILIA (*to* 2nd DRUNK). And you are Meme?

1st DRUNK. No, I'm Meme. (*Pointing to* 2nd DRUNK:) He's Coco.

SILIA. Oh yes, of course. Coco — Meme (*To the* 3rd DRUNK:) And you?

3rd DRUNK (*with a silly, sly look*). Moi? Moi . . . *Je ne sais pas, mon petit chou.*

SILIA. Well, it doesn't matter. One is enough.

2nd DRUNK. But we all want to be in it. We all want . . .

3rd DRUNK. . . . an absolutely Spanish night!

1st DRUNK. Personally, I don't actually propose to do anything, but I should love to see you dance, Pepita . . . You know, with castanets . . . Ta trrrra ti ta ti, ta trrra ti ta ti . . . (*He breaks into 'Habanera' from the opera Carmen.*)

2nd DRUNK. Yes, yes. Dance first . . . And *then* . . .

MIGLIORITI. But not dressed like that!

3rd DRUNK. Why dressed at all, gentlemen?

2nd DRUNK (*rising and staggering up to* SILIA). Yes, that's right! Without a stitch!

> MIGLIORITI *and the others crowd round* SILIA *as if to strip her.*

ALL. Yes, stripped . . . in the altogether. That's the idea! Splendid! Without a stitch. Splendid!

SILIA (*freeing herself*). But not in here, gentlemen, please. Naked, if you like. But not here.

3rd DRUNK. Where then?

SILIA. Down in the square.

MIGLIORITI (*very still, sobering up a little*). In the square?

1st DRUNK (*quietly*). Naked in the square?

SILIA. Of course! Why not? It's the ideal place. The moon is shining — there won't be anyone about . . . just the statue of the king on horseback. And you four gentlemen . . . in evening dress.

> At this point tenants of the floors above and below rush in with CLARA, *shouting confusedly. One elderly gentleman holds a little riding crop in his hand as a weapon.*

THE TENANTS. What's the matter? What's happened? Who are they? What's going on here? What have they done to her? Has she been assaulted?

CLARA. There they are! There they are!

SILIA (*suddenly changing her tone and demeanour*). I've been assaulted! Assaulted in my own home! They forced their way in, knocked me down, and pulled me about, as you can see. They've molested me and insulted me in every possible way, the cowards!

A TENANT (*trying to chase them out*). Get out of here! Get out!

A TENANT. Stand back! Leave her alone!

A TENANT. Come along! Get out of here.

1st DRUNK. All right! Keep calm! Keep calm!

A TENANT. Go on! Get out!

A WOMAN TENANT. What scoundrels.

MIGLIORITI. Well, this is an open house isn't it? Anybody can come in, surely?

1st DRUNK. Spain is doing a brisk trade!

A WOMAN TENANT. Well . . . Really!!!

A WOMAN TENANT. Get out, you disgusting drunken lot, you!

3rd DRUNK. Oh, I say, there's no need to make such a fuss, you know.

MIGLIORITI. Dear Pepita. . .

A TENANT. Pepita?

A WOMAN TENANT. Pepita! This isn't Pepita, young man. This is Signora Gala.

A TENANT. Of course. Signora Gala.

MIGLIORITI & the 3 DRUNKS. Signora Gala.

3rd DRUNK. No Pepita?

A TENANT. Certainly not! Signora Gala.

A WOMAN TENANT. You ought to be ashamed of yourselves. Good for nothing, drunken hooligans, that's what you are!

2nd DRUNK. Oh, well . . . In that case, we'll apologise to the Signora for our mistake.

ALL THE TENANTS. Go along now! Get out! Leave this place at once!

1st DRUNK. *Doucement . . . doucement, s'il vous plait!*

2nd DRUNK. We thought she was Pepita.

3rd DRUNK. Yes, and we wanted to do homage to Spain. To-reador, tum, tum-ti, tumti, tummm . . . (*He starts to sing Habanera again*).

A TENANT. That's quite enough, now! Get out!

2nd DRUNK. No! First we must beg the Signora's pardon.

A TENANT. Stop it. That'll do now. Go home.

MIGLIORITI. Yes — very well. But, look here, all of you, look here. (*He kneels in front of* SILIA.) Down on our knees, we offer you our humble apologies.

ALL DRUNKS. That's right . . . on our knees. Go on, Coco . . . down you go . . . etc.

SILIA. Oh, no! That's not good enough. Marquis, I have your name, and you and your friends will have to answer for the outrage you have done to me in my own home.

MIGLIORITI. But, Signora — if we beg your pardon . . .

SILIA. I accept no apologies.

MIGLIORITI (*rising, much sobered*). Very well. You have my card . . . and I'm quite ready to answer —

SILIA. Now get out of my flat — at once!

> The FOUR DRUNKS, *who nevertheless feel compelled to bow, are driven out by the* TENANTS, *and accompanied to the door by* CLARA.

(*to the* TENANTS:) Thank you all very much indeed. I'm awfully sorry to have bothered you all.

A TENANT. Not at all, Signora Gala.

A TENANT. Don't mention it.

A WOMAN TENANT. After all, we're neighbours — and if neighbours don't help each other . . .

A TENANT. What scoundrels!

A WOMAN TENANT. We can't be safe even in our homes these days.

A TENANT. But perhaps, Signora Gala — seeing that they begged your pardon. . .

SILIA. Oh, no! They were told several times that this was a respectable place, and in spite of that . . . Really, you wouldn't believe the improper suggestions they dared to make to me.

A TENANT. Yes, you were quite right to take no excuses, Signora Gala.

A TENANT. Oh, you've done the right thing, there's no doubt about that.

A TENANT. They must be given a good lesson. You poor dear! Horsewhipping would be too good for them.

SILIA. I know the name of one of them. He gave me his card.

A TENANT. Who is he?

SILIA (*showing the card*). Marquis Aldo Miglioriti.

A WOMAN TENANT. Oh! Marquis Miglioriti!

A WOMAN TENANT. A Marquis!

ALL. He ought to be ashamed of himself! Disgraceful! A marquis
to behave like that! That makes his behaviour all the worse!
(*etc.*)

SILIA. You agree then that I had every right to be annoyed?

A WOMAN TENANT. Oh, yes! You're perfectly justified in
teaching them a lesson, Signora Gala.

A WOMAN TENANT. They must be shown up, Signora. Shown
up!

A TENANT. And punished!

A TENANT. They ought to be publicly disgraced!

A TENANT. But don't be too upset, Signora Gala.

A WOMAN TENANT. You ought to rest a little.

A WOMAN TENANT. Yes. It would do you good . . . after such
an experience!

A WOMAN TENANT. Yes, we'll leave you now, dear.

ALL TENANTS. Good-night, Signora Gala . . . (*etc.*)

> *They leave.*

> *As soon as the* TENANTS *have gone,* SILIA *looks radiantly
> at* MIGLIORITI'S *card, and laughs with gleeful, excited and
> malicious triumph. Meanwhile* GUIDO *is hammering on the
> door, right, with his fists.*

SILIA. All right! All right! All right! I'm coming!

> SILIA *runs and unlocks the door.*
> GUIDO, *trembling with rage and indignation.*

GUIDO. Why did you lock me in? I was longing to get my hands
on them. My God, if I could only have got at those ruffians!

SILIA. Oh, yes, it only needed you to come dashing to my
defence out of my bedroom to compromise me and . . . (*With
a mad glint in her eyes*:) . . . spoil everything! (*Showing him*
MIGLIORITI'S *card*:) Look. I've got it! I've got it!

GUIDO. What?

SILIA. One of their visiting cards!

GUIDO (*reading it — with surprise*). Marquis Miglioriti? I know him well. But what do you propose to do?

SILIA. I've got it, and I'm going to give it to my husband!

GUIDO. To Leone? (*He looks at her in terrified astonishment.*) But, Silia!

He tries to take the card from her.

SILIA (*preventing him*). I want to see if I can't cause him (*Sarcastically*:) just the 'slightest little bit of bother.'

GUIDO. But do you realise who this man is?

SILIA. Marquis Aldo Miglioriti.

GUIDO. Silia, listen to me! For goodness sake get this idea out of your head.

SILIA. I'll do nothing of the sort. *You* needn't worry. He'll realise that my lover couldn't possibly have come forward to defend me.

GUIDO. No, no, Silia, I tell you. You mustn't! I'll stop you at all costs!

SILIA. You'll stop nothing! In the first place, you can't . . .

GUIDO. Yes I can, and will! You'll see!

SILIA. We'll see about that tomorrow. (*Imperiously*:) I've had enough of this. I'm tired.

GUIDO (*in a threatening tone*). Very well. I'm going.

SILIA (*imperiously*). No! (*She pauses, then changes her tone.*) Come here, Guido!

GUIDO (*not altering his attitude, but going nearer to her*). What do you want?

SILIA. I want . . . I want you to stop being such a silly spoil-sport.

Pause. She laughs to herself, remembering.

Those poor boys! You know, I really did treat them rather badly.

GUIDO. As a matter of fact you did. After all, they admitted they'd made a mistake. And they begged your pardon.

SILIA (*curt and imperious again, admitting no discussion on the point*). That'll do, I tell you. I don't want to hear any more about that. I'm thinking of how funny they looked, poor boys. (*With a sigh of heart-felt envy*:) Such wonderful fantasies men get hold of at night! What fun they have! Moonlight, and . . . Do you know, Guido, they wanted to see me dance . . . in the square . . . (*Very softly, almost in his ear*:) Naked.

GUIDO. Silia!!!

SILIA (*leaning her head back and tickling his face with her hair*). Guido . . . do you remember calling me a wayward child? (*Seductively*:) I want to be your wayward child.

GUIDO (*embracing her*). Silia . . .

Curtain

Act Two

A room in LEONE GALA'S *flat.*

It is an unusual room, fitted up to be at the same time a dining-room and a study. There is a dining table laid for lunch — and a writing desk covered with books, papers and writing material. There are glass-fronted cabinets filled with sumptuous silver epergnes and cruets, a fine porcelain dinner service, and valuable wine glasses — and bookshelves lined with solid-looking volumes. In fact, all the furniture accentuates the dual function of the room, with the exception of a third, occasional table on which there are a vase of flowers, a cigar box and an ash tray.

At the back, a door connects this room with LEONE'S *bedroom.*

To the left, a door leads to the kitchen.

To the right is the main door into the room from the hall.

Time: The next morning.

When the curtain rises, LEONE, *in cook's cap and apron is busy beating an egg in a bowl with a wooden spoon.* PHILIP, *also dressed as a cook, is beating another.* GUIDO VENANZI, *seated, is listening to* LEONE.

LEONE. Yes, my dear Venanzi, he's so rude to me sometimes. You must wonder why I put up with him.

PHILIP (*surly and bored*). Don't talk so much — and carry on beating that egg.

LEONE. Do you hear that, Venanzi? Anyone would think he was the master and I the servant. But he amuses me. Philip is my 'tame devil.'

PHILIP. I wish the devil would fly away with you.

LEONE. Tt, tt . . . Now he's swearing. You see? I can hardly talk to him!

PHILIP. There's no need to talk. Keep quiet.

LEONE *laughs*.

GUIDO. Really, Socrates!

PHILIP. Now, don't *you* start calling me Socrates. I've had enough of it from the master. To hell with Socrates. I don't even know who he is.

LEONE. What! (*Laughing*:) You don't know him?

PHILIP. No, Signore! And I don't want to have anything to do with him. Keep an eye on that egg.

LEONE. All right! I'm watching it.

PHILIP. How are you beating it?

LEONE. With a spoon, of course.

PHILIP. Yes, yes! But which side of the spoon are you using?

LEONE. Oh, the back. Don't worry!

PHILIP. You'll poison that gentleman at lunch, I tell you, if you don't stop chattering.

GUIDO. No, no, Philip. Let him go on. I'm enjoying myself.

LEONE. I'm emptying him out of himself a bit, to give him an appetite.

PHILIP. But you're disturbing *me*.

LEONE (*laughing*). And 'me' is the only one who matters! Now we've come to the point!

PHILIP. You've hit it. What are you doing now?

LEONE. What am I doing?

PHILIP. Go on beating that egg, for goodness' sake! You mustn't slacken or you'll ruin it.

LEONE. All right, all right!

PHILIP. Have I got to keep my eyes on what he's doing, my ears on what he's saying, and my mind — that's already in a whirl — on all the tomfoolery that comes out of his mouth? I'm off to the kitchen!

LEONE. No, Philip — don't be a fool. Stay here. I'll be quiet. (*To* GUIDO, *sotto voce, but so that* PHILIP *can hear*:) He used not to be like this. Bergson has done for him.

PHILIP. Now he's trotting out that Bergson again!

LEONE. Yes, and why not? (*To* GUIDO:) D'you know, Venanzi,

since I expounded to him Bergson's theory of intuition, he's become a different man. He used to be a powerful thinker . . .

PHILIP. I've never been a thinker, for your information! And if you go on like this, I'll drop everything here and leave you, once and for all. Then you'll really be in the soup!

LEONE (*to* GUIDO). You see? And I'm not allowed to say Bergson has ruined him! Mark you, I quite agree with what you say about his views on reason . . .

PHILIP. Well, if you agree there's nothing more to be said! Beat that egg!

LEONE. I'm beating it, I'm beating it! But listen a moment: according to Bergson, anything in reality that is fluid, living, mobile and indeterminate, lies beyond the scope of reason . . . (*To* GUIDO, *as though in parenthesis*:) though how it manages to escape reason, I don't know, seeing that Bergson is able to say it does. What makes him say so if it isn't his reason? And in that case, it seems to me it can't be *beyond* reason. What do you say?

PHILIP. Beat that egg! (*He is exasperated.*)

LEONE. I am beating it, can't you see? Listen Venanzi . . .

GUIDO. Oh, do stop calling me by surname; everyone calls me Guido.

LEONE (*with a strange smile*). I prefer to think of you as Venanzi. Anyway, listen: it's a fine game reason plays with Bergson, making him think she has been dethroned and slighted by him, to the infinite delight of all the feather-brained philosophising females in Paris! He maintains that reason can consider only the identical and constant aspects and characteristics of matter. She has geometrical and mechanical habits. Reality is a ceaseless flow of perpetual newness, which reason breaks down into so many static and homogeneous particles . . .

> During this speech, LEONE, *as he gets worked up, gradually forgets his egg-beating, and finally stops.* PHILIP *always watching him and beating his own egg, approaches him stealthily.*

PHILIP (*leaning forward and almost shouting at him*). And what are you doing now?

LEONE (*with a start, beginning to beat again*). Right you are!
I'm beating the egg! Look!

PHILIP. You're not concentrating! All this talk about reason is
taking your mind off what you're supposed to be doing.

LEONE. How impatient you are, my dear fellow! I'm perfectly
well aware of the necessity of beating eggs. (*He beats rapidly.*)
As you see, I accept and obey this necessity. But am I not
allowed to use my mind for anything else?

GUIDO (*laughing*). You really are wonderful! The pair of you!

LEONE. No, no! You're wrong there! I'm wonderful if you like.
But *he*, for a long time now — since he has been corrupted by
Bergson, in fact . . .

PHILIP. No one has corrupted me, if you don't mind!

LEONE. Oh yes, my dear chap! You've become so deplorably
human that I don't recognise you any more.

> PHILIP *is about to remonstrate.*

LEONE. Do let me finish what I'm saying, for goodness' sake.
We must have a little more emptiness to make room for all this
batter. Look! I've filled the bowl with my energetic beating!

> *There is a loud ring at the front door.* PHILIP *puts down
> his bowl and goes towards the door on the right.*

LEONE (*putting down his bowl*). Wait. Wait. Come here. Untie
this apron for me first.

> PHILIP *does so.*

And take this into the kitchen too. (*He takes off his cap and
gives it to* PHILIP.)

PHILIP. You've done it an honour, I must say!

> *He goes off to the left, leaving the apron and cap in the
> kitchen, and returns a moment later, during the ensuing
> conversation between* LEONE *and* GUIDO, *to collect the
> two bowls of batter and take them into the kitchen. He
> forgets to answer the bell.*

> GUIDO *gets up, very worried and perplexed at the sound*

of the bell.)

GUIDO. Did . . . did someone ring?

LEONE (*noting his perturbation*). Yes. Why? What's the matter?

GUIDO. Good God, Leone. It must be Silia.

LEONE. Silia? Here?

GUIDO. Yes. Listen, for heaven's sake. I came early like this, to tell you . . . (*He hesitates.*)

LEONE. What?

GUIDO. About something that happened last night . . .

LEONE. To Silia?

GUIDO. Yes, but it's nothing, really. Just something rather silly. That's why I haven't said anything to you. I hoped that after sleeping on it she would have forgotten all about it.

Renewed, louder ringing at the door.

GUIDO. But there she is — that must be Silia!

LEONE (*calmly, turning towards the door on the left*). Socrates! For goodness' sake go and open the door!

GUIDO. Just a minute. (*To* PHILIP, *as he enters*). Wait! (*To* LEONE:) I warn you, Leone, that your wife intends to do something really crazy . . .

LEONE. That's nothing new!

GUIDO. . . . at *your* expense. She wants to make you suffer for it.

LEONE. Make me suffer, eh? (*To* PHILIP:) Let her in. Go and open the door! (*To* GUIDO:) My dear Venanzi, my wife is always sure of a welcome when she comes to visit me on that sort of business!

PHILIP, *more irritated than ever, goes to open the door.*

GUIDO. But you don't know what it is!

LEONE. It doesn't matter what it is! Let her go ahead. You'll see! Remember what I do with the egg? I catch it, I pierce it, and I suck the yolk out of it.

GUIDO. Oh, damn your eggs!

SILIA *enters like a whirlwind.*

SILIA. Oh, so you're here, Guido! I suppose you came to warn him.

SILIA (*looking closely at* LEONE). I can see he knows.

LEONE. I don't know anything. (*Assuming a light, gay tone*:) Good morning!

SILIA (*quivering with rage*). Good morning, indeed! If you've told him Guido, I'll never . . .

LEONE. No, no, Silia. You can say what you've come to say without any fear of losing the effect of complete surprise you've been looking forward to. He's told me nothing. However, go out if you like, and make your entry again, in order to come upon me unexpectedly.

SILIA. Look here, Leone, I've not come here for fun! (*To* GUIDO:) What are you doing here, then?

GUIDO. Well, I came . . .

LEONE. Tell her the truth. He came to warn me, sure enough, of some crazy plan or other of yours.

SILIA (*exploding*). Crazy plan, you call it!

GUIDO. Yes, Silia.

LEONE. But he hasn't told me. I must admit I wasn't really interested to know.

GUIDO. I hoped you wouldn't come here . . .

LEONE. . . . so he didn't say a word about it, you see!

SILIA. How do you know it's 'one of my crazy plans,' then?

LEONE. Oh, that I could imagine for myself. But, really . . .

GUIDO. I did tell him that much — that it was a crazy plan! And I stick to it!

SILIA (*exasperated to the utmost*). Will you keep quiet! No one has given you the right to criticise the way I feel about things! (*She pauses, then, turning to* LEONE, *as though shooting him in the chest*:) You've been challenged!

LEONE. I've been challenged?

GUIDO. Impossible.

SILIA. Yes, you have.

LEONE. Who has challenged me?

GUIDO. It's impossible, I tell you.

SILIA. Well, I don't really know whether he's challenged you, or whether you have to challenge him. I don't understand these things. But I do know that I've got the wretched man's card . . . (*She takes it out of her bag.*) Here it is. (*She gives it to*

LEONE.) You must get dressed at once, and go and find two seconds.

LEONE. Hold on. Not so fast!

SILIA. No, you must do it now. Don't pay any attention to what *he* says! He only wants to make you think this is 'one of my crazy plans' because that would suit him.

LEONE. Oh, it would suit him, would it?

GUIDO (*furiously indignant*). What do you mean?

SILIA. Of course it suits you to put that idea into his head. Otherwise you'd still be making the same excuses for that . . . that scoundrel!

LEONE (*looking at the card*). Who is he?

GUIDO. Marquis Aldo Miglioriti.

LEONE. Do you know him?

GUIDO. Very well indeed. He's one of the best swordsmen in town.

SILIA. Ah, so that's why!

GUIDO (*pale, quavering*). That's why what? What do you mean?

SILIA (*As though to herself, scornfully, disdainfully*). That's why! That's why!

LEONE. Am I going to be allowed to know what's happened? Why should I be challenged? Or why should I challenge anybody?

SILIA (*in a rush*). Because I've been insulted, and outraged and indecently assaulted — in my own home, too! And all through you — because I was alone and defenceless! Grossly insulted! They put their hands on me, and mauled me about — (*touching her breast:*) here, do you understand? Because they thought I was . . . Oh! (*She covers her face with her hands and breaks out in harsh, convulsive sobs of shame and rage*).

LEONE. But I don't understand. Did this Marquis . . .

SILIA. There were four of them. You saw them yourself as you were leaving the house.

LEONE. Oh, those four men who were by the front door?

SILIA. Yes. They came up and forced the door.

GUIDO. But they were tight. They didn't know what they were doing!

LEONE (*his voice heavy with mock astonishment*). Hello! Were you still there?

> *The question puts* SILIA *and* GUIDO *at a loss. There is a pause.*

GUIDO. Yes . . . but . . . I wasn't . . .

SILIA (*suddenly plucking up courage again, aggressively*). Why should he have protected me? Was it his job to do so when my husband had just that very moment turned his back, leaving me exposed to the attack of four ruffians, who, if Guido had come forward . . .

GUIDO (*interrupting*). I was in the . . . next room, you see, and . . .

SILIA. In the dining-room . . .

LEONE (*very calmly*). Having another liqueur?

SILIA (*in a furious outburst*). But do you know what they said to me? They said, 'If you've got a gentleman in there, carry on, don't mind us.' It only needed him to show himself, for me to be finally compromised! Thank goodness he had enough sense to realise that and keep out of sight!

LEONE. I understand, I understand! But I am surprised, Silia, — more than surprised — absolutely amazed to find that your pretty little head could ever have been capable of such clear discernment!

SILIA (*tonelessly, not understanding*). What discernment?

LEONE. Why, that it was up to *me* to protect you, because, after all, I am your husband, while Venanzi here . . . If he had attempted to stop those four drunks . . . By the way, he must have been more than a little drunk himself . . .

GUIDO. Nonsense! I tell you I didn't come in because I thought it more discreet not to!

LEONE. And you were quite right not to, my dear chap! What is so wonderful is that that pretty little head was able to understand that 'discretion' of yours, and could grasp that you would have compromised her if you had shown yourself. So she didn't call you to her aid, though she was being attacked by four dangerous drunks!

SILIA (*quickly, almost childishly*). They were crowding round me, all of them, clutching at me and trying to tear my clothes off . . .

LEONE (*to* GUIDO). And yet she actually managed to think
matters out calmly and decide that this was something which
concerned me! That is such a miracle that I am absolutely
ready, here and now, to do without further delay, everything
that can be expected of me!

GUIDO (*quickly*). What? You'll do it?

SILIA (*stupefied, turning pale, hardly believing her ears*). Do you
mean that?

LEONE (*softly and calmly, smiling*). Of course I'll do it!
Naturally! I'm sorry, but you're not logical!

GUIDO (*in a stupor*). Who? Me?

LEONE. Yes, you, you! Don't you see that my doing it is the
exact and inevitable consequence of your 'discretion?'

SILIA (*triumphant*). You can't deny that's true!

GUIDO. How? (*Bewildered:*) I don't understand. Why is it the
consequence of my discretion?

LEONE (*gravely*). Just think a bit! If she was outraged like this,
and you were quite right to act so discreetly, it obviously
follows that I must be the one to issue the challenge!

GUIDO. Not at all. Not at all. Because my discretion was due to
. . . because . . . because I realized that I should have had to
deal with four men who were so drunk that they didn't know
what they were doing!

SILIA. That's a lie!

GUIDO. Listen, Leone. They were drunk and they mistook the
door. Anyway, they apologized.

SILIA. I didn't accept their apologies. It's easy to make excuses
afterwards. I couldn't accept. But by the way Guido's talking
anybody would think they had apologized to him! As though
he was the one who'd been insulted! While all the time he kept
himself well out of it, 'because he thought it would be more
discreet!'

LEONE (*to* GUIDO). There! Now you're spoiling everything,
my dear fellow.

SILIA. It was *me* they insulted. Me!

LEONE (*to* GUIDO). It was her. (*To* SILIA:) And you immediately
thought of your husband, didn't you? (*To* GUIDO:) I'm
sorry Venanzi. It's obvious you don't think things out properly.

GUIDO (*exasperated, noting* SILIA'S *perfidy*). Why should I think things out? I kept out of it last night, and you can leave me out of it now!

LEONE (*conceding the point and continuing in the same solemn tone*). Yet you were right, you know, quite right to say that you would have compromised her. But not because they were drunk! That might, if anything, be an excuse for *me* . . . a reason why I should not challenge them, and call upon them to make amends for their behaviour . . .

SILIA (*dismayed*). What?

LEONE (*quickly*). I said 'if anything', don't worry! (*To* GUIDO:) But it can't possibly be an excuse for your discretion, because . . . well, if they were drunk you could perfectly well have been less 'discreet.'

SILIA. Of course he could! Men in their condition wouldn't have been shocked to find me entertaining a man in my flat. It wasn't yet midnight, after all!

GUIDO (*roused*). Good Lord, Silia. Now you have the impertinence to suggest I ought to have done what you prevented!

LEONE (*precipitately*). No, no, no, no! He acted quite rightly — you said so yourself, Silia. Just as *you* were right to think of me! After all, Venanzi, when a lady is being assaulted by drunks, her mental processes may be a little unpredictable. No, you both acted perfectly correctly.

GUIDO. Look, just leave me out of it, will you? There isn't one consistent argument in the whole affair.

LEONE. That's where you're wrong, my dear friend. Silia's behaviour was perfectly consistent. After all, I am her husband — just as she is still my wife. And you . . . Why, of course, you are going to be 'The Second'.

GUIDO (*exploding*). Oh no, I'm not! You can get that idea out of your head!

LEONE. Why not, pray?

GUIDO. Because I flatly refuse!

LEONE. You do?

GUIDO. Yes.

LEONE. But you are bound to accept. You can't help yourself.

GUIDO. I tell you I won't do it.

SILIA (*bitingly*). Another sample of his 'discretion.'

GUIDO (*exasperated*). Silia!!!

LEONE (*conciliating*). Come now, please! Let us discuss the matter calmly. (*To* GUIDO:) Now, Venanzi, do you deny that everybody calls upon your services in affairs of honour? Not a month passes without your having a duel on your hands. Why, you're a professional second! Come now, it would be ridiculous. What would people say — those who know you're such a close friend of mine and so experienced in these matters — if I, of all people, should turn to someone else!

GUIDO. There's absolutely no occasion for a duel at all.

LEONE. That's not for you to say!

GUIDO. Well, I'm saying it. I'm not going to do it.

SILIA. I forced that man to leave me his card, and I showed it to everybody.

LEONE. Oh? The entertainment had an audience then?

SILIA. They heard me shouting for help. And they all said it would be a good thing to teach the Marquis a lesson.

LEONE (*to* GUIDO). There! You see! A public scandal! (*To* SILIA:) You're right! (*To* GUIDO:) Come, come. It's no use arguing, my dear chap. Besides, you have so much experience in these affairs. Everyone calls upon your services when they want a second.

> GUIDO *gives up the position he has been maintaining, in the hope of getting on the right side of* SILIA *once more.*

GUIDO. Oh, all right then! I'll cart you off to the slaughter, if you insist!

SILIA (*beginning to think better of it, since she finds herself left alone*). Oh, Guido! Don't exaggerate now!

GUIDO. To the slaughter, Silia! He will have it, so I shall take him off to the slaughter.

LEONE. No . . . Really, you know, my wishes don't come into it. You're the one who *will* have it.

SILIA. But it isn't necessary to fight a duel to the death.

GUIDO. That's where you are wrong, Silia. You either fight or you don't fight. If there is a duel, it has to be fought in deadly earnest.

LEONE. Of course, of course!

SILIA. Why?

GUIDO. Because the mere fact of my going to demand a meeting would show that we don't consider they were drunk.

LEONE. Quite right.

GUIDO. And the insult they did to you becomes doubly serious.

LEONE. Exactly.

SILIA. But it's up to you to suggest the terms — and you can make them easier.

GUIDO. How can I?

LEONE. Quite right. (*To* SILIA:) He can't.

GUIDO. Moreover, if Miglioriti finds we are making no allowance for the state he was in, or for his apology . . .

LEONE. Yes, yes!

GUIDO. . . . he'll be so angry . . .

LEONE. Naturally enough!

GUIDO. . . . that he'll insist on the severest possible terms!

LEONE. It will seem a great provocation to him — a swordsman!

GUIDO. One of our best swordsmen, as I told you. Consider that point very carefully! And you don't even know what a sword looks like!

LEONE. That's your worry. You don't expect me to concern myself with details like that, do you?

GUIDO. What do you mean, my worry?

LEONE. Because I'm certainly not going to worry about it.

GUIDO. You mean . . . It's my responsibility . . . to . . .

LEONE. It's all yours! And a very serious one. I feel sorry for you. But you must play your part, just as I am playing mine. It's all in the game. Even Silia has grasped that! Each of us must play his part through to the end. And you may rest assured that I shan't budge from my anchorage, come what may! I'm watching us all play our roles — and I find it vastly entertaining.

> *The doorbell rings again.* PHILIP *enters from the left. He crosses the stage in a furious temper and goes out to the right.*

All that interests me is to get the whole thing over quickly.

You go ahead and arrange everything . . . Oh, by the way,
do you need any money?

GUIDO. Money? Good Lord, no! Why?

LEONE. I've been told these affairs are expensive.

GUIDO. Well, we'll go into that later. Not now.

LEONE. Very well, we'll settle up afterwards.

GUIDO. Will Barelli suit you as a witness?

LEONE. Oh, yes . . . Barelli . . . or anyone you please.

PHILIP *comes in again with* DR SPIGA.

Ah — Doctor Spiga. Come in, come in! (*To* GUIDO *who has
approached* SILIA *and is pale and agitated*:) Look, Venanzi,
we've even got the Doctor here. How convenient!

GUIDO. Good morning, Doctor.

LEONE. If you have confidence in him . . .

GUIDO. But really . . .

LEONE. He's a good chap, you know. First rate surgeon. But I
don't want to put him to too much trouble, so I'm wondering
— (*He turns to* GUIDO *who is talking to* SILIA). I say, do
listen! You've left us standing here like a couple of hermits in
the wilderness! I was going to say, the orchard is conveniently
near, we could do it there, early tomorrow morning.

GUIDO. Yes, all right, leave it to me, leave it to me! Don't interfere! (*He bows to* SILIA.) Good-bye, Doctor. (*To* LEONE:)
I'll be back soon. No, wait, though! I shall have a lot to do. I'll
send Barelli to you. I'll see you this evening. Good-bye.

He goes out to the right.

SPIGA. What's all this about?

PHILIP. I say, don't you think it's about time . . .

LEONE. One moment, Socrates. Come over here, Spiga. First, let
me introduce you to my wife . . .

SPIGA (*puzzled*). Oh, but . . .

LEONE (*to* SILIA). Doctor Spiga, my friend, fellow tenant, and
intrepid opponent in philosophical arguments!

SPIGA. Charmed, Signora. (*To* LEONE:) So, you two have . . .
(*'Made up' is understood.*) . . . Well, I congratulate you; though,
no doubt, to me it will mean the loss of a valued companionship

to which I had become accustomed.

LEONE. Oh, no! What are you thinking?

SPIGA. That you and your wife have . . .

LEONE. A reconciliation? But my dear fellow! We've never quarrelled. We live in perfect harmony — apart!

SPIGA. Oh . . . Well, in that case, I beg your pardon. I . . . I must confess I couldn't see what my being a surgeon had to do with a reconciliation.

PHILIP *comes forward, unable to contain any longer his furious indignation against his master.*

PHILIP. It has a lot to do with it, Doctor. And your surgery is only one of the absurd, mad things that go on here!

LEONE. Really, Philip, I . . .

PHILIP. Oh, I'm off, I'm off! I'm leaving you right here and now!

He goes to the kitchen, slamming the door.

LEONE. Spiga, go with him and try to calm him, will you? Bergson, my dear fellow, Bergson! Disastrous effect! As you said when I gave him the book, 'Once he starts studying logic and reason, there'll be no living with him'.

SPIGA *laughs, then, pushed by* LEONE *towards the door on the left, turns to bow to* SILIA, *then looks at* LEONE.

SPIGA. But I still don't see how my surgery comes into it!

LEONE. Go on, go on! He'll explain it to you!

SPIGA. Hm! (*He leaves*).

LEONE *goes to* SILIA *and stands behind the low chair in which she is sitting, absorbed. He leans over and looks down at her.*

LEONE (*gently*). Well, Silia? Have you something else to say to me?

SILIA (*speaking with difficulty*). I never . . . never imagined . . . that you . . .

LEONE. That I?

SILIA . . . would say 'yes'.

LEONE. You know very well that I have always said 'yes' to you.

> SILIA *jumps to her feet, a prey to the most disordered feelings. Irritation with her husband's docility, remorse for what she has done, disdain for the shuffling perfidy of her lover. She is distracted to the point of weeping.*

SILIA. I can't stand it! I can't stand it!

LEONE (*pretending not to understand*). What? My having said 'yes?'

SILIA. Yes, that too! Everything . . . all this . . . (*Alluding to GUIDO:*) It will be your fault if it turns out to Guido's advantage!

LEONE. My fault?

SILIA. Yes yours! Through your insufferable, limitless apathy!

LEONE. Do you mean apathy in general — or towards you?

SILIA. Your complete indifference, always! But especially now!

LEONE. You think he has taken advantage of it?

SILIA. Didn't you see him just now? Changing sides at every moment — but at the end, he still goes off to commit you to a duel.

LEONE. Aren't you being a little unfair to him?

SILIA. But I did tell him to try to make the terms easier, and not to go too far now . . .

LEONE But at first you egged him on.

SILIA. Because he denied everything!

LEONE. That's true. He did. But, you see, he thought your attitude mistaken.

SILIA. And you? What do you think?

LEONE (*with a shrug*). I agreed to the duel.

SILIA. I suppose you think I exaggerated, too. Perhaps I did a little — but that was only because of the way he behaved.

LEONE. But wasn't that what you wanted?

SILIA (*distracted*). Yes . . . No . . . Oh, I can hardly remember now what it was I did want!

LEONE. You see, Silia, you always let emotion get the upper hand.

SILIA (*after a pause, looking at him in stupefaction*). And you?

Still unmoved?

LEONE. You must allow me to protect myself as best I can.

SILIA. Do you really think this indifference of yours can help
you?

LEONE. Certainly! I know it can.

SILIA. But he's an expert swordsman!

LEONE. Let Signor Guido Venanzi worry about that! What does
it matter to me what this fellow is?

SILIA. You don't even know how to hold a sword!

LEONE. It would be useless to me. This indifference will be
weapon enough for me, be sure of that! There I have an
inexhaustible source of courage — not merely to face one
man, that's nothing — but to face the whole world, always.
I live in a realm where no anxieties can trouble me, my dear.
I don't have to worry about anything — not even death —
or life! Just look at the ridiculous absurdity of men and their
miserable, petty opinions! Don't you worry! I understand the
game.

The voice of PHILIP *is heard in the kitchen.*

PHILIP. Well, go in your birthday suit, then!

SPIGA *comes in, left.*

SPIGA (*as he enters*). In my birthday suit, indeed! Damned
insolence! Oh . . . I beg your pardon, Signora. Leone, that
manservant of yours is an absolute demon.

LEONE (*laughing*). What's the matter?

SPIGA. What's all this I hear about a duel? Are you really
involved in one?

LEONE. Do you find that difficult to believe?

SPIGA (*glancing at* SILIA, *embarrassed*). Well . . . er . . . no! To
tell you the truth, I really don't know what the devil that
fellow has been telling me. You've actually sent the challenge,
have you?

LEONE. Yes.

SPIGA. Because you considered . . .

LEONE . . . that I had to, of course. My wife has been insulted.

SPIGA (*to* SILIA). Oh, in that case — your pardon, Signora. I
didn't realise. I . . . I . . . won't interfere. (*To* LEONE:) As
a matter of fact, you know, I . . . I've never been present at
a duel!

LEONE. Neither have I. So that makes two of us. It will be a new
experience for you.

SPIGA. Yes, but . . . I mean . . . What about the formalities?
How should I dress, for example?

LEONE (*laughing*). Oh, now I understand! That's what you were
asking Socrates?

SPIGA. He told me to go naked. I shouldn't like to cut a poor
figure.

LEONE. My poor friend, I'm afraid I can't tell you what doctors
wear at duels. We'll ask Venanzi. He'll know.

SPIGA. And I must bring my surgical instruments, I suppose?

Philip *comes in from the left.*

LEONE. Certainly you must.

SPIGA. It's on . . . serious terms, Philip tells me.

LEONE. So it seems.

SPIGA. Swords?

LEONE. I believe so.

SPIGA. If I bring my little bag . . . That'll be enough, eh?

LEONE. Listen — it's going to take place only a stone's throw
away — in the orchard — so you can easily bring anything you
feel you may need.

The doorbell rings. PHILIP *leaves to answer it.*

SILIA. Surely that can't be Guido back so soon?

SPIGA. Venanzi? Oh, good. Then I can get him to tell me what I
should wear.

PHILIP *comes in again and crosses the stage towards the
door on the left.*

LEONE. Who was it?

PHILIP (*loudly, drily and with an ill grace*). I don't know. Some
man or other with a sword.

PHILIP goes to the kitchen. BARELLI enters, right, with two swords in a green baize cover under his arm, and a case containing a pair of pistols.

BARELLI. Good morning.

LEONE (*going to meet* BARELLI). Come in, come in, Barelli. What's all this arsenal for?

BARELLI (*indignantly puffing*). Oh, I say, you know, look here, my dear Leone: this is absolute madness! Sheer raving lunacy!

He sees LEONE *pointing to* SILIA.

Eh? What? What's that?

LEONE. May I introduce you to my wife? (*To* SILIA:) This is Barelli — a formidable marksman!

BARELLI (*bowing*). Signora.

LEONE (*to* BARELLI). Doctor Spiga.

BARELLI. How do you do?

SPIGA. Delighted. (*He shakes* BARELLI'S *hand, then, without releasing it, turns to* LEONE.) May I ask him?

LEONE. Not now. Later.

BARELLI. I've never heard of such a preposterous business in all my life. (*To* SILIA:) You must excuse me, Signora, but if I didn't say so I should be neglecting my plain duty. (*To* LEONE:) You don't mean to tell me you've actually sent an unconditional challenge?!

LEONE. What does that mean?

BARELLI. What!!! You've issued one without even knowing what it is?

LEONE. How on earth should I know anything about such matters!

SILIA. Please — what is an unconditional challenge?

BARELLI. One that can't be discussed. It gives us no chance to try and settle the difference without fighting. It's against all the rules and quite illegal — prohibited under the severest penalties. And there are those two maniacs with the terms fixed up already — almost before they've set eyes on each other. By the way they were carrying on, it's a wonder they haven't decided on bombs and cannon as well.

SPIGA. Cannon?

SILIA. What do you mean?

BARELLI. Oh, the whole thing's crazy enough for that! First an
   exchange with pistols.

SILIA. Pistols?

LEONE (*to* SILIA). Perhaps he's arranged that to avoid swords,
   you know. I expect Miglioriti is not so clever with a pistol.

BARELLI. Who, Miglioriti? Why that fellow shoots the pip off
   the ace of spades at twenty paces!

SILIA. Was it Venanzi who suggested pistols?

BARELLI. Yes, Venanzi. What's the matter with him? Has he
   gone mad?

SILIA. Oh, my God!

SPIGA. But . . . excuse me, I don't follow. Where does the ace
   of spades come in?

BARELLI. What ace of spades?

LEONE. Quiet, quiet, Spiga. You and I don't understand these
   things.

BARELLI. First there's to be an exchange of two shots with
   pistols. Then you fall to with swords!

SILIA. Swords as well? Pistols weren't enough for him!

BARELLI. No, Signora — swords were chosen by agreement.
   Pistols were thrown in as an extra — out of bravado, as it were.

SILIA. But this is murder!

BARELLI. Yes, Signora. that's just what it is. But, if I may say
   so, it's up to you to stop it.

SILIA. Up to me? No! He's the one who can say the word! My
   husband. I never wanted it to become so serious.

LEONE. That's enough, Barelli. There's no point in starting a
   discussion with my wife now.

BARELLI. But, you don't understand! The whole town is full of
   this affair. They're talking about nothing else.

LEONE. Already.

SILIA. And I suppose they all say *I* am to blame.

BARELLI. No, no. Not you. Guido Venanzi, Signora. You
   understand, Leone, nothing is being said against you. You
   don't come into it at all, in fact. Miglioriti's furious against
   Guido since he found out that Guido was in the flat the whole

time — hiding in the bedroom. (*To* LEONE, *with pained sympathy*:) Sorry, old boy! If he'd only come out and told Miglioriti it was all a mistake . . . After all, they were only drunk, you know . . . They'd have had a good laugh and there'd be no need for all this scandal. You need never have known, Leone . . . Or, at least you'd have been offered the chance to blink an eye. Instead of which, that damned fool lets the entire block of flats be called in to witness. And now he has the audacity to turn up at Miglioriti's as the bearer of a challenge!

SPIGA. Listen, Leone, perhaps — as a friend of both parties — I could do something . . .

LEONE (*in a sudden outburst*). Don't interfere, Spiga.

SPIGA. But, surely . . . since it is to take place so near here . . .

BARELLI. Yes, in the orchard — at seven tomorrow morning. Look, I have brought two swords.

LEONE (*quickly, pretending not to understand*). Have I to pay you for them?

BARELLI. Pay? Good Lord, no! They're mine. I want to give you a little elementary instruction, and let you get the feel of it.

LEONE (*calmly*). You want *me* to practise?

BARELLI. Of course! Who else? Me?

LEONE (*laughing*). No, no, no, no, thank you. It's quite unnecessary.

BARELLI. But I doubt if you've ever seen a sword, let alone handled one. (*He takes out one of the swords*).

SILIA (*trembling at the sight of the sword*). Please! Please!

LEONE (*loudly*). That will do, Barelli! Let's have no more of these jokes.

BARELLI. Jokes?! You must at least learn how to hold the damn thing!

LEONE. That will do, I tell you. (*Firmly*:) Listen, all of you. I don't want to appear rude, but I'd like to be left alone now.

BARELLI. Yes, of course, you must conserve your nervous energy. It's most important that you should keep calm.

LEONE. Oh, I shall keep calm, all right. When Guido comes back you two can amuse yourselves with those gadgets while I watch. Will that do? Meanwhile leave them here — and don't be annoyed if I ask you to go.

BARELLI. Only trying to help, old chap.

LEONE. You too, doctor, if you don't mind.

SPIGA. But won't you let me . . . ?

LEONE (*interrupting*). You'll be able to ask Barelli for all the information you want.

BARELLI (*bowing to* SILIA). Goodbye, Signora. Terribly sorry!

SILIA *barely inclines her head.*

SPIGA. Goodbye, dear lady. (*He shakes her hand. To* LEONE:) Calm, you understand . . . calm . . . !

LEONE. Yes, all right. Goodbye.

BARELLI. Till this evening, then.

LEONE. Goodbye.

BARELLI *and* SPIGA *leave.*

LEONE. Thank heaven they've gone.

SILIA. Do you . . .

LEONE. No, you stay if you like — provided you don't speak to me about this business.

SILIA. That wouldn't be possible. And then you'd never be sure of what I may do if Guido comes back, as he may at any moment.

LEONE *laughs loud and long.*

SILIA. Don't laugh. Don't laugh!

LEONE. I'm laughing because I'm genuinely amused. You can't imagine how much I am enjoying watching you chop and change like this.

SILIA (*on the point of weeping*). But doesn't it seem natural to you?

LEONE. Yes, and that's just why I'm enjoying it: because you're so natural!

SILIA (*promptly, furiously*). But *you* are not!

LEONE. Isn't that a good thing?

SILIA. I don't understand you! I don't understand you! I don't understand you! (*She says this, first with almost wild anguish, then with wonder, then in an almost supplicating tone.*)

LEONE (*gently, approaching*). You can't, my dear! But it's better so, believe me. (*Pause. Then, in a low voice:*) I understand!

SILIA (*scarcely raising her eyes to look at him, terrified*). What do you understand?

LEONE (*calmly*). What it is you want.

SILIA. What do I want?

LEONE. You know— and yet you don't know what you want.

SILIA. I think I must be going mad!

LEONE. Mad? Oh, no!

SILIA. Yes. I must have been mad last night. I'm terrified.

LEONE. Don't be afraid! I'm here.

SILIA. What are you going to do?

LEONE. What I have always intended to do ever since you made me see the necessity.

SILIA. I?

LEONE. You.

SILIA. What necessity?

LEONE (*softly, after a pause*). To kill you! Do you think you haven't given me the motive to do it, more than once? Yes, of course you have! But it was a motive that sprang from a feeling— first of love, then of hate. I had to disarm those two feelings — to empty myself of them. And because I *have* emptied myself of them, now I can let the motive drop, and permit you to live. Not as you want to live — you don't know that yourself — but as you *can* live, and are bound to, seeing that it is impossible for you to do as I do.

SILIA. What do you do?

LEONE (*with a vague sad gesture, after a pause*). I set myself apart. (*Pause.*) Do you imagine that impulses and feelings don't arise in me too? They do, indeed they do. But I don't let them loose. I cage them, like wild beasts at a fair. And I am their tamer. Yet I laugh at myself sometimes as I watch myself playing this self-imposed role of tamer of my feelings. At times, I confess, a desire comes upon me to let myself be mangled by one of those wild beasts — and, by you, looking at me now so meekly, so contritely. But that would be the last trick in the game: that would take away for ever the pleasure of all the rest.

SILIA (*hesitant, as though offering herself*). Do you want me to stay?

LEONE. Why?

SILIA. Or shall I come back tonight, when all the others have gone?

LEONE. No, no, thank you. I shall need all my strength.

SILIA. I mean, to be near you . . . To help you . . .

LEONE. I shall sleep . . . As I always do, without dreams.

SILIA (*with profound grief*). That's why everything's hopeless, you see! You won't believe it, but in bed my real love is sleep — sleep that quickly brings me dreams!

LEONE. Oh, yes, I believe you.

SILIA. But it never happens now. I can't sleep. And imagine what it will be like tonight! (*She breaks off.*) Well — I shall be here in the morning.

LEONE. Oh, no, no! You mustn't come. I don't want you to.

SILIA. You're joking!

LEONE. I forbid you to come.

SILIA. You can't stop me.

LEONE. Very well. Do as you please.

At this point PHILIP *enters, left — with the lunch tray.*

PHILIP (*in a hollow, surly, imperious voice*). Hey! Lunch is ready!

SILIA. Till tomorrow morning, then.

She gazes at him with deep longing. If he were only to give a sign, she'd be prepared to become his again forever. But he is as impassive as ever.

LEONE (*submissively*). Till tomorrow morning . . .

SILIA *goes out.* LEONE *closes the door behind her and stands for a moment, lost in thought. Then he moves slowly towards the table and seats himself at the end of it, absently unrolling his napkin.*

Curtain

Act Three

LEONE'S *flat early the next morning.*

When the curtain rises, the stage is empty and almost dark.

The front door bell rings.

PHILIP *enters left, and crosses the stage.*

PHILIP. Who the devil's calling on us at this hour? What a day!

> *He goes out, right. After a moment he enters with Dr SPIGA, who is dressed in frock coat and top hat, and carries two large bags full of surgical instruments.*

SPIGA. Good morning, Philip.

PHILIP. 'Morning, Doctor.

SPIGA (*surprised at not seeing* LEONE). How is he?

PHILIP. He's still asleep, so don't talk so loudly.

SPIGA. Good God, he's still asleep and I haven't shut my eyes all night!

PHILIP. What have you got there? (*He points to the two bags.*)

SPIGA. All my instruments — everything! (*He goes to the dining-table which PHILIP has already partly laid.*) Now . . . Take off this table-cloth.

PHILIP. What for?

SPIGA. I brought my own. (*He takes a surgical sheet of white American cloth out of one of the bags.*)

PHILIP. What are you going to do with that?

SPIGA. I'm going to get everything laid out in readiness here.

PHILIP. Oh, no, you're not! You're not touching this table. I'm just laying it for breakfast.

SPIGA. Breakfast? Lord, man! This is no time to be thinking about breakfast!

PHILIP. You leave this table alone!

SPIGA (*turning to the writing desk*). Well, clear the desk then.

PHILIP. Are you joking? If the police find out about the duel, don't you know that these two tables can talk?

SPIGA (*testily*). Oh, yes! I know all about that. Don't you start quoting *him* at me! I've heard it before! Two symbols: writing desk and dining table; books and cooking utensils; the void and the counter balance! I know, I know. But haven't you realized that in half an hour from now all those nonsensical ideas of his may be snuffed out like a candle?

PHILIP. I suppose you've ordered his coffin, too! You look like an undertaker.

SPIGA (*exasperated*). My God, what an unfeeling brute you are! They told me to dress like this. This is really the limit. Heaven alone knows what a night I've had . . .

PHILIP. Not so loud! You'll wake him up!

SPIGA (*softly*). . . . I haven't time to argue with you. Clear this other little table for me then. (*He points to the third, smaller one.*) And get a move on.

PHILIP. Oh, I don't mind your using *that* one. It won't take long. (*He removes a cigar-box and a vase of flowers.*) There you are — cleared.

SPIGA. At last.

> SPIGA *spreads his cloth on the table and begins to get out his instruments. At the same time* PHILIP *goes on laying the breakfast table, occasionally disappearing into the kitchen to fetch things. The conversation continues meantime.*

SPIGA (*to himself, checking his instruments*). Scalpels . . . bone saw . . . forceps . . . dissectors . . . compressors . . .

PHILIP. What do you want all the butcher's shop for?

SPIGA. What do I want it for! Don't you realize he's going to fight a duel? Suppose he gets shot in a leg or an arm? We may have to amputate.

PHILIP. Oh, I see. Why haven't you brought a wooden leg, then?

SPIGA. You never know what may happen with firearms; you have to be prepared for anything. Look, I've brought these other little gadgets for bullet extraction. Probe . . . mirror . . .

electric torch . . . scissors . . . two types of extractor . . .
Look at this one! English model — a beauty isn't it? Now,
where did I put the needles? Let . . . me . . . see . . . Hm . . .
(*He looks in one of the bags.*) Ah, here they are! I think
that's everything. (*Looks at the clock*). I say, it's twenty-
five past six! The seconds will be here any minute!

PHILIP. So what? It's got nothing to do with me!

SPIGA. I was thinking of him — suppose he isn't awake yet!

PHILIP. It's too early for him.

SPIGA. It's no good trying to keep him to his timetable today!
He made the appointment for seven o'clock.

PHILIP. Then he'll have to wake himself up.

SPIGA. Perhaps he's up already. You might go and see!

PHILIP. Look . . . I'm his clock on ordinary days and I know
the hours I've got to keep . . . and I'm not putting myself a
minute fast or slow, today or any other day. Reveille, seven
thirty . . .

SPIGA. Good God man! Don't you realise that at seven-thirty
today he may be dead?

PHILIP. . . . . and at eight I bring him his breakfast!

There is a ring at the front door bell.

SPIGA. There! You see? That'll be the seconds.

PHILIP *goes out. He comes back shortly after with*
GUIDO *and* BARELLI.

GUIDO (*as he enters*). Ah, good morning, Doctor.

BARELLI (*ditto*). Good morning, Doctor.

SPIGA. Good morning. Good morning.

GUIDO. Are we all ready?

SPIGA. *I* am, quite ready!

BARELLI (*laughing at the sight of all the surgical armoury laid
out on the table*). He certainly has got everything ready!

GUIDO (*irritated*). Well, good God there's nothing to laugh at!

BARELLI (*with amused curiosity as he picks up an instrument*).
What on earth's this?

SPIGA *sharply takes away the object.*

SPIGA (*rather crossly*). Well, it *was* sterilized. (*He replaces it, but away from the others*).

GUIDO (*with a shudder*). Terrifying collection! Has *he* seen it?

SPIGA. Who? Excuse me . . . '*Quod abundat non vitiat*'.

GUIDO. I'm asking you whether Leone has seen these intruments. (*To* BARELLI:) You know, he must be absolutely calm, but if he sees . . .

SPIGA. Oh, no, he hasn't seen anything yet!

GUIDO. Where is he?

SPIGA. Well . . . I think he's not up yet.

BARELLI. What?

GUIDO. Not up yet?

SPIGA. I *think*, I said. I don't *know*. He hasn't been in here.

GUIDO. Well, we can't stand about here like this. We have only a quarter of an hour left. He must be up. (*To* PHILIP:) Go and tell him we are here.

BARELLI. What a man!

GUIDO (*To* PHILIP, *who has remained motionless, frowning*) Get a move on!

PHILIP. At seven-thirty!

GUIDO. Oh, go to blazes! I'll call him myself. (*He rushes to the door at the back*.)

SPIGA. He's bound to be up.

BARELLI. He really is amazing, upon my word!

> GUIDO (*knocking loudly on the door, centre and listens with his ear to it.*)

GUIDO. What can he be doing? Surely he isn't still asleep? (*He knocks again, louder and calls:*) Leone! Leone! (*He listens*) He is still asleep! My God, he's still asleep! (*He knocks again and tries to open the door.*) Leone? Leone!

BARELLI. He really is amazing, you know — quite amazing!

GUIDO. How does he lock himself in?

PHILIP. With the bolt.

GUIDO. But why?

PHILIP. I don't know.

BARELLI. Does he always sleep as soundly as this?

PHILIP. Like a log! Two minutes, it takes me to wake him, every morning.

GUIDO. Well, I'll wake him if I have to smash the door in! Leone! Leone! Ah, he's awake at last! (*Speaking through the door:*) Get dressed quickly. Hurry up. Hurry up. It's almost seven already.

BARELLI. Would you believe it!

SPIGA. What a sound sleeper!

PHILIP. Yes, he's always the same. He has to drag himself out of his sleep as if he was hauling himself up from the bottom of a well!

GUIDO. Oh, is there any danger of his falling back again? (*He turns back to look at* LEONE'S *door.*)

BARELLI (*hearing a noise*). No, listen. He's opening the door.

SPIGA (*placing himself in front of the table with his instruments*). I'll keep him away from here!

> LEONE *appears, perfectly placid and still rather sleepy, in pyjamas and slippers.*

LEONE. Good morning.

GUIDO. Go and get dressed at once. You haven't a minute to lose.

LEONE. Why, may I ask?

GUIDO. He asks why!

BARELLI. Have you forgotten you've a duel to fight?

LEONE. I? Fight a duel?

SPIGA. He's still asleep!

GUIDO. The duel, man! The duel! At seven o'clock.

BARELLI. In less than ten minutes.

LEONE. Don't get excited, I heard.

GUIDO (*absolutely dumbfounded*). Well then?

LEONE. Well then what?

BARELLI (*also dumbfounded*). What do you mean 'what'?! You've got to get dressed and go and fight!

LEONE (*placidly*). Have I?

SPIGA (*as though to himself*). He must have gone out of his mind!

LEONE. No, Doctor! I'm perfectly '*Compos mentis*'.

GUIDO. You have to fight.

LEONE. I have to fight, too, have I?

BARELLI. 'Too'? What do you mean?

LEONE. Oh, no, my friends. You're mistaken!

GUIDO. Do you want to withdraw?

BARELLI. Don't you want to fight, now?

LEONE. I? Withdraw? But you know perfectly well that I
always firmly maintain my position.

GUIDO. I find you like this, and yet . . .

BARELLI. But, if you say . . .

LEONE. How do you find me? What do I say? I say that you and
my wife upset my whole day yesterday, Venanzi, trying to
make me do what I admitted all the time was my duty.

GUIDO. But . . . but . . .

BARELLI. You're going to fight!

LEONE. That's not my duty.

BARELLI. Whose is it, then?

LEONE (*pointing to* GUIDO). His!

BARELLI. Guido's?

LEONE. Yes, his.

He goes to GUIDO, *who has turned pale.*

LEONE. And you know it. (*To* BARELLI:) He knows it! I, the
husband, issued the challenge, because he couldn't for my
wife's sake. But as for fighting the duel, oh no! As for fighting
the duel . . . (*To* GUIDO *softly, pulling one of the lapels of his
jacket, and stressing every word:*) . . . you know quite well, don't
you, that that is no concern of mine, because I never fight
against anybody. You're the one who fights!

GUIDO, *in a cold sweat, passes a hand across his brow.*

BARELLI. This is fantastic!

LEONE. No, Barelli, perfectly normal, I assure you! Quite in
accordance with the rules of the game. I'm playing my part:
he's playing his. I am not going to budge from my anchorage.
And his opponent looks at it as I do. You said yourself,
Barelli, that the marquis is really angry with him, not with

me. Because they all know, and you better than any of them, what he wanted to do to me. Yes, Venanzi, you and Silia really did want to cart me off to the slaughter, didn't you?

GUIDO (*protesting vigorously*). No, *I* didn't! *I* didn't!

LEONE. Oh, yes, yesterday, you and my wife were like two children bouncing up and down on a see-saw. And I was in the middle, balancing myself and you two into the bargain.

GUIDO. Leone, I assure you . . .

LEONE. You thought you'd have a little game with me, didn't you? You thought between you, you could win my life from me? Well, you've lost the game, my friends. I have outplayed you.

GUIDO. No! You are my witness that yesterday, right from the beginning, I tried . . .

LEONE. Oh yes, you *tried* to be discreet. Very discreet!

GUIDO. What do you mean? What are you insinuating?

LEONE. You must admit, my dear fellow, that you didn't carry your discretion quite far enough — did you? At a certain point — for reasons which I understand quite well; indeed, I feel quite sorry for you — at a certain point your discretion failed you. And now, I regret to say, you are about to suffer the consequences.

GUIDO. Because you're not going to fight?

LEONE. Exactly. It's not my business.

GUIDO. Very well, then. Is it mine?

BARELLI (*rising*). 'Very well', do you say?!

GUIDO (*to* Barelli). Wait! (*To* LEONE:) What are you going to do?

LEONE. I'm going to have breakfast.

BARELLI. But this is fantastic!

GUIDO. No, I mean . . . Don't you realise that if I take your place . . .

LEONE. No, no, my dear Venanzi! Not mine. Your own!

GUIDO. Very well, if I take *my* place, don't you realize that *you* will be dishonoured!

BARELLI. Disgraced! We shall be forced to expose your dishonour!

LEONE *laughs loudly.*

BARELLI. How can you laugh? You'll be dishonoured, dishonoured!

LEONE. I understand, my friends, and I can still laugh. Don't you see how and where I live? Why should I worry my head about honour?

GUIDO. Don't let's waste any more time. Let's go.

BARELLI. But are you really going to fight this duel?

GUIDO. Yes, I am. Don't you understand?

BARELLI. No, I don't!

LEONE. Yes, it really is his business, you know, Barelli!

BARELLI. You're being cynical!

LEONE. No, Barelli, I'm being rational! When one has emptied oneself of every passion and . . .

GUIDO (*interrupting and gripping* BARELLI *by the arm*:) Come, Barelli. It's no use arguing now. And you too Doctor — you'd better come with us.

SPIGA. I'm coming! I'm coming!

> *At this moment,* SILIA *enters, right. There is a short silence, during which she stands still, perplexed and amazed.*

> GUIDO (*comes forward, very pale, and grasps her hand.*)

GUIDO. Goodbye, Silia. (*He turns to* LEONE:) Goodbye.

> GUIDO *rushes out, right, followed by* BARELLI *and* SPIGA.

SILIA. Why did he say goodbye like that?

LEONE. I told you, dear, that it was quite useless for you to come here. But you were determined to.

SILIA. But . . . What are you doing here?

LEONE. Don't you know? I live here!

SILIA. And what is Guido doing? Isn't . . . Isn't the duel going to take place?

LEONE. Oh, it will take place, I suppose. It may be taking place now!

SILIA. But . . . How can it be? If you're still here?

LEONE. Oh, yes, I am here. But he has gone. Didn't you see him?

SILIA. But then . . . That means . . . Oh, God! Why has he gone? Has he gone to fight for you?

LEONE. Not for me — for you!

SILIA. For me? Oh, God! Did you do this?

> LEONE *comes close to her, with the commanding, disdainful air of a cruel judge.*

LEONE. Did I do this? You have the impertinence to suggest that I am responsible?

SILIA. But you have . . .

LEONE (*in a low voice, gripping her arm*) I have punished you both!

SILIA (*as though biting him*) I see! But at the price of your own dishonour!

LEONE. You are my dishonour.

SILIA. And all this time . . . God, what can be happening to him? It's horrible. Is he down there fighting? Fighting on *those* terms!

LEONE (*quickly*). Upon which he himself insisted.

> SILIA *suddenly laughs hysterically.*

SILIA. Oh, it's perfect, perfect! And you let him have his way. I swear he never intended to fight, not he! You are the devil! The devil incarnate! Where are they fighting? Tell me! Down there? In the orchard? (*She looks for a window*).

LEONE. It's no good, you know. There aren't any windows overlooking the orchard. You must either go down or climb up onto the roof.

> At this point, DR SPIGA, *pale and dishevelled in grotesque discomposure, dashes in; flings himself at his surgical instruments laid out on the table, rolls them up in the cloth, and rushes out without saying a word.*

SILIA. Doctor! Tell me . . . Tell me . . . What's happened? (*Not believing her own presentiments*:) Dead? (*Running out after him*:) Tell me! Is he dead? Tell me?

LEONE *remains motionless, absorbed in deep, serious thought. A long pause.   PHILIP enters, left, with the breakfast tray and puts it down on the table.*

PHILIP (*calling in a hollow voice*). Hey!

LEONE *barely turns his head.* PHILIP *indicates the breakfast with a vague gesture.*

Breakfast time!

LEONE, *as though he has not heard, does not move.*

Curtain

SIX CHARACTERS
IN SEARCH OF AN AUTHOR

Translated by John Linstrum

Introduction

Time acts upon a translation in a way that it does not upon the original, so that a translation made a quarter of a century ago might be almost as distant from us as the original itself and in criticising the effectiveness of the play we may find ourselves judging and reacting to a translation and not the work that is translated. The modernisation of a translation is not only acceptable but necessary in order to preserve a sense of freshness as language itself changes. An original work possesses a natural elasticity of language that allows it to accommodate these changes more easily than a translation which is inevitably limited by attempts to be both lucid and faithful to an original.

My aim has been to offer an accurate, new translation that sensitively adjusts the language to suit a new age of audience, not to tamper with the quality and form of the play or to offer a totally restructured version. Above all, I hope to have given actors who perform the play lines to speak that they find entirely appropriate and comfortable.

This play is of some importance in the development of the theatre of the twentieth century and deserves better than to be relegated to the status of a period-piece: in 1921, when the play was first performed, it was far ahead of its time, not only in its form but because the central thought was so original and astonishing. Imagined but uncompleted characters burst in to reality from an author's creative mind with an explosive, dynamic power; that is both a startling and a timeless event. However, despite its ageless theme, embedded in this remarkable play there are factors that compel us to leave it in a period rather earlier than today. If we show The Actors in jeans, jerseys, modern jewellery, the fashionable undress of today, we shall also have to give them a style of language and behaviour to match and this would be destructive of the relationship that Pirandello needed between The Characters and The Actors. The details of the family life of The Characters with its disruption, adultery,

prostitution, illegitimacy, nudity and potential incest would be
reduced in their effectiveness in a late 20th-century setting. With
that in mind I have retained the title Producer and Prompter
rather than change them to Director and DSM as in current
theatrical practice. The older forms suggest a theatrical hierarchy
which is no longer so obvious but which is contained in the
attitudes of the people in the play. It would be tempting to
compose a totally new version in which the frame-work, the style
and the language are altered, but that would be to rewrite the
play not translate it, and it would, I suspect, lose more that it
gained.

John Linstrum
Penarth. 1984

The Characters

THE FATHER
THE MOTHER
THE STEPDAUGHTER
THE SON
THE BOY (non-speaking)
THE LITTLE GIRL (non-speaking)
MADAME PACE

The Actors

THE PRODUCER
THE LEADING ACTRESS
THE LEADING ACTOR
THE SECOND ACTRESS
THE YOUNG ACTRESS
THE YOUNG ACTOR
OTHER ACTORS AND ACTRESSES (a variable number)
THE STAGE MANAGER
THE PROMPTER
THE PROPERTY MAN
THE STAGE-HAND
THE PRODUCER'S SECRETARY
THE DOORKEEPER
OTHER THEATRE STAFF

The action of the play takes place on the stage of a theatre. There are no act or scene divisions, but there are two interruptions: when the Producer and the Characters go to the office to write the scenario, giving the Actors a break in rehearsal, and when a stage-hand lowers the front curtain by mistake.

References to 'prompt-box', 'curtains' and 'letting down trees' will need to be altered if they are not appropriate to the theatre where the performance is taking place.

This translation was first presented at the Greenwich Theatre, London, in June 1979, with the following cast:

The Characters

FATHER	Philip Stone
MOTHER	Mona Bruce
STEPDAUGHTER	Pauline Moran
SON	Nick Dunning
BOY	Stuart Wilde
LITTLE GIRL	Clare Barnes/
	Charlotte Levitt/
	Rachel Quarmby
MADAME PACE	Claire Davenport

The Company

THE DIRECTOR	Michael Jackson
THE STAGE STAFF	Deborah Blake
	Jeannie Crowther
	Mark Preston
THE ACTORS	David Beale
	Sally Nesbitt
	Christopher Saul
	Erica Stevens
	Joanna Wake

Directed by Phil Young
Designed by Bernard Culshaw

Act One

When the audience enters, the curtain is already up and the stage is just as it would be during the day. There is no set; it is empty, in almost total darkness. This is so that from the beginning the audience will have the feeling of being present, not at a performance of a properly rehearsed play, but at a performance of a play that happens spontaneously. Two small sets of steps, one on the right and one on the left, lead up to the stage from the auditorium. On the stage, the top is off the PROMPTER's *box and is lying next to it. Downstage, there is a small table and a chair with arms for the* PRODUCER: *it is turned with its back to the audience.*

Also downstage there are two small tables, one a little bigger than the other, and several chairs, ready for the rehearsal if needed. There are more chairs scattered on both left and right for the ACTORS: *to one side at the back and nearly hidden is a piano.*

When the houselights go down the STAGE HAND *comes on through the back door. He is in blue overalls and carries a tool bag. He brings some pieces of wood on, comes to the front, kneels down and starts to nail them together.*

The STAGE MANAGER *rushes on from the wings.*

STAGE MANAGER. Hey! What are you doing?

STAGE HAND. What do you think I'm doing? I'm banging nails in.

STAGE MANAGER. Now? (*He looks at his watch.*) It's half-past ten already. The Producer will be here in a moment to rehearse.

STAGE HAND. I've got to do my work some time, you know.

STAGE MANAGER. Right — but not now.

STAGE HAND. When?

STAGE MANAGER. When the rehearsal's finished. Come on, get all this out of the way and let me set for the second act of 'The Rules of the Game'.

The STAGE HAND *picks up his tools and wood and goes off, grumbling and muttering. The* ACTORS *of the company come in through the door, men and women, first one then another, then two together and so on: there will be nine or ten, enough for the parts for the rehearsal of a play by Pirandello, 'The Rules of the Game', today's rehearsal. They come in, say their 'Good-mornings' to the* STAGE MANAGER *and each other. Some go off to the dressing-rooms; others, among them the* PROMPTER *with the text rolled up under his arm, scatter about the stage waiting for the* PRODUCER *to start the rehearsal. Meanwhile, sitting or standing in groups, they chat together; some smoke, one complains about his part, another one loudly reads something from 'The Stage'. It would be as well if the* ACTORS *and* ACTRESSES *were dressed in colourful clothes, and this first scene should be improvised naturally and vivaciously. After a while somebody might sit down at the piano and play a song; the younger* ACTORS *and* ACTRESSES *start dancing.*

STAGE MANAGER (*clapping his hands to call their attention*). Come on everybody! Quiet please. The Producer's here.

The piano and the dancing both stop. The ACTORS *turn to look out into the theatre and through the door at the back comes the* PRODUCER; *he walks down the gangway between the seats and, calling 'Good-morning' to the* ACTORS, *climbs up one of the sets of stairs onto the stage. The* SECRETARY *gives him the post, a few magazines, a script. The* ACTORS *move to one side of the stage.*

PRODUCER. Any letters?
SECRETARY. No. That's all the post there is. (*Giving him the script.*)
PRODUCER. Put it in the office. (*Then looking round and turning to the* STAGE MANAGER.) I can't see a thing here. Let's have some lights please.
STAGE MANAGER. Right. (*Calling.*) Workers please!

In a few seconds the side of the stage where the ACTORS *are standing is brilliantly lit with white light. The*

PROMPTER *has gone into his box and spread out his script.*

PRODUCER. Good. (*Clapping hands.*) Well then, let's get started. Anybody missing?

STAGE MANAGER (*heavily ironic*). Our leading lady.

PRODUCER. Not again! (*Looking at his watch.*) We're ten minutes late already. Send her a note to come and see me. It might teach her to be on time for rehearsals. (*Almost before he has finished, the* LEADING ACTRESS's *voice is heard from the auditorium.*)

LEADING ACTRESS. Morning everybody. Sorry I'm late. (*She is very expensively dressed and is carrying a lap-dog. She comes down the aisle and goes up on to the stage.*)

PRODUCER. You're determined to keep us waiting, aren't you?

LEADING ACTRESS. I'm sorry. I just couldn't find a taxi anywhere. But you haven't started yet and I'm not on at the opening anyhow. (*Calling the* STAGE MANAGER, *she gives him the dog.*) Put him in my dressing-room for me will you?

PRODUCER. And she's even brought her lap-dog with her! As if we haven't enough lap-dogs here already. (*Clapping his hands and turning to the* PROMPTER.) Right then, the second act of 'The Rules of the Game'. (*Sits in his arm-chair.*) Quiet please! Who's on?

The ACTORS *clear from the front of the stage and sit to one side, except for three who are ready to start the scene — and the* LEADING ACTRESS. *She has ignored the* PRODUCER *and is sitting at one of the little tables.*

PRODUCER. Are you in this scene, then?

LEADING ACTRESS. No — I've just told you.

PRODUCER (*annoyed*). Then get off, for God's sake. (*The* LEADING ACTRESS *goes and sits with the others. To the* PROMPTER.) Come on then, let's get going.

PROMPTER (*reading his script*). 'The house of Leone Gala. A peculiar room, both dining-room and study.'

PRODUCER (*to the* STAGE MANAGER). We'll use the red set.

STAGE MANAGER (*making a note*). The red set — right.

PROMPTER (*still reading*). 'The table is laid and there is a desk

with books and papers. Bookcases full of books and china
cabinets full of valuable china. An exit at the back leads to
Leone's bedroom. An exit to the left leads to the kitchen. The
main entrance is on the right.'

PRODUCER. Right. Listen carefully everybody: there, the
main entrance, there, the kitchen. (*To the* LEADING ACTOR
who plays Socrates.) Your entrances and exits will be from
there. (*To the* STAGE MANAGER.) We'll have the French
windows there and put the curtains on them.

STAGE MANAGER (*making a note*). Right.

PROMPTER (*reading*). 'Scene One. Leone Gala, Guido Venanzi,
and Filippo, who is called Socrates.' (*To* PRODUCER.) Have
I to read the directions as well?

PRODUCER. Yes, you have! I've told you a hundred times.

PROMPTER (*reading*). 'When the curtain rises, Leone Gala, in a
cook's hat and apron, is beating an egg in a dish with a little
wooden spoon. Filippo is beating another and he is dressed
as a cook too. Guido Venanzi is sitting listening.'

LEADING ACTOR. Look, do I really have to wear a cook's hat?

PRODUCER (*annoyed by the question*). I expect so! That's
what it says in the script. (*Pointing to the script.*)

LEADING ACTOR. If you ask me it's ridiculous.

PRODUCER (*leaping to his feet furiously*). Ridiculous? It's
ridiculous, is it? What do you expect me to do if nobody
writes good plays any more and we're reduced to putting on
plays by Pirandello? And if you can understand them you must
be very clever. He writes them on purpose so nobody enjoys
them, neither actors nor critics nor audience. (*The* ACTORS
laugh. Then crosses to LEADING ACTOR *and shouts at him.*)
A cook's hat and you beat eggs. But don't run away with the
idea that that's all you are doing — beating eggs. You must
be joking! You have to be symbolic of the shells of the eggs
you are beating. (*The* ACTORS *laugh again and start making
ironical comments to each other.*) Be quiet! Listen carefully
while I explain. (*Turns back to* LEADING ACTOR.) Yes, the
shells, because they are symbolic of the empty form of
reason, without its content, blind instinct! You are reason
and your wife is instinct: you are playing a game where you
have been given parts and in which you are not just yourself

but the puppet of yourself. Do you see?

LEADING ACTOR (*spreading his hands*). Me? No.

PRODUCER (*going back to his chair*). Neither do I! Come on, let's get going; you wait till you see the end! You haven't seen anything yet! (*Confidentially.*) By the way, I should turn almost to face the audience if I were you, about three-quarters face. Well, what with the obscure dialogue and the audience not being able to hear you properly in any case, the whole lot'll go to hell. (*Clapping hands again.*) Come on. Let's get going!

PROMPTER. Excuse me, can I put the top back on the prompt-box? There's a bit of a draught.

PRODUCER. Yes, yes, of course. Get on with it.

> *The* STAGE DOORKEEPER, *in a braided cap, has come into the auditorium, and he comes all the way down the aisle to the stage to tell the* PRODUCER *the* SIX CHARACTERS *have come, who, having come in after him, look about them a little puzzled and dismayed. Every effort must be made to create the effect that the* SIX CHARACTERS *are very different from the* ACTORS *of the company. The placings of the two groups, indicated in the directions, once the* CHARACTERS *are on the stage, will help this; so will using different coloured lights. But the most effective idea is to use masks for the* CHARACTERS, *masks specially made of a material that will not go limp with perspiration and light enough not to worry the actors who wear them: they should be made so that the eyes, the nose and the mouth are all free. This is the way to bring out the deep significance of the play. The* CHARACTERS *should not appear as ghosts, but as created realities, timeless creations of the imagination, and so more real and consistent than the changeable realities of the* ACTORS. *The masks are designed to give the impression of figures constructed by art, each one fixed forever in its own fundamental emotion; that is, Remorse for the* FATHER, *Revenge for the* STEPDAUGHTER, *Scorn for the* SON, *Sorrow for the* MOTHER. *Her mask should have wax tears in the corners of the eyes and down the cheeks like the*

sculptured or painted weeping Madonna in a church. Her dress should be of a plain material, in stiff folds, looking almost as if it were carved and not of an ordinary material you can buy in a shop and have made up by a dressmaker.

The FATHER *is about fifty: his reddish hair is thinning at the temples, but he is not bald: he has a full moustache that almost covers his young-looking mouth, which often opens in an uncertain and empty smile. He is pale, with a high forehead: he has blue oval eyes, clear and sharp: he is dressed in light trousers and a dark jacket: his voice is sometimes rich, at other times harsh and loud.*

The MOTHER *appears crushed by an intolerable weight of shame and humiliation. She is wearing a thick black veil and is dressed simply in black; when she raises her veil she shows a face like wax, but not suffering, with her eyes turned down humbly.*

The STEPDAUGHTER, *who is eighteen years old, is defiant, even insolent. She is very beautiful, dressed in mourning as well, but with striking elegance. She is scornful of the timid, suffering, dejected air of her* YOUNG BROTHER, *a grubby little boy of fourteen, also dressed in black; she is full of a warm tenderness, on the other hand, for the* LITTLE SISTER, *a girl of about four, dressed in white with a black silk sash round her waist.*

The SON *is twenty-two, tall, almost frozen in an air of scorn for the* FATHER *and indifference to the* MOTHER: *he is wearing a mauve overcoat and a long green scarf round his neck.*

DOORMAN. Excuse me, sir.

PRODUCER (*angrily*). What the hell is it now?

DOORMAN. There are some people here — they say they want to see you, sir.

The PRODUCER *and the* ACTORS *are astonished and turn to look out into the auditorium.*

PRODUCER. But I'm rehearsing! You know perfectly well that no-one's allowed in during rehearsals. (*Turning to face out front.*) Who are you? What do you want?

FATHER (*coming forward, followed by the others, to the foot of one of the sets of steps).* We're looking for an author.

PRODUCER (*angry and astonished*). An author? Which author?

FATHER. Any author will do, sir.

PRODUCER. But there isn't an author here because we're not rehearsing a new play.

STEPDAUGHTER (*excitedly as she rushes up the steps*). That's better still, better still! We can be your new play.

ACTORS (*lively comments and laughter from the* ACTORS). Oh, listen to that, etc.

FATHER (*going up on the stage after the* STEPDAUGHTER). Maybe, but if there isn't an author here . . . (*To the* PRODUCER.) Unless you'd like to be . . .

> *Hand in hand, the* MOTHER *and the* LITTLE GIRL, *followed by the* LITTLE BOY, *go up on the stage and wait. The* SON *stays sullenly behind.*

PRODUCER. Is this some kind of joke?

FATHER. Now, how can you think that? On the contrary, we are bringing you a story of anguish.

STEPDAUGHTER. We might make your fortune for you!

PRODUCER. Do me a favour, will you? Go away. We haven't time to waste on idiots.

FATHER (*hurt but answering gently*). You know very well, as a man of the theatre, that life is full of all sorts of odd things which have no need at all to pretend to be real because they are actually true.

PRODUCER. What the devil are you talking about?

FATHER. What I'm saying is that you really must be mad to do things the opposite way round: to create situations that obviously aren't true and try to make them seem to be really happening. But then I suppose that sort of madness is the only reason for your profession.

> *The* ACTORS *are indignant.*

PRODUCER (*getting up and glaring at him*). Oh, yes? So ours is a profession of madmen, is it?

FATHER. Well, if you try to make something look true when it obviously isn't, especially if you're not forced to do it, but do it for a game . . . Isn't it your job to give life on the stage to imaginary people?

PRODUCER (*quickly answering him and speaking for the* ACTORS *who are growing more indignant*). I should like you to know, sir, that the actor's profession is one of great distinction. Even if nowadays the new writers only give us dull plays to act and puppets to present instead of men, I'd have you know that it is our boast that we have given life, here on this stage, to immortal works.

> The ACTORS, *satisfied, agree with and applaud the* PRODUCER.

FATHER (*cutting in and following hard on his argument*). There! You see? Good! You've given life! You've created living beings with more genuine life than people have who breathe and wear clothes! Less real, perhaps, but nearer the truth. We are both saying the same thing.

> The ACTORS *look at each other, astonished.*

PRODUCER. But just a moment! You said before . . .
FATHER. I'm sorry, but I said that before, about acting for fun, because you shouted at us and said you'd no time to waste on idiots, but you must know better than anyone that Nature uses human imagination to lift her work of creation to even higher levels.
PRODUCER. All right then: but where does all this get us?
FATHER. Nowhere. I want to try to show that one can be thrust into life in many ways, in many forms: as a tree or a stone, as water or a butterfly — or as a woman. It might even be as a character in a play.
PRODUCER (*ironic, pretending to be annoyed*). And you, and these other people here, were thrust into life, as you put it, as characters in a play?
FATHER. Exactly! And alive, as you can see.

> The PRODUCER *and the* ACTORS *burst into laughter as if at a joke.*

FATHER. I'm sorry you laugh like that, because we carry in us, as I said before, a story of terrible anguish as you can guess from this woman dressed in black.

> *Saying this, he offers his hand to the* MOTHER *and helps*

her up the last steps and, holding her still by the hand, leads
her with a sense of tragic solemnity across the stage which
is suddenly lit by a fantastic light.

The LITTLE GIRL *and the* BOY *follow the* MOTHER:
then the SON *comes up and stands to one side in the*
background: then the STEPDAUGHTER *follows and leans*
against the proscenium arch: the ACTORS *are astonished*
at first, but then, full of admiration for the 'entrance', they
burst into applause — just as if it were a performance
specially for them.

PRODUCER (*at first astonished and then indignant*). My God!
Be quiet all of you. (*Turns to the* CHARACTERS.) And you
lot get out! Clear off! (*To the* STAGE MANAGER.) Jesus!
Get them out of here.

STAGE MANAGER (*comes forward but stops short as if held
back by something strange*). Go on out! Get out!

FATHER (*to* PRODUCER). Oh no, please, you see, we . . .

PRODUCER (*shouting*). We came here to work, you know.

LEADING ACTOR. We really can't be messed about like this.

FATHER (*resolutely, coming forward*). I'm astonished! Why
don't you believe me? Perhaps you are not used to seeing
the characters created by an author spring into life up here on
the stage face to face with each other. Perhaps it's because
we're not in a script? (*He points to the* PROMPTER's *box.*)

STEPDAUGHTER (*coming down to the* PRODUCER, *smiling
and persuasive*). Believe me, sir, we really are six of the most
fascinating characters. But we've been neglected.

FATHER. Yes, that's right, we've been neglected. In the sense
that the author who created us, living in his mind,
wouldn't or couldn't make us live in a written play for the
world of art. And that really is a crime sir, because whoever
has the luck to be born a character can laugh even at death.
Because a character will never die! A man will die, a writer,
the instrument of creation: but what he has created will never
die! And to be able to live for ever you don't need to have
extraordinary gifts or be able to do miracles. Who was Sancho
Panza? Who was Prospero? But they will live for ever because
— living seeds — they had the luck to find a fruitful soil, an

imagination which knew how to grow them and feed them, so
that they will live for ever.

PRODUCER. This is all very well! But what do you want here?

FATHER. We want to live, sir.

PRODUCER (*ironically*). For ever!

FATHER. No, no: only for a few moments — in you.

AN ACTOR. Listen to that!

LEADING ACTRESS. They want to live in us!

YOUNG ACTOR (*pointing to the* STEPDAUGHTER). I don't
mind . . . so long as I get her.

FATHER. Listen, listen: the play is all ready to be put together
and if you and your actors would like to, we can work it out
now between us.

PRODUCER (*annoyed*). But what exactly do you want to do?
We don't make up plays like that here! We present comedies
and tragedies here.

FATHER. That's right, we know that of course. That's why we've
come.

PRODUCER. And where's the script?

FATHER. It's in us, sir. (*The* ACTORS *laugh.*) The play is in us:
we are the play and we are impatient to show it to you: the
passion inside us is driving us on.

STEPDAUGHTER (*scornfully, with the tantalising charm of
deliberate impudence*). My passion, if only you knew! My
passion for him! (*She points at the* FATHER *and suggests
that she is going to embrace him: but stops and bursts into a
screeching laugh.*)

FATHER (*with sudden anger*). You keep out of this for the
moment! And stop laughing like that!

STEPDAUGHTER. Really? Then with your permission, ladies
and gentlemen; even though it's only two months since I
became an orphan, just watch how I can sing and dance.

> The ACTORS, *especially the younger, seem strangely
> attracted to her while she sings and dances and they edge
> closer and reach out their hands to catch hold of her.* * *She*

---

*   Suggested songs: Eartha Kitt's *Old Fashioned Millionaire*; Theme Song
from *The Moon is Blue*, *I'm Gonna Wash That Man Right Out Of My
Hair* from *South Pacific*.

eludes them, and when the ACTORS *applaud her and the*
PRODUCER *speaks sharply to her she stays still quite
removed from them all.*

ACTOR 1: Very good! etc.

PRODUCER (*angrily*). Be quiet! Do you think this is a night-
club? (*Turns to* FATHER *and asks with some concern.*) Is she
a bit mad?

FATHER. Mad? Oh no — it's worse than that.

STEPDAUGHTER (*suddenly running to the* PRODUCER). Yes.
It's worse, much worse! Listen please! Let's put this play on
at once, because you'll see that at a particular point I — when
this darling little girl here — (*Taking the* LITTLE GIRL *by the
hand from next to the* MOTHER *and crossing with her to the*
PRODUCER.) Isn't she pretty? (*Takes her in her arms.*)
Darling! Darling! (*Puts her down again and adds, moved very
deeply but almost without wanting to.*) Well, this lovely little
girl here, when God suddenly takes her from this poor Mother:
and this little idiot here (*Turning to the* LITTLE BOY *and
seizing him roughly by the sleeve.*) does the most stupid thing,
like the half-wit he is, — then you will see me run away! Yes,
you'll see me rush away! But not yet, not yet! Because, after
all the intimate things there have been between him and me
(*In the direction of the* FATHER, *with a horrible vulgar
wink.*) I can't stay with them any longer, to watch the insult
to this mother through that supercilious cretin over there.
(*Pointing to the* SON.) Look at him! Look at him!
Condescending, stand-offish, because he's the legitimate son,
him! Full of contempt for me, for the boy and for the little
girl: because we are bastards. Do you understand? Bastards.
(*Running to the* MOTHER *and embracing her.*) And this poor
mother — she — who is the mother of all of us — he doesn't
want to recognise her as his own mother — and he looks down
on her, he does, as if she were only the mother of the three
of us who are bastards — the traitor. (*She says all this quickly,
with great excitement, and after having raised her voice on
the word 'bastards' she speaks quietly, half-spitting the word
'traitor'.*)

MOTHER (*with deep anguish to the* PRODUCER). Sir, in the
name of these two little ones, I beg you . . . (*Feels herself*

grow faint and sways.) Oh, my God.

FATHER (*rushing to support her with almost all the* ACTORS *bewildered and concerned*). Get a chair someone . . . quick, get a chair for this poor widow.

> One of the ACTORS *offers a chair: the others press urgently around. The* MOTHER, *seated now, tries to stop the* FATHER *lifting her veil.*

ACTORS. Is it real? Has she really fainted? etc.

FATHER. Look at her, everybody, look at her.

MOTHER. No, for God's sake, stop it.

FATHER. Let them look!

MOTHER (*lifting her hands and covering her face, desperately*). Oh, please, I beg you, stop him from doing what he is trying to do; it's hateful.

PRODUCER (*overwhelmed, astounded*). It's no use, I don't understand this any more. (*To the* FATHER.) Is this woman your wife?

FATHER (*at once*). That's right, she is my wife.

PRODUCER. How is she a widow, then, if you're still alive?

> The ACTORS *are bewildered too and find relief in a loud laugh.*

FATHER (*wounded, with rising resentment*). Don't laugh! Please don't laugh like that! That's just the point, that's her own drama. You see, she had another man. Another man who ought to be here.

MOTHER. No, no! (*Crying out.*)

STEPDAUGHTER. Luckily for him he died. Two months ago, as I told you: we are in mourning for him, as you can see.

FATHER. Yes, he's dead: but that's not the reason he isn't here. He isn't here because — well just look at her, please, and you'll understand at once — hers is not a passionate drama of the love of two men, because she was incapable of love, she could feel nothing — except, perhaps a little gratitude (but not to me, to him). She's not a woman; she's a mother. And her drama — and, believe me, it's a powerful one — her drama is focused completely on these four children of the two men she had.

MOTHER. I had them? How dare you say that I had them, as if I wanted them myself? It was him, sir! He forced the other man on me. He made me go away with him!

STEPDAUGHTER (*leaping up, indignantly*). It isn't true!

MOTHER (*bewildered*). How isn't it true?

STEPDAUGHTER. It isn't true, it just isn't true.

MOTHER. What do you know about it?

STEPDAUGHTER. It isn't true. (*To the* PRODUCER.) Don't believe it! Do you know why she said that? She said it because of him, over there. (*Pointing to the* SON.) She tortures herself, she exhausts herself with worry and all because of the indifference of that son of hers. She wants to make him believe that she abandoned him when he was two years old because the Father made her do it.

MOTHER (*passionately*). He did! He made me! God's my witness. (*To the* PRODUCER.) Ask him if it isn't true. (*Pointing to the* FATHER.) Make him tell our son it's true. (*Turning to the* STEPDAUGHTER.) You don't know anything about it.

STEPDAUGHTER. I know that when my father was alive you were always happy and contented. You can't deny it.

MOTHER. No, I can't deny it.

STEPDAUGHTER. He was always full of love and care for you. (*Turning to the* LITTLE BOY *with anger.*) Isn't it true? Admit it. Why don't you say something, you little idiot?

MOTHER. Leave the poor boy alone! Why do you want to make me appear ungrateful? You're my daughter. I don't in the least want to offend your father's memory. I've already told him that it wasn't my fault or even to please myself that I left his house and my son.

FATHER. It's quite true. It was my fault.

LEADING ACTOR (*to other actors*). Look at this. What a show!

LEADING ACTRESS. And we're the audience.

YOUNG ACTOR. For a change.

PRODUCER (*beginning to be very interested*). Let's listen to them! Quiet! Listen!

> *He goes down the steps into the auditorium and stands there as if to get an idea of what the scene will look like from the audience's viewpoint.*

SON (*without moving, coldly, quietly, ironically*). Yes, listen to his little scrap of philosophy. He's going to tell you all about the Daemon of Experiement.

FATHER. You're a cynical idiot, and I've told you so a hundred times. (*To the* PRODUCER *who is now in the stalls.*) He sneers at me because of this expression I've found to defend myself.

SON. Words, words.

FATHER. Yes words, words! When we're faced by something we don't understand, by a sense of evil that seems as if it's going to swallow us, don't we all find comfort in a word that tells us nothing but that calms us?

STEPDAUGHTER. And dulls your sense of remorse, too. That more than anything.

FATHER. Remorse? No, that's not true. It'd take more than words to dull the sense of remorse in me.

STEPDAUGHTER. It's taken a little money too, just a little money. The money that he was going to offer as payment, gentlemen.

> The ACTORS *are horrified.*

SON (*contemptuously to his stepsister*). That's a filthy trick.

STEPDAUGHTER. A filthy trick? There it was in a pale blue envelope on the little mahogany table in the room behind the shop at Madame Pace's. You know Madame Pace, don't you? One of those Madames who sell 'Robes et Manteaux' so that they can attract poor girls like me from decent families into their workroom.

SON. And she's bought the right to tyrannise over the whole lot of us with that money — with what he was going to pay her: and luckily — now listen carefully — he had no reason to pay it to her.

STEPDAUGHTER. But it was close!

MOTHER (*rising up angrily*). Shame on you, daughter! Shame!

STEPDAUGHTER. Shame? Not shame, revenge! I'm desperate, desperate to live that scene! The room . . . over here the show-case of coats, there the divan, there the mirror, and the screen, and over there in front of the window, that little mahogany table with the pale blue envelope and the money in it. I can see it all quite clearly. I could pick it up! But you should turn your faces

away, gentlemen: because I'm nearly naked! I'm not blushing any
longer — I leave that to him. *(Pointing at the* FATHER.) But I tell
you he was very pale, very pale then. *(To the* PRODUCER.)
Believe me.

PRODUCER. I don't understand any more.

FATHER. I'm not surprised when you're attacked like that!
Why don't you put your foot down and let me have my say
before you believe all these horrible slanders she's so viciously
telling about me.

STEPDAUGHTER. We don't want to hear any of your long
winded fairy-stories.

FATHER. I'm not going to tell any fairy-stories! I want to explain
things to him.

STEPDAUGHTER. I'm sure you do. Oh, yes! In your own
special way.

The PRODUCER *comes back up on stage to take control.*

FATHER. But isn't that the cause of all the trouble? Words!
We all have a world of things inside ourselves and each one of
us has his own private world. How can we understand each
other if the words I use have the sense and the value that I
expect them to have, but whoever is listening to me
inevitably thinks that those same words have a different sense
and value, because of the private world he has inside himself
too. We think we understand each other: but we never do.
Look! All my pity, all my compassion for this woman
(Pointing to the MOTHER.) she sees as ferocious cruelty.

MOTHER. But he turned me out of the house!

FATHER. There, do you hear? I turned her out! She really
believed that I had turned her out.

MOTHER. You know how to talk. I don't . . . But believe me,
sir, *(Turning to the* PRODUCER.) after he married me . . . I
can't think why! I was a poor, simple woman.

FATHER. But that was the reason! I married you for your
simplicity, that's what I loved in you, believing — *(He
stops because she is making gestures of contradiction. Then,
seeing the impossibility of making her understand, he throws
his arms wide in a gesture of desperation and turns back to*

the PRODUCER.) No, do you see? She says no! It's terrifying, sir, believe me, terrifying, her deafness, her mental deafness. (*He taps his forehead.*) Affection for her children, oh yes. But deaf, mentally deaf, deaf, sir, to the point of desperation.

STEPDAUGHTER. Yes, but make him tell you what good all his cleverness has brought us.

FATHER. If only we could see in advance all the harm that can come from the good we think we are doing.

> *The* LEADING ACTRESS, *who has been growing angry watching the* LEADING ACTOR *flirting with the* STEPDAUGHTER, *comes forward and snaps at the* PRODUCER.

LEADING ACTRESS. Excuse me, are we going to go on with our rehearsal?

PRODUCER. Yes, of course. But I want to listen to this first.

YOUNG ACTOR. It's such a new idea.

YOUNG ACTRESS. It's fascinating.

LEADING ACTRESS. For those who are interested. (*She looks meaningfully at the* LEADING ACTOR.)

PRODUCER (*to the* FATHER). Look here, you must explain yourself more clearly. (*He sits down.*)

FATHER. Listen then. You see, there was a rather poor fellow working for me as my assistant and secretary, very loyal: he understood her in everything. (*Pointing to the* MOTHER.) But without a hint of deceit, you must believe that: he was good and simple, like her: neither of them was capable even of thinking anything wrong, let alone doing it.

STEPDAUGHTER. So instead he thought of it for them and did it too!

FATHER. It's not true! What I did was for their good — oh yes and mine too, I admit it! The time had come when I couldn't say a word to either of them without there immediately flashing between them a sympathetic look: each one caught the other's eye for advice, about how to take what I had said, how not to make me angry. Well, that was enough, as I'm sure you'll understand, to put me in a bad temper all the time, in a state of intolerable exasperation.

PRODUCER. Then why didn't you sack this secretary of yours?

FATHER. Right! In the end I did sack him! But then I had to watch this poor woman wandering about in the house on her own, forlorn, like a stray animal you take in out of pity.

MOTHER. It's quite true.

FATHER (*suddenly, turning to her, as if to stop her*). And what about the boy? Is that true as well?

MOTHER. But first he tore my son from me, sir.

FATHER. But not out of cruelty! It was so that he could grow up healthy and strong, in touch with the earth.

STEPDAUGHTER (*pointing to the* SON *jeeringly*). And look at the result!

FATHER (*quickly*). And is it my fault, too, that he's grown up like this? I took him to a nurse in the country, a peasant, because his mother didn't seem strong enough to me, although she is from a humble family herself. In fact that was what made me marry her. Perhaps it was superstitious of me; but what was I to do? I've always had this dreadful longing for a kind of sound moral healthiness.

> The STEPDAUGHTER *breaks out again into noisy laughter.*

Make her stop that! It's unbearable.

PRODUCER. Stop it will you? Let me listen, for God's sake.

> When the PRODUCER *has spoken to her, she resumes her previous position . . . absorbed and distant, a half-smile on her lips. The* PRODUCER *comes down into the auditorium again to see how it looks from there.*

FATHER. I couldn't bear the sight of this woman near me. (*Pointing to the* MOTHER.) Not so much because of the annoyance she caused me, you see, or even the feeling of being stifled, being suffocated that I got from her, as for the sorrow, the painful sorrow that I felt for her.

MOTHER. And he sent me away.

FATHER. With everything you needed, to the other man, to set her free from me.

MOTHER. And to set yourself free!

FATHER. Oh, yes, I admit it. And what terrible things came out of it. But I did it for the best, and more for her than

...it! (*Folds his arms: then turns suddenly to the*
...never lost sight of you did I? Until that fellow,
...knowing it, suddenly took you off to another
...day. He was idiotically suspicious of my interest in
...genuine interest, I assure you, without any ulterior
...at all. I watched the new little family growing up
round her with unbelievable tenderness, she'll confirm that.
(*He points to the* STEPDAUGHTER.)

STEPDAUGHTER. Oh yes, I can indeed. I was a pretty little
girl, you know, with plaits down to my shoulders and my little
frilly knickers showing under my dress — so pretty — he used
to watch me coming out of school. He came to see how I was
maturing.

FATHER. That's shameful! It's monstrous.

STEPDAUGHTER. No it isn't! Why do you say it is?

FATHER. It's monstrous! Monstrous. (*He turns excitedly to the*
PRODUCER *and goes on in explanation.*) After she'd gone
away (*Pointing to the* MOTHER.), my house seemed empty.
She'd been like a weight on my spirit but she'd filled the house
with her presence. Alone in the empty rooms I wandered
about like a lost soul. This boy here, (*Indicating the* SON.)
growing up away from home — whenever he came back to the
home — I don't know — but he didn't seem to be mine any
more. We needed the mother between us, to link us together,
and so he grew up by himself, apart, with no connection to
me either through intellect or love. And then — it must seem
odd, but it's true — first I was curious about and then strongly
attracted to the little family that had come about because of
what I'd done. And the thought of them began to fill all the
emptiness that I felt around me. I needed, I really needed to
believe that she was happy, wrapped up in the simple cares
of her life, lucky because she was better off away from the
complicated torments of a soul like mine. And to prove it,
I used to watch that child coming out of school.

STEPDAUGHTER. Listen to him! He used to follow me along
the street; he used to smile at me and when we came near the
house he'd wave his hand — like this! I watched him, wide-
eyed, puzzled. I didn't know who he was. I told my mother
about him and she knew at once who it must be. (MOTHER

nods agreement.) At first, she didn't let me go to school again, at any rate for a few days. But when I did go back, I saw him standing near the door again — looking ridiculous — with a brown paper bag in his hand. He came close and petted me: then he opened the bag and took out a beautiful straw hat with a hoop of rosebuds round it — for me!

PRODUCER. All this is off the point, you know.

SON (*contemptuously*). Yes . . . literature, literature.

FATHER. What do you mean, literature? This is real life: real passions.

PRODUCER. That may be! But you can't put it on the stage just like that.

FATHER. That's right you can't. Because all this is only leading up to the main action. I'm not suggesting that this part should be put on the stage. In any case, you can see for yourself, (*Pointing at the* STEPDAUGHTER.) she isn't a pretty little girl any longer with plaits down to her shoulders.

STEPDAUGHTER. — and with frilly knickers showing under her frock.

FATHER. The drama begins now: and it's new and complex.

STEPDAUGHTER (*coming forward, fierce and brooding*). As soon as my father died . . .

FATHER (*quickly, not giving her time to speak*). They were so miserable. They came back here, but I didn't know about it because of the Mother's stubbornness. (*Pointing to the* MOTHER.) She can't really write you know; but she could have got her daughter to write, or the boy, or tell me that they needed help.

MOTHER. But tell me, sir, how could I have known how he felt?

FATHER. And hasn't that always been your fault? You've never known anything about how I felt.

MOTHER. After all the years away from him and after all that had happened.

FATHER. And was it my fault if that fellow took you so far away? (*Turning back to the* PRODUCER.) Suddenly, overnight, I tell you, he'd found a job away from here without my knowing anything about it. I couldn't possibly trace them; and then, naturally I suppose, my interest in them grew less over the years. The drama broke out, unexpected and violent, when they came back: when I was driven in misery by the needs of my flesh, still alive with desire . . . and it is misery, you know, unspeakable misery for the man who lives alone and who detests sordid, casual affairs; not old enough to do without women, but not young enough to be able to go and look for one without shame! Misery? Is that what I called it. It's horrible, it's revolting, because there isn't a woman who will give her love to him any more. And when he realises this, he should do without . . . It's easy to say though. Each of us, face to face with other men, is clothed with some sort of dignity, but we know only too well all the unspeakable things that go on in the heart. We surrender, we give in to temptation: but afterwards we rise up out of it very quickly, in a desperate hurry to rebuild our dignity, whole and firm as if it were a gravestone that would cover every sign and memory of our shame, and hide it from even our own eyes. Everyone's like that, only some of us haven't the courage to talk about it.

STEPDAUGHTER. But they've all got the courage to do it!

FATHER. Yes! But only in secret! That's why it takes more courage to talk about it! Because if a man does talk about it — what happens then? — everybody says he's a cynic. And it's simply not true; he's just like everybody else; only better perhaps, because he's not afraid to use his intelligence to point out the blushing shame of human bestiality, that man, the beast, shuts his eyes to, trying to pretend it doesn't exist. And what about woman — what is she like? She looks at you invitingly, teasingly. You take her in your arms. But as soon as she feels your arms round her she closes her eyes. It's the sign of her mission, the sign by which she says to a man, 'Blind yourself — I'm blind!'

STEPDAUGHTER. And when she doesn't close her eyes any more? What then? When she doesn't feel the need to hide from herself any more, to shut her eyes and hide her own shame. When she can see instead, dispassionately and dry-eyed this blushing shame of a man who has blinded himself, who is without love. What then? Oh, then what disgust, what utter disgust she feels for all these intellectual complications, for all this philosophy that points to the bestiality of man and

then tries to defend him, to excuse him . . . I can't listen to
him, sir. Because when a man says he needs to 'simplify' life
like this — reducing it to bestiality — and throws away every
human scrap of innocent desire, genuine feeling, idealism,
duty, modesty, shame, then there's nothing more
contemptible and nauseating than his remorse — crocodile
tears!

PRODUCER. Let's get to the point, let's get to the point. This is
all chat.

FATHER. Right then! But a fact is like a sack — it won't stand
up if it's empty. To make it stand up, first you have to put
in it all the reasons and feelings that caused it in the first place.
I couldn't possibly have known that when that fellow died
they'd come back here, that they were desperately poor and
that the Mother had gone out to work as a dressmaker, nor
that she'd gone to work for Madame Pace, of all people.

STEPDAUGHTER. She's a very high-class dressmaker — you
must understand that. She apparently has only high-class
customers, but she has arranged things carefully so that these
high-class customers in fact serve her — they give her a respectable
front . . . without spoiling things for the other ladies at the shop,
who are not quite so high-class at all.

MOTHER. Believe me, sir, the idea never entered my head that
the old hag gave me work because she had an eye on my
daughter . . .

STEPDAUGHTER. Poor Mummy! Do you know what that
woman would do when I took back the work that my mother
had been doing? She would point out how the dress had been
ruined by giving it to my mother to sew: she bargained, she
grumbled. So, you see, I paid for it, while this poor woman
here thought she was sacrificing herself for me and these two
children, sewing dresses all night for Madame Pace.

The ACTORS *make gestures and noises of disgust.*

PRODUCER (*quickly*). And there one day, you met . . .

STEPDAUGHTER (*pointing at the* FATHER). Yes, him. Oh,
he was an old customer of hers! What a scene that's going to
be, superb!

FATHER. With her, the mother, arriving —

STEPDAUGHTER (*quickly, viciously*). — Almost in time!

FATHER (*crying out*). — No, just in time, just in time!
Because, luckily, I found out who she was in time. And I
took them all back to my house, sir. Can you imagine the
situation now, for the two of us living in the same house? She,
just as you see her here: and I, not able to look her in the face.

STEPDAUGHTER. It's so absurd! Do you think it's possible
for me, sir, after what happened at Madame Pace's, to pretend
that I'm a modest little miss, well brought up and virtuous
just so that I can fit in with his damned pretensions to a
'sound moral healthiness'?

FATHER. This is the real drama for me; the belief that we all,
you see, think of ourselves as one single person: but it's not
true: each of us is several different people, and all these people
live inside us. With one person we seem like this and with
another we seem very different. But we always have the
illusion of being the same person for everybody and of always
being the same person in everything we do. But it's not true!
It's not true! We find this out for ourselves very clearly when
by some terrible chance we're suddenly stopped in the middle
of doing something and we're left dangling there, suspended.
We realise then, that every part of us was not involved in
what we'd been doing and that it would be a dreadful
injustice of other people to judge us only by this one action
as we dangle there, hanging in chains, fixed for all eternity,
as if the whole of one's personality were summed up in that
single, interrupted action. Now do you understand this girl's
treachery? She accidentally found me somewhere I shouldn't
have been, doing something I shouldn't have been doing! She
discovered a part of me that shouldn't have existed for her:
and now she wants to fix on me a reality that I should never have
had to assume for her: it came from a single brief and shameful
moment in my life. This is what hurts me most of all. And
you'll see that the play will make a tremendous impact from
this idea of mine. But then, there's the position of the others.
His . . . (*Pointing to the* SON.)

SON (*shrugging his shoulders scornfully*). Leave me out of it.
I don't come into this.

FATHER. Why don't you come into this?

SON. I don't come into it and I don't want to come into it, because you know perfectly well that I wasn't intended to be mixed up with you lot.

STEPDAUGHTER. We're vulgar, common people, you see! He's a fine gentleman. But you've probably noticed that every now and then I look at him contemptuously, and when I do, he lowers his eyes — he knows the harm he's done me.

SON (*not looking at her*). I have?

STEPDAUGHTER. Yes, you. It's your fault, dearie, that I went on the streets! Your fault! (*Movement of horror from the* ACTORS.) Did you or didn't you, with your attitude, deny us — I won't say the intimacy of your home — but that simple hospitality that makes guests feel comfortable? We were intruders who had come to invade the country of your 'legitimacy'! (*Turning to the* PRODUCER.) I'd like you to have seen some of the little scenes that went on between him and me, sir. He says that I tyrannised over everyone. But don't you see? It was because of the way he treated us. He called it 'vile' that I should insist on the right we had to move into his house with my mother — and she's his mother too. And I went into the house as its mistress.

SON (*slowly coming forward*). They're really enjoying themselves, aren't they, sir? It's easy when they all gang up against me. But try to imagine what happened: one fine day, there is a son sitting quietly at home and he sees arrive as bold as brass, a young woman like this, who cheekily asks for his father, and heaven knows what business she has with him. Then he sees her come back with the same brazen look in her eye accompanied by that little girl there: and he sees her treat his father — without knowing why — in a most ambiguous and insolent way — asking him for money in a tone that leads one to suppose he really ought to give it, because he is obliged to do so.

FATHER. But I was obliged to do so: I owed it to your mother.

SON. And how was I to know that? When had I ever seen her before? When had I ever heard her mentioned? Then one day I see her come in with her (*Pointing at the* STEPDAUGHTER.), that boy and that little girl: they say to me, 'Oh, didn't you know? This is your mother, too.' Little by little I began to understand, mostly from her attitude (*Points to* STEPDAUGHTER.) why they'd come to live in the house so suddenly. I can't and I won't say what I feel, and what I think. I wouldn't even like to confess it to myself. So I can't take any active part in this. Believe me, sir, I am a character who has not been fully developed dramatically, and I feel uncomfortable, most uncomfortable, in their company. So please leave me out of it.

FATHER. What! But it's precisely because you feel like this . . .

SON (*violently exasperated*). How do you know what I feel? When have you ever bothered yourself about me?

FATHER. All right! I admit it! But isn't that a situation in itself? This withdrawing of yourself, it's cruel to me and to your mother: when she came back to the house, seeing you almost for the first time, not recognising you, but knowing that you're her own son . . . (*Turning to point out the* MOTHER *to the* PRODUCER.) There, look at her: she's weeping.

STEPDAUGHTER (*angrily, stamping her foot*). Like the fool she is!

FATHER (*quickly pointing at the* STEPDAUGHTER *to the* PRODUCER). She can't stand that young man, you know. (*Turning and referring to the* SON.) He says that he doesn't come into it, but he's really the pivot of the action! Look here at this little boy, who clings to his mother all the time, frightened, humiliated. And it's because of him over there! Perhaps this little boy's problem is the worst of all: he feels an outsider, more than the others do; he feels so mortified, so humiliated just being in the house, — because it's charity, you see. (*Quietly.*) He's like his father: timid; he doesn't say anything . . .

PRODUCER. It's not a good idea at all, using him: you don't know what a nuisance children are on the stage.

FATHER. He won't need to be on the stage for long. Nor will the little girl — she's the first to go.

PRODUCER. That's good! Yes. I tell you all this interests me — it interests me very much. I'm sure we've the material here for a good play.

STEPDAUGHTER (*trying to push herself in*). With a character like me you have!

FATHER (*driving her off, wanting to hear what the* PRODUCER
has decided). You stay out of it!

PRODUCER (*going on, ignoring the interruption*). It's new,
yes.

FATHER. Oh, it's absolutely new!

PRODUCER. You've got a nerve, though, haven't you, coming
here and throwing it at me like this?

FATHER. I'm sure you understand. Born as we are for the
stage . . .

PRODUCER. Are you amateur actors?

FATHER. No! I say we are born for the stage because . . .

PRODUCER. Come on now! You're an old hand at this, at
acting!

FATHER. No I'm not. I only act, as everyone does, the part in
life that he's chosen for himself, or that others have chosen
for him. And you can see that sometimes my own passion
gets a bit out of hand, a bit theatrical, as it does with all of
us.

PRODUCER. Maybe, maybe . . . But you do see, don't you,
that without an author . . . I could give you someone's
address . . .

FATHER. Oh no! Look here! You do it.

PRODUCER. Me? What are you talking about?

FATHER. Yes, you. Why not?

PRODUCER. Because I've never written anything!

FATHER. Well, why not start now, if you don't mind my
suggesting it? There's nothing to it. Everybody's doing it.
And your job is even easier, because we're here, all of us, alive
before you.

PRODUCER. That's not enough.

FATHER. Why isn't it enough? When you've seen us live our
drama . . .

PRODUCER. Perhaps so. But we'll still need someone to write
it.

FATHER. Only to write it down, perhaps, while it happens in
front of him — live — scene by scene. It'll be enough to
sketch it out simply first and then run through it.

PRODUCER (*coming back up, tempted by the idea*). Do you

know I'm almost tempted . . . just for fun . . . it might work.

FATHER. Of course it will. You'll see what wonderful scenes will come right out of it! I could tell you what they will be!

PRODUCER. You tempt me . . . you tempt me! We'll give it a chance. Come with me to the office. (*Turning to the* ACTORS.) Take a break: but don't go far away. Be back in a quarter of an hour or twenty minutes. (*To the* FATHER.) Let's see, let's try it out. Something extraordinary might come out of this.

FATHER. Of course it will! Don't you think it'd be better if the others came too? (*Indicating the other* CHARACTERS.)

PRODUCER. Yes, come on, come on. (*Going, then turning to speak to the* ACTORS.) Don't forget: don't be late: back in a quarter of an hour.

> The PRODUCER *and the* SIX CHARACTERS *cross the stage and go. The* ACTORS *look at each other in astonishment.*

LEADING ACTOR. Is he serious? What's he going to do?

YOUNG ACTOR. I think he's gone round the bend.

ANOTHER ACTOR. Does he expect to make up a play in five minutes?

YOUNG ACTOR. Yes, like the old actors in the commedia del'arte!

LEADING ACTRESS. Well if he thinks I'm going to appear in that sort of nonsense . . .

YOUNG ACTOR. Nor me!

FOURTH ACTOR. I should like to know who they are.

THIRD ACTOR. Who do you think? They're probably escaped lunatics — or crooks.

YOUNG ACTOR. And is he taking them seriously?

YOUNG ACTRESS. It's vanity. The vanity of seeing himself as an author.

LEADING ACTOR. I've never heard of such a thing! If the theatre, ladies and gentlemen, is reduced to this . . .

FIFTH ACTOR. I'm enjoying it!

THIRD ACTOR. Really? We shall have to wait and see what happens next I suppose.

Talking, they leave the stage. Some go out through the
back door, some to the dressing-rooms.
The Curtain stays up.
The interval lasts twenty minutes.

Act Two

The theatre warning-bell sounds to call the audience back. From the dressing-rooms, the door at the back and even from the auditorium, the ACTORS, *the* STAGE MANAGER, *the* STAGE HANDS, *the* PROMPTER, *the* PROPERTY MAN *and the* PRODUCER, *accompanied by the* SIX CHARACTERS *all come back on to the stage.*

The house lights go out and the stage lights come on again.

PRODUCER. Come on, everybody! Are we all here? Quiet now! Listen! Let's get started! Stage manager?

STAGE MANAGER. Yes, I'm here.

PRODUCER. Give me that little parlour setting, will you? A couple of plain flats and a door flat will do. Hurry up with it!

> *The* STAGE MANAGER *runs off to order someone to do this immediately and at the same time the* PRODUCER *is making arrangements with the* PROPERTY MAN, *the* PROMPTER, *and the* ACTORS: *the two flats and the door flat are painted in pink and gold stripes.*

PRODUCER (*to* PROPERTY MAN). Go see if we have a sofa in stock.

PROPERTY MAN. Yes, there's that green one.

STEPDAUGHTER. No, no, not a green one! It was yellow, yellow velvet with flowers on it: it was enormous! And so comfortable!

PROPERTY MAN. We haven't got one like that.

PRODUCER. It doesn't matter! Give me whatever there is.

STEPDAUGHTER. What do you mean, it doesn't matter? It was Mme. Pace's famous sofa.

PRODUCER. It's only for a rehearsal! Please, don't interfere. (*To the* STAGE MANAGER.) Oh, and see if there's a shop window, will you — preferably a long, low one.

STEPDAUGHTER. And a little table, a little mahogany table for the blue envelope.

STAGE MANAGER (*to the* PRODUCER). There's that little gold one.

PRODUCER. That'll do — bring it.

FATHER. A mirror!

STEPDAUGHTER. And a screen! A screen, please, or I won't be able to manage, will I?

STAGE MANAGER. All right. We've lots of big screens, don't you worry.

PRODUCER (*to* STEPDAUGHTER). Then don't you want some coat-hangers and some clothes racks?

STEPDAUGHTER. Yes, lots of them, lots of them.

PRODUCER (*to the* STAGE MANAGER). See how many there are and have them brought up.

STAGE MANAGER. Right, I'll see to it.

The STAGE MANAGER *goes off to do it: and while the* PRODUCER *is talking to the* PROMPTER, *the* CHARACTERS *and the* ACTORS, *the* STAGE MANAGER *is telling the* SCENE SHIFTERS *where to set up the furniture they have brought.*

PRODUCER (*to the* PROMPTER). Now you, go sit down, will you? Look, this is an outline of the play, act by act. (*He hands him several sheets of paper.*) But you'll need to be on your toes.

PROMPTER. Shorthand?

PRODUCER (*pleasantly surprised*). Oh, good! You know shorthand?

PROMPTER. I don't know much about prompting, but I do know about shorthand.

PRODUCER. Thank God for that anyway! (*He turns to a* STAGE HAND.) Go fetch me some paper from my office — lots of it — as much as you can find!

The STAGE HAND *goes running off and then comes back shortly with a bundle of paper that he gives to the* PROMPTER.

PRODUCER (*crossing to the* PROMPTER). Follow the scenes, one after another, as they are played and try to get the lines down . . . at least the most important ones. (*Then turning to the* ACTORS.) Get out of the way everybody! Here, go over to the prompt side (*Pointing to stage left.*) and pay attention!

LEADING ACTRESS. But, excuse me, we . . .

PRODUCER (*anticipating her*). You won't be expected to improvise, don't worry!

LEADING ACTOR. Then what are we expected to do?

PRODUCER. Nothing! Just go over there, listen and watch. You'll all be given your parts later written out. Right now we're going to rehearse, as well as we can. And they will be doing the rehearsal. (*He points to the* CHARACTERS.)

FATHER (*rather bewildered, as if he had fallen from the clouds into the middle of the confusion on the stage*). We are? Excuse me, but what do you mean, a rehearsal?

PRODUCER. I mean a rehearsal — a rehearsal for the benefit of the actors. (*Pointing to the* ACTORS.)

FATHER. But if we are the characters . . .

PRODUCER. That's right, you're 'the characters': but characters don't act here, my dear chap. It's actors who act here. The characters are there in the script — (*Pointing to the* PROMPTER.) that's when there is a script.

FATHER. That's the point! Since there isn't one and you have the luck to have the characters alive in front of you . . .

PRODUCER. Great! You want to do everything yourselves, do you? To act your own play, to produce your own play!

FATHER. Well yes, just as we are.

PRODUCER. That would be an experience for us, I can tell you!

LEADING ACTOR. And what about us? What would we be doing then?

PRODUCER. Don't tell me you think you know how to act! Don't make me laugh! (*The* ACTORS *in fact laugh.*) There you are, you see, you've made them laugh. (*Then remembering.*) But let's get back to the point! We need to cast the play. Well, that's easy: it almost casts itself. (*To the* SECOND ACTRESS.) You, the mother. (*To the* FATHER.) You'll need to give her a name.

FATHER. Amalia.

PRODUCER. But that's the real name of your wife isn't it? We can't use her real name.

FATHER. But why not? That is her name . . . But perhaps if this lady is to play the part . . . (*Indicating the* ACTRESS *vaguely with a wave of his hand.*) I think of her as Amalia . . . (*Pointing to the* MOTHER.) But do as you like . . . (*A little confused.*) I don't know what to say . . . I'm already starting to . . . how can I explain it . . . to sound false, my own words sound like someone else's.

PRODUCER. Now don't worry yourself about it, don't worry about it at all. We'll work out the right tone of voice. As for the name, if you want it to be Amalia, then Amalia it shall be: or we can find another. For the moment we'll refer to the characters like this: (*To the* YOUNG ACTOR, *the juvenile lead.*) you are The Son. (*To the* LEADING ACTRESS.) You, of course, are The Stepdaughter.

STEPDAUGHTER (*excitedly*). What did you say? That woman is me? (*Bursts into laughter.*)

PRODUCER (*angrily*). What are you laughing at?

LEADING ACTRESS (*indignantly*). Nobody has ever dared to laugh at me before! Either you treat me with respect or I'm walking out! (*Starting to go.*)

STEPDAUGHTER. I'm sorry. I wasn't really laughing at you.

PRODUCER (*to the* STEPDAUGHTER). You should feel proud to be played by . . .

LEADING ACTRESS (*quickly, scornfully*). . . . that woman!

STEPDAUGHTER. But I wasn't thinking about her, honestly. I was thinking about me: I can't see myself in you at all . . . you're not a bit like me!

FATHER. Yes, that's right: you see, our meaning . . .

PRODUCER. What are you talking about, 'our meaning'? Do you think you have exclusive rights to what you represent? Do you think it can only exist inside you? Not a bit of it!

FATHER. What? Don't we even have our own meaning?

PRODUCER. Not a bit of it! Whatever you mean is only material here, to which the actors give form and body, voice and gesture, and who, through their art, have given expression to much better material than what you have to offer: yours is really very trivial and if it stands up on the stage, the credit, believe me, will all be due to my actors.

FATHER. I don't dare to contradict you. But you for your part, must believe me — it doesn't seem trivial to us. We are suffering terribly now, with these bodies, these faces . . .

PRODUCER (*interrupting impatiently*). Yes, well, the make-up will change that, make-up will change that, at least as far as the faces are concerned.

FATHER. Yes, but the voices, the gestures . . .

PRODUCER. That's enough! You can't come on the stage here as yourselves. It is our actors who will represent you here: and let that be the end of it!

FATHER. I understand that. But now I think I see why our author who saw us alive as we are here now, didn't want to put us on the stage. I don't want to offend your actors. God forbid that I should! But I think that if I saw myself represented . . . by I don't know whom . . .

LEADING ACTOR (*rising majestically and coming forward, followed by a laughing group of* YOUNG ACTRESSES). By me, if you don't object.

FATHER (*respectfully, smoothly*). I shall be honoured, sir. (*He bows.*) But I think, that no matter how hard this gentleman works with all his will and all his art to identify himself with me . . . (*He stops, confused.*)

LEADING ACTOR. Yes, go on.

FATHER. Well, I was saying the performance he will give, even if he is made up to look like me . . . I mean with the difference in our appearance . . . (*All the* ACTORS *laugh.*) it will be difficult for it to be a performance of me as I really am. It will be more like — well, not just because of his figure — it will be more an interpretation of what I am, what he believes me to be, and not how I know myself to be. And it seems to me that this should be taken into account by those who are going to comment on us.

PRODUCER. So you are already worrying about what the critics will say, are you? And I'm still waiting to get this thing started! The critics can say what they like: and we'll worry about putting on the play. If we can! (*Stepping out of the group and looking around.*) Come on, come on! Is the scene set for us yet? (*To the* ACTORS *and* CHARACTERS.)

Out of the way! Let's have a look at it. (*Climbing down off the stage.*) Don't let's waste any more time. (*To the* STEPDAUGHTER.) Does it look all right to you?

STEPDAUGHTER. What? That? I don't recognise it at all.

PRODUCER. Good God! Did you expect us to reconstruct the room at the back of Mme. Pace's shop here on the stage? (*To the* FATHER.) Did you say the room had flowered wallpaper?

FATHER. White, yes.

PRODUCER. Well it's not white: it's striped. That sort of thing doesn't matter at all! As for the furniture, it looks to me as if we have nearly everything we need. Move that little table a bit further downstage. (*A* STAGE HAND *does it. To the* PROPERTY MAN.) Go and fetch an envelope, pale blue if you can find one, and give it to that gentleman there. (*Pointing to the* FATHER.)

STAGE HAND. An envelope for letters?

PRODUCER)
 FATHER   )   Yes, an envelope for letters!

STAGE HAND. Right. (*He goes off.*)

PRODUCER. Now then, come on! The first scene is the young lady's. (*The* LEADING ACTRESS *comes to the centre.*) No, no, not yet. I said the young lady's. (*He points to the* STEPDAUGHTER.) You stay there and watch.

STEPDAUGHTER (*adding quickly*). . . . how I bring it to life.

LEADING ACTRESS (*resenting this*). I shall know how to bring it to life, don't you worry, when I am allowed to.

PRODUCER (*his head in his hands*). Ladies, please, no more arguments! Now then. The first scene is between the young lady and Mme Pace. Oh! (*Worried, turning round and looking out into the auditorium.*) Where is Mme. Pace?

FATHER. She isn't here with us.

PRODUCER. So what do we do now?

FATHER. But she is real. She's real too!

PRODUCER. All right. So where is she?

FATHER. May I deal with this? (*Turns to the* ACTRESSES.) Would each of you ladies be kind enough to lend me a hat, a coat, a scarf or something?

ACTRESSES (*some are surprised or amused*). What? My scarf?

A coat? What's he want my hat for? What are you wanting to do with them? (*All the* ACTRESSES *are laughing.*)

FATHER. Oh, nothing much, just hang them up here on the racks for a minute or two. Perhaps someone would be kind enough to lend me a coat?

ACTORS. Just a coat? Come on, more! The man must be mad.

AN ACTRESS. What for? Only my coat?

FATHER. Yes, to hang up here, just for a moment. I'm very grateful to you. Do you mind?

ACTRESSES (*taking off various hats, coats, scarves, laughing and going to hang them on the racks*). Why not? Here you are. I really think it's crazy. Is it to dress the set?

FATHER. Yes, exactly. It's to dress the set.

PRODUCER. Would you mind telling me what you are doing?

FATHER. Yes, of course: perhaps, if we dress the set better, she will be drawn by the articles of her trade and, who knows, she may even come to join us . . . (*He invites them to watch the door at the back of the set.*) Look! Look!

> The door at the back opens and MME. PACE *takes a few steps downstage: she is a gross old harridan wearing a ludicrous carroty-coloured wig with a single red rose stuck in at one side, Spanish fashion: garishly made-up: in a vulgar but stylish red silk dress, holding an ostrich-feather fan in one hand and a cigarette between two fingers in the other. At the sight of this Apparition, the* ACTORS *and the* PRODUCER *immediately jump off the stage with cries of fear, leaping down into the auditorium and up the aisles. The* STEPDAUGHTER, *however, runs across to* MME. PACE, *and greets her respectfully, as if she were the mistress.*

STEPDAUGHTER (*running across to her*). Here she is! Here she is!

FATHER (*smiling broadly*). It's her! What did I tell you? Here she is!

PRODUCER (*recovering from his shock, indignantly*). What sort of trick is this?

LEADING ACTOR (*almost at the same time as the others*). What the hell is happening?

JUVENILE LEAD. Where on earth did they get that extra from?
YOUNG ACTRESS. They were keeping her hidden!
LEADING ACTRESS. It's a game, a conjuring trick!
FATHER. Wait a minute! Why do you want to spoil a miracle
   by being factual. Can't you see this is a miracle of reality,
   that is born, brought to life, lured here, reproduced, just
   for the sake of this scene, with more right to be alive here
   than you have? Perhaps it has more truth than you have
   yourselves. Which actress can improve on Mme. Pace there?
   Well? That is the real Mme. Pace. You must admit that the
   actress who plays her will be less true than she is herself —
   and there she is in person! Look! My daughter recognised her
   straight away and went to meet her. Now watch — just
   watch this scene.

> *Hesitantly, the* PRODUCER *and the* ACTORS *move back
> to their original places on the stage.*
>   *But the scene between the* STEPDAUGHTER *and* MME.
> PACE *has already begun while the* ACTORS *were
> protesting and the* FATHER *explaining: it is being played
> under their breaths, very quietly, very naturally, in a way
> that is obviously impossible on stage. So when the*
> ACTORS' *attention is recalled by the* FATHER *they turn
> and see that* MME. PACE *has just put her hand under the*
> STEPDAUGHTER'*s chin to make her lift her head up:
> they also hear her speak in a way that is unintelligible
> to them. They watch and listen hard for a few moments,
> then they start to make fun of them.*

PRODUCER. Well?
LEADING ACTOR. What's she saying?
LEADING ACTRESS. Can't hear a thing!
JUVENILE LEAD. Louder! Speak up!
STEPDAUGHTER (*leaving* MME. PACE *who has an astonishing
   smile on her face, and coming down to the* ACTORS). Louder?
   What do you mean, 'Louder'? What we're talking about you
   can't talk about loudly. I could shout about it a moment ago
   to embarrass him (*Pointing to the* FATHER.) to shame him
   and to get my own back on him! But it's a different matter
   for Mme. Pace. It would mean prison for her.

PRODUCER. What the hell are you on about? Here in the theatre you have to make yourself heard! Don't you see that? We can't hear you even from here, and we're on the stage with you! Imagine what it would be like with an audience out front! You need to make the scene go! And after all, you would speak normally to each other when you're alone, and you will be, because we shan't be here anyway. I mean we're only here because it's a rehearsal. So just imagine that there you are in the room at the back of the shop, and there's no one to hear you.

The STEPDAUGHTER, *with a knowing smile, wags her finger and her head rather elegantly, as if to say no.*

PRODUCER. Why not?

STEPDAUGHTER (*mysteriously, whispering loudly*). Because there is someone who will hear if she speaks normally. (*Pointing to* MME. PACE.)

PRODUCER (*anxiously*). You're not going to make someone else appear are you?

The ACTORS *get ready to dive off the stage again.*

FATHER. No, no. She means me. I ought to be over there, waiting behind the door: and Mme. Pace knows I'm there, so excuse me will you: I'll go there now so that I shall be ready for my entrance.

He goes towards the back of the stage.

PRODUCER (*stopping him*). No, no wait a minute! You must remember the stage conventions! Before you can go on to that part . . .

STEPDAUGHTER (*interrupts him*). Oh yes, let's get on with that part. Now! Now! I'm dying to do that scene. If he wants to go through it now, I'm ready!

PRODUCER (*shouting*). But before that we must have, clearly stated, the scene between you and her. (*Pointing to* MME. PACE.) Do you see?

STEPDAUGHTER. Oh God! She's only told me what you already know, that my mother's needlework is badly done again, the dress is spoilt and that I shall have to be patient if

I want her to go on helping us out of our mess.
MME. PACE (*coming forward, with a great air of importance*).
Ah, yes, sir, for that I do not wish to make a profit, to make
advantage.
PRODUCER (*half frightened*). What? Does she really speak like
that?

All the ACTORS *burst out laughing.*

STEPDAUGHTER (*laughing too*). Yes, she speaks like that, half
in Spanish, in the silliest way imaginable!
MME. PACE. Ah it is not good manners that you laugh at me
when I make myself to speak, as I can, English, senor.
PRODUCER. No, no, you're right! Speak like that, please speak
like that, madam. It'll be marvellous. Couldn't be better! It'll
add a little touch of comedy to a rather crude situation.
Speak like that! It'll be great!
STEPDAUGHTER. Great! Why not? When you hear a proposition
made in that sort of accent, it'll almost seem like a joke, won't
it? Perhaps you'll want to laugh when you hear that there's
an 'old senor' who wants to 'amuse himself with me' — isn't
that right, Madame?
MME. PACE. Not so old . . . but not quite young, no? But if he
is not to your taste . . . he is, how you say, discreet!

The MOTHER *leaps up, to the astonishment and dismay
of the* ACTORS *who had not been paying any attention
to her, so that when she shouts out they are startled and
then smilingly restrain her: however she has already
snatched off* MME. PACE's *wig and flung it on the floor.*

MOTHER. You witch! Witch! Murderess! Oh, my daughter!
STEPDAUGHTER (*running across and taking hold of the*
MOTHER). No! No! Mother! Please!
FATHER (*running across to her as well*). Calm yourself, calm
yourself! Come and sit down.
MOTHER. Get her away from here!
STEPDAUGHTER (*to the* PRODUCER *who has also crossed to
her*). My mother can't bear to be in the same place with her.
FATHER (*also speaking quietly to the* PRODUCER). They can't

possibly be in the same place! That's why she wasn't with
us when we first came, do you see! If they meet, everything's
given away from the very beginning.

PRODUCER. It's not important, that's not important! This is
only a first run-through at the moment! It's all useful stuff,
even if it is confused. I'll sort it all out later. (*Turning to the*
MOTHER *and taking her to sit down on her chair.*) Come on
my dear, take it easy, take it easy: come and sit down again.

STEPDAUGHTER. Go on, Mme. Pace.

MME. PACE (*offended*). Oh no, thank-you! I no longer do
nothing here with your mother present.

STEPDAUGHTER. Get on with it, bring in this 'old senor' who
wants to 'amuse himself with me'! (*Turning majestically to
the others.*) You see, this next scene has got to be played out
— we must do it now. (*To* MME. PACE.) Oh, you can go!

MME. PACE. Ah, I go, I go — I go! Most probably I go!

> *She leaves banging her wig back into place, glaring furiously
> at the* ACTORS *who applaud her exit, laughing loudly.*

STEPDAUGHTER (*to the* FATHER). Now you come on! No,
you don't need to go off again! Come back! Pretend you've
just come in! Look, I'm standing here with my eyes on the
ground, modestly — well, come on, speak up! Use that special
sort of voice, like somebody who has just come in. 'Good
afternoon, my dear.'

PRODUCER (*off the stage by now*). Look here, who's the director
here, you or me? (*To the* FATHER *who looks uncertain and
bewildered.*) Go on, do as she says: go upstage — no, no
don't bother to make an entrance. Then come down stage
again.

> *The* FATHER *does as he is told, half mesmerised. He is
> very pale but already involved in the reality of his
> recreated life, smiles as he draws near the back of the stage,
> almost if he genuinely is not aware of the drama that is
> about to sweep over him. The* ACTORS *are immediately
> intent on the scene that is beginning now.*

The Scene

FATHER (*coming forward with a new note in his voice*). Good afternoon, my dear.

STEPDAUGHTER (*her head down trying to hide her fright*). Good afternoon.

FATHER (*studying her a little under the brim of her hat which partly hides her face from him and seeing that she is very young, he exclaims to himself a little complacently and a little guardedly because of the danger of being compromised in a risky adventure*). Ah . . . but . . . tell me, this won't be the first time, will it? The first time you've been here?

STEPDAUGHTER. No, sir.

FATHER. You've been here before? (*And after the* STEP-DAUGHTER *has nodded an answer.*) More than once? (*He waits for her reply: tries again to look at her under the brim of her hat: smiles: then says.*) Well then . . . it shouldn't be too . . . May I take off your hat?

STEPDAUGHTER (*quickly, to stop him, unable to conceal her shudder of fear and disgust*). No, don't! I'll do it!

> She takes it off unsteadily.
> The MOTHER *watches the scene intently with the* SON *and the two smaller children who cling close to her all the time: they make a group on one side of the stage opposite the* ACTORS. *She follows the words and actions of the* FATHER *and the* STEPDAUGHTER *in this scene with a variety of expressions on her face — sadness, dismay, anxiety, horror: sometimes she turns her face away and sobs.*

MOTHER. Oh God! Oh God!

FATHER (*he stops as if turned to stone by the sobbing: then he goes on in the same tone of voice*). Here, give it to me. I'll hang it up for you. (*He takes the hat in his hand.*) But such a pretty, dear little head like yours should have a much smarter hat than this! Would you like to help me choose one, then, from these hats of Madame's hanging up here? Would you?

YOUNG ACTRESS (*interrupting*). Be careful! Those are our hats!

PRODUCER (*quickly and angrily*). For God's sake, shut up! Don't try to be funny! We're rehearsing! (*Turns back to the* STEPDAUGHTER.) Please go on, will you, from where you were interrupted.

STEPDAUGHTER (*going on*). No, thank you, sir.

FATHER. Oh, don't say no to me please! Say you'll have one — to please me. Isn't this a pretty one — look! And then it will please Madame too, you know. She's put them out here on purpose, of course.

STEPDAUGHTER. No, look, I could never wear it.

FATHER. Are you thinking of what they would say at home when you went in wearing a new hat? Goodness me! Don't you know what to do? Shall I tell you what to say at home?

STEPDAUGHTER (*furiously, nearly exploding*). That's not why! I couldn't wear it because . . . as you can see: you should have noticed it before. (*Indicating her black dress.*)

FATHER. You're in mourning! Oh, forgive me. You're right, I see that now. Please forgive me. Believe me, I'm really very sorry.

STEPDAUGHTER (*gathering all her strength and making herself overcome her contempt and revulsion*). That's enough. Don't go on, that's enough. I ought to be thanking you and not letting you blame yourself and get upset. Don't think any more about what I told you, please. And I should do the same. (*Forcing herself to smile and adding.*) I should try to forget that I'm dressed like this.

PRODUCER (*interrupting, turning to the* PROMPTER *in the box and jumping up on the stage again*). Hold it, hold it! Don't put that last line down, leave it out. (*Turning to the* FATHER *and the* STEPDAUGHTER.) It's going well! It's going well! (*Then to the* FATHER *alone.*) Then we'll put in there the bit that we talked about. (*To the* ACTORS.) That scene with the hats is good, isn't it?

STEPDAUGHTER. But the best bit is coming now! Why can't we get on with it?

PRODUCER. Just be patient, wait a minute. (*Turning and moving across to the* ACTORS.) Of course, it'll all have to be made a lot more light-hearted.

LEADING ACTOR. We shall have to play it a lot quicker, I think.

LEADING ACTRESS. Of course: there's nothing particularly
  difficult in it. (*To the* LEADING ACTOR.) Shall we run
  through it now?
LEADING ACTOR. Yes right . . . Shall we take it from my
  entrance? (*He goes to his position behind the door upstage.*)
PRODUCER (*to the* LEADING ACTRESS). Now then, listen,
  imagine the scene between you and Mme. Pace is finished.
  I'll write it up myself properly later on. You ought to be over
  here I think – (*She goes the opposite way.*) Where are you
  going now?
LEADING ACTRESS. Just a minute, I want to get my hat –
  (*She crosses to take her hat from the stand.*)
PRODUCER. Right, good, ready now? You are standing here
  with your head down.
STEPDAUGHTER (*very amused*). But she's not dressed in
  black!
LEADING ACTRESS. Oh, but I shall be, and I'll look a lot
  better than you do, darling.
PRODUCER (*to the* STEPDAUGHTER). Shut up, will you!
  Go over there and watch! You might learn something!
  (*Clapping his hands.*) Right! Come on! Quiet please! Take it
  from his entrance.

> *He climbs off stage so that he can see better. The door
> opens at the back of the set and the* LEADING ACTOR
> *enters with the lively, knowing air of an ageing rouet. The
> playing of the following scene by the* ACTORS *must
> seem from the very beginning to be something quite
> different from the earlier scene, but without having the
> faintest air of parody in it.*
>
> *Naturally the* STEPDAUGHTER *and the* FATHER,
> *unable to see themselves in the* LEADING ACTOR *and*
> LEADING ACTRESS, *hearing their words said by them,
> express their reactions in different ways, by gestures, or
> smiles or obvious protests so that we are aware of their
> suffering, their astonishment, their disbelief.*
>
> *The* PROMPTER's *voice is heard clearly between every
> line in the scene, telling the* ACTORS *what to say next.*

LEADING ACTOR. Good afternoon, my dear.

FATHER (*immediately, unable to restrain himself*). Oh, no!

> The STEPDAUGHTER, *watching the* LEADING ACTOR *enter this way, bursts into laughter.*

PRODUCER (*furious*). Shut up, for God's sake! And don't you dare laugh like that! We're never going to get anywhere at this rate.

STEPDAUGHTER (*coming to the front*). I'm sorry, I can't help it! The lady stands exactly where you told her to stand and she never moved. But if it were me and I heard someone say good afternoon to me in that way and with a voice like that I should burst out laughing — so I did.

FATHER (*coming down a little too*). Yes, she's right, the whole manner, the voice . . .

PRODUCER. To hell with the manner and the voice! Get out of the way, will you, and let me watch the rehearsal!

LEADING ACTOR (*coming down stage*). If I have to play an old man who has come to a knocking shop —

PRODUCER. Take no notice, ignore them. Go on please! It's going well, it's going well! (*He waits for the* ACTOR *to begin again*). Right, again!

LEADING ACTOR. Good afternoon, my dear.

LEADING ACTRESS. Good afternoon.

LEADING ACTOR (*copying the gestures of the* FATHER, *looking under the brim of the hat, but expressing distinctly the two emotions, first, complacent satisfaction and then anxiety*). Ah! But tell me . . . this won't be the first time I hope.

FATHER (*instinctively correcting him*). Not 'I hope' — 'will it', 'will it'.

PRODUCER. Say 'will it' — and it's a question.

LEADING ACTOR (*glaring at the* PROMPTER). I distinctly heard him say 'I hope'.

PRODUCER. So what? It's all the same, 'I hope' or 'isn't it'. It doesn't make any difference. Carry on, carry on. But perhaps it should still be a little bit lighter; I'll show you — watch me! (*He climbs up on the stage again, and going back to the entrance, he does it himself.*) Good afternoon, my dear.

LEADING ACTRESS. Good afternoon.

PRODUCER. Ah, tell me . . . (*He turns to the* LEADING ACTOR *to make sure that he has seen the way he has demonstrated of looking under the brim of the hat.*) You see — surprise . . . anxiety and self-satisfaction. (*Then, starting again, he turns to the* LEADING ACTRESS.) This won't be the first time, will it? The first time you've been here? (*Again turns to the* LEADING ACTOR, *questioningly.*) Right? (*To the* LEADING ACTRESS.) And then she says, 'No, sir'. (*Again to* LEADING ACTOR.) See what I mean? More subtlety. (*And he climbs off the stage.*)

LEADING ACTRESS. No, sir.

LEADING ACTOR. You've been here before? More than once?

PRODUCER. No, no, no! Wait for it, wait for it. Let her answer first. 'You've been here before?'

> The LEADING ACTRESS *lifts her head a little, her eyes closed in pain and disgust, and when the* PRODUCER *says 'Now' she nods her head twice.*

STEPDAUGHTER (*involuntarily*). Oh, my God! (*And she immediately claps her hand over her mouth to stifle her laughter.*)

PRODUCER. What now?

STEPDAUGHTER (*quickly*). Nothing, nothing!

PRODUCER (*to* LEADING ACTOR). Come on, then, now it's you.

LEADING ACTOR. More than once? Well then, it shouldn't be too . . . May I take off your hat?

> The LEADING ACTOR *says this last line in such a way and adds to it such a gesture that the* STEPDAUGHTER, *even with her hand over her mouth trying to stop herself laughing, can't prevent a noisy burst of laughter.*

LEADING ACTRESS (*indignantly turning*). I'm not staying any longer to be laughed at by that woman!

LEADING ACTOR. Nor am I! That's the end — no more!

PRODUCER (*to* STEPDAUGHTER, *shouting*). Once and for all, will you shut up! Shut up!

STEPDAUGHTER. Yes, I'm sorry . . . I'm sorry.

PRODUCER. You're an ill-mannered little bitch! That's what

you are! And you've gone too far this time!

FATHER (*trying to interrupt*). Yes, you're right, she went too far, but please forgive her . . .

PRODUCER (*jumping on the stage*). Why should I forgive her? Her behaviour is intolerable!

FATHER. Yes, it is, but the scene made such a peculiar impact on us . . .

PRODUCER. Peculiar? What do you mean peculiar? Why peculiar?

FATHER. I'm full of admiration for your actors, for this gentleman (*To the* LEADING ACTOR.) and this lady. (*To the* LEADING ACTRESS.) But, you see, well . . . they're not us!

PRODUCER. Right! They're not! They're actors!

FATHER. That's just the point — they're actors. And they are acting our parts very well, both of them. But that's what's different. However much they want to be the same as us, they're not.

PRODUCER. But why aren't they? What is it now?

FATHER. It's something to do with . . . being themselves, I suppose, not being us.

PRODUCER. Well we can't do anything about that! I've told you already. You can't play the parts yourselves.

FATHER. Yes, I know, I know . . .

PRODUCER. Right then. That's enough of that. (*Turning back to the* ACTORS.) We'll rehearse this later on our own, as we usually do. It's always a bad idea to have rehearsals with authors there! They're never satisfied. (*Turns back to the* FATHER *and the* STEPDAUGHTER.) Come on, let's get on with it; and let's see if it's possible to do it without laughing.

STEPDAUGHTER. I won't laugh any more, I won't really. My best bit's coming up now, you wait and see!

PRODUCER. Right: when you say 'Don't think any more about what I told you, please. And I should do the same'. (*Turning to the* FATHER.) then you come in immediately with the line 'I understand, ah yes, I understand' and then you ask . . .

STEPDAUGHTER (*interrupting*). Ask what? What does he ask?

PRODUCER. Why you're in mourning.

STEPDAUGHTER. No! No! That's not right! Look: when I said that I should try not to think about the way I was dressed, do you know what he said? 'Well then, let's take it off, we'll take it off at once, shall we, your little black dress.'

PRODUCER. That's great! That'll be wonderful! That'll bring the house down!

STEPDAUGHTER. But it's the truth!

PRODUCER. The truth! Do me a favour will you? This is the theatre you know! Truth's all very well up to a point but . . .

STEPDAUGHTER. What do you want to do then?

PRODUCER. You'll see! You'll see! Leave it all to me.

STEPDAUGHTER. No. No I won't. I know what you want to do! Out of my feeling of revulsion, out of all the vile and sordid reasons why I am what I am, you want to make a sugary little sentimental romance. You want him to ask me why I'm in mourning and you want me to reply with the tears running down my face that it is only two months since my father died. No. No. I won't have it! He must say to me what he really did say. 'Well then, let's take it off, we'll take it off at once, shall we, your little black dress.' And I, with my heart still grieving for my father's death only two months before, I went behind there, do you see? Behind that screen and with my fingers trembling with shame and loathing I took off the dress, unfastened my bra . . .

PRODUCER (*his head in his hands*). For God's sake! What are you saying!

STEPDAUGHTER (*shouting excitedly*). The truth! I'm telling you the truth!

PRODUCER. All right then. Now listen to me. I'm not denying it's the truth. Right. And believe me I understand your horror, but you must see that we can't really put a scene like that on the stage.

STEPDAUGHTER. You can't? Then thanks very much. I'm not stopping here.

PRODUCER. No, listen . . .

STEPDAUGHTER. No, I'm going. I'm not stopping. The pair of you have worked it all out together, haven't you, what to put in the scene. Well, thank you very much! I understand everything now! He wants to get to the scene where he can talk about his spiritual torments but I want to show you my drama! Mine!

PRODUCER (*shaking with anger*). Now we're getting to the

real truth of it, aren't we? Your drama — yours! But it's not
only yours, you know. It's drama for the other people as
well! For him (*Pointing to the* FATHER.) and for your
mother! You can't have one character coming on like you're
doing, trampling over the others, taking over the play.
Everything needs to be balanced and in harmony so that we
can show what has to be shown! I know perfectly well that
we've all got a life inside us and that we all want to parade it
in front of other people. But that's the difficulty, how to
present only the bits that are necessary in relation to the
other characters: and in the small amount we show, to hint
at all the rest of the inner life of the character! I agree, it
would be so much simpler, if each character, in a soliloquy
or in a lecture could pour out to the audience what's
bubbling away inside him. But that's not the way we work.
(*In an indulgent, placating tone.*) You must restrain yourself,
you see. And believe me, it's in your own interests: because
you could so easily make a bad impression, with all this
uncontrollable anger, this disgust and exasperation. That
seems a bit odd, if you don't mind my saying so, when you've
admitted that you'd been with other men at Mme. Pace's
and more than once.

STEPDAUGHTER. I suppose that's true. But you know, all the
other men were all him as far as I was concerned.

PRODUCER (*not understanding*). Uum — ? What? What are you
talking about?

STEPDAUGHTER. If someone falls into evil ways, isn't the
responsibility for all the evil which follows to be laid at the
door of the person who caused the first mistake? And in my
case, it's him, from before I was even born. Look at him: see
if it isn't true.

PRODUCER. Right then! What about the weight of remorse he's
carrying? Isn't that important? Then, give him the chance to
show it to us.

STEPDAUGHTER. But how? How on earth can he show all his
long-suffering remorse, all his moral torments as he calls
them, if you don't let him show his horror when he finds me
in his arms one fine day, after he had asked me to take my
dress off, a black dress for my father who had just died: and

he finds that I'm the child he used to go and watch as she
came out of school, me, a woman now, and a woman he could
buy. (*She says these last words in a voice trembling with
emotion.*)

> The MOTHER, *hearing her say this, is overcome and at
> first gives way to stifled sobs: but then she bursts out into
> uncontrollable crying. Everyone is deeply moved. There is
> a long pause.*

STEPDAUGHTER (*as soon as the MOTHER has quietened
herself she goes on, firmly and thoughtfully*). At the moment
we are here on our own and the public doesn't know about
us. But tomorrow you will present us and our story in
whatever way you choose, I suppose. But wouldn't you
like to see the real drama? Wouldn't you like to see it explode
into life, as it really did?

PRODUCER. Of course, nothing I'd like better, then I can use
as much of it as possible.

STEPDAUGHTER. Then persuade my mother to leave.

MOTHER (*rising and her quiet weeping changing to a loud cry*).
No! No! Don't let her! Don't let her do it!

PRODUCER. But they're only doing it for me to watch — only
for me, do you see?

MOTHER. I can't bear it, I can't bear it!

PRODUCER. But if it's already happened, I can't see what's the
objection.

MOTHER. No! It's happening now, as well: it's happening all
the time. I'm not acting my suffering! Can't you understand
that? I'm alive and here now but I can never forget that
terrible moment of agony, that repeats itself endlessly and
vividly in my mind. And these two little children here, you've
never heard them speak have you? That's because they don't
speak any more, not now. They just cling to me all the time:
they help to keep my grief alive, but they don't really exist for
themselves any more, not for themselves. And she (*Indicating
the* STEPDAUGHTER.) . . . she has gone away, left me
completely, she's lost to me, lost . . . you see her here for
one reason only: to keep perpetually before me, always real,
the anguish and the torment I've suffered on her account.

FATHER. The eternal moment, as I told you, sir. She is here (*Indicating the* STEPDAUGHTER.) to keep me too in that moment, trapped for all eternity, chained and suspended in that one fleeting shameful moment of my life. She can't give up her role and you cannot rescue me from it.

PRODUCER. But I'm not saying that we won't present that bit. Not at all! It will be the climax of the first act, when she (*He points to the* MOTHER.) surprises you.

FATHER. That's right, because that is the moment when I am sentenced: all our suffering should reach a climax in her cry. (*Again indicating the* MOTHER.)

STEPDAUGHTER. I can still hear it ringing in my ears! It was that cry that sent me mad! You can have me played just as you like: it doesn't matter! Dressed, too, if you want, so long as I can have at least an arm — only an arm — bare, because, you see, as I was standing like this (*She moves across to the* FATHER *and leans her head on his chest.*) with my head like this and my arms round his neck, I saw a vein, here in my arm, throbbing: and then it was almost as if that throbbing vein filled me with a shivering fear, and I shut my eyes tightly like this, like this and buried my head in his chest. (*Turning to the* MOTHER.) Scream, Mummy, scream. (*She buries her head in the* FATHER's *chest, and with her shoulders raised as if to try not to hear the scream, she speaks with a voice tense with suffering.*) Scream, as you screamed then!

MOTHER (*coming forward to pull them apart*). No! She's my daughter! My daughter! (*Tearing her from him.*) You brute, you animal, she's my daughter! Can't you see she's my daughter?

PRODUCER (*retreating as far as the footlights while the* ACTORS *are full of dismay*). Marvellous! Yes, that's great! And then curtain, curtain!

FATHER (*running downstage to him, excitedly*). That's it, that's it! Because it really was like that!

PRODUCER (*full of admiration and enthusiasm*). Yes, yes, that's got to be the curtain line! Curtain! Curtain!

   At the repeated calls of the PRODUCER, *the* STAGE MANAGER *lowers the curtain, leaving on the apron in front, the* PRODUCER *and the* FATHER.

PRODUCER (*looking up to heaven with his arms raised*). The idiots! I didn't mean now! The bloody idiots — dropping it in on us like that! (*To the* FATHER, *and lifting up a corner of the curtain.*) That's marvellous! Really marvellous! A terrific effect! We'll end the act like that! It's the best tag line I've heard for ages. What a First Act ending! I couldn't have done better if I'd written it myself!

   They go through the curtain together.

Act Three

When the curtain goes up we see that the STAGE MANAGER *and* STAGE HANDS *have struck the first scene and have set another, a small garden fountain.*

From one side of the stage the ACTORS *come on and from the other the* CHARACTERS. *The* PRODUCER *is standing in the middle of the stage with his hand over his mouth, thinking.*

PRODUCER (*after a short pause, shrugging his shoulders*). Well, then: let's get on to the second act! Leave it all to me, and everything will work out properly.

STEPDAUGHTER. This is where we go to live at his house (*Pointing to the* FATHER.) in spite of the objections of him over there. (*Pointing to the* SON.)

PRODUCER (*getting impatient*). All right, all right! But leave it all to me, will you?

STEPDAUGHTER. Provided that you make it clear that he objected!

MOTHER (*from the corner, shaking her head*). That doesn't matter! The worse it was for us, the more he suffered from remorse.

PRODUCER (*impatiently*). I know, I know! I'll take it all into account. Don't worry!

MOTHER (*pleading*). To set my mind at rest, sir, please do make sure it's clear that I tried all I could —

STEPDAUGHTER (*interrupting her scornfully and going on*). — to pacify me, to persuade me that this despicable creature wasn't worth making trouble about! (*To the* PRODUCER.) Go on, set her mind at rest, because it's true, she tried very hard. I'm having a whale of a time now! You can see, can't you, that the meeker she was and the more she tried to worm her way into his heart, the more lofty and distant he became! How's that for a dramatic situation!

PRODUCER. Do you think that we can actually begin the Second Act?

STEPDAUGHTER. I won't say another word! But you'll see that it won't be possible to play everything in the garden, like you want to do.

PRODUCER. Why not?

STEPDAUGHTER (*pointing to the* SON). Because to start with, he stays shut up in his room in the house all the time! And then all the scenes for this poor little devil of a boy happen in the house. I've told you once.

PRODUCER. Yes, I know that! But on the other hand we can't put up a notice to tell the audience where the scene is taking place, or change the set three or four times in each Act.

LEADING ACTOR. That's what they used to do in the good old days.

PRODUCER. Yes, when the audience was about as bright as that little girl over there!

LEADING ACTRESS. And it makes it easier to create an illusion.

FATHER (*leaping up*). An illusion? For pity's sake don't talk about illusions! Don't use that word, it's especially hurtful to us!

PRODUCER (*astonished*). And why, for God's sake?

FATHER. It's so hurtful, so cruel! You ought to have realised that!

PRODUCER. What else should we call it? That's what we do here — create an illusion for the audience . . .

LEADING ACTOR. With our performance . . .

PRODUCER. A perfect illusion of reality!

FATHER. Yes, I know that, I understand. But on the other hand, perhaps you don't understand us yet. I'm sorry! But you see, for you and for your actors what goes on here on the stage is, quite rightly, well, it's only a game.

LEADING ACTRESS (*interrupting indignantly*). A game! How dare you! We're not children! What happens here is serious!

FATHER. I'm not saying that it isn't serious. And I mean, really, not just a game but an art, that tries, as you've just said, to create the perfect illusion of reality.

PRODUCER. That's right!

FATHER. Now try to imagine that we, as you see us here, (*He indicates himself and the other* CHARACTERS.) that we have no other reality outside this illusion.

PRODUCER (*astonished and looking at the* ACTORS *with the same sense of bewilderment as they feel themselves*).What the hell are you talking about now?

FATHER (*after a short pause as he looks at them, with a faint smile*). Isn't it obvious? What other reality is there for us? What for you is an illusion you create, for us is our only reality. (*Brief pause. He moves towards the* PRODUCER *and goes on.*) But it's not only true for us, it's true for others as well, you know. Just think about it. (*He looks intently into the* PRODUCER's *eyes.*) Do you really know who you are? (*He stands pointing at the* PRODUCER.)

PRODUCER (*a little disturbed but with a half smile*). What? Who I am? I am me!

FATHER. What if I told you that that wasn't true: what if I told you that you were me?

PRODUCER. I would tell you that you were mad!

The ACTORS *laugh.*

FATHER. That's right, laugh! Because everything here is a game! (*To the* PRODUCER.) And yet you object when I say that it is only for a game that the gentleman there (*Pointing to the* LEADING ACTOR.) who is 'himself' has to be 'me', who, on the contrary, am 'myself'. You see, I've caught you in a trap.

The ACTORS *start to laugh.*

PRODUCER. Not again! We've heard all about this a little while ago.

FATHER. No, no. I didn't really want to talk about this. I'd like you to forget about your game, (*Looking at the* LEADING ACTRESS *as if to anticipate what she will say.*) I'm sorry — your artistry! Your art! — that you usually pursue here with your actors; and I am going to ask you again in all seriousness, who are you?

PRODUCER (*turning with a mixture of amazement and annoyance, to the* ACTORS). Of all the bloody nerve!A fellow who claims he is only a character comes and asks me who I am!

FATHER (*with dignity but without annoyance*). A character, my dear sir, can always ask a man who he is, because a character really has a life of his own, a life full of his own specific qualities, and because of these he is always 'someone'. While a man — I'm not speaking about you personally, of course, but man in general — well, he can be an absolute 'nobody'.

PRODUCER. All right, all right! Well, since you've asked me, I'm the Director, the Producer — I'm in charge! Do you understand?

FATHER (*half smiling, but gently and politely*). I'm only asking to try to find out if you really see yourself now in the same way that you saw yourself, for instance, once upon a time in the past, with all the illusions you had then, with everything inside and outside yourself as it seemed then — and not only seemed, but really was! Well then, look back on those illusions, those ideas that you don't have any more, on all those things that no longer seem the same to you. Don't you feel that not only this stage is falling away from under your feet but so is the earth itself, and that all these realities of today are going to seem tomorrow as if they had been an illusion?

PRODUCER. So? What does that prove?

FATHER. Oh, nothing much. I only want to make you see that if we (*Pointing to himself and the other* CHARACTERS.) have no other reality outside our own illusion, perhaps you ought to distrust your own sense of reality: because whatever is a reality today, whatever you touch and believe in and that seems real for you today, is going to be — like the reality of yesterday — an illusion tomorrow.

PRODUCER (*deciding to make fun of him*). Very good! So now you're saying that you as well as this play you're going to show me here, are more real than I am?

FATHER (*very seriously*). There's no doubt about that at all.

PRODUCER. Is that so?

FATHER. I thought you'd realised that from the beginning.

PRODUCER. More real than I am?

FATHER. If your reality can change between today and tomorrow —

PRODUCER. But everybody knows that it can change, don't
    they? It's always changing! Just like everybody else's!
FATHER (*crying out*). But ours doesn't change! Do you see?
    That's the difference! Ours doesn't change, it can't change,
    it can never be different, never, because it is already
    determined, like this, for ever, that's what's so terrible! We
    are an eternal reality. That should make you shudder to
    come near us.
PRODUCER (*jumping up, suddenly struck by an idea, and
    standing directly in front of the* FATHER). Then I should like
    to know when anyone saw a character step out of his part
    and make a speech like you've done, proposing things,
    explaining things. Tell me when, will you? I've never seen it
    before.
FATHER. You've never seen it because an author usually hides
    all the difficulties of creating. When the characters are alive,
    really alive and standing in front of their author, he has only
    to follow their words, the actions that they suggest to him:
    and he must want them to be what they want to be: and it's
    his bad luck if he doesn't do what they want! When a character
    is born he immediately assumes such an independence even
    of his own author that everyone can imagine him in scores
    of situations that his author hadn't even thought of putting
    him in, and he sometimes acquires a meaning that his author
    never dreamed of giving him.
PRODUCER. Of course I know all that.
FATHER. Well, then. Why are you surprised by us? Imagine what
    a disaster it is for a character to be born in the imagination
    of an author who then refuses to give him life in a written
    script. Tell me if a character, left like this, suspended,
    created but without a final life, isn't right to do what we are
    doing now, here in front of you. We spent such a long time,
    such a very long time, believe me, urging our author,
    persuading him, first me, then her, (*Pointing to the*
    STEPDAUGHTER.) then this poor Mother . . .
STEPDAUGHTER (*coming down the stage as if in a dream*).
    It's true, I would go, would go and tempt him, time after
    time, in his gloomy study just as it was growing dark, when he
    was sitting quietly in an armchair not even bothering to switch

a light on but leaving the shadows to fill the room: the
shadows were swarming with us, we had come to tempt him.
(*As if she could see herself there in the study and is annoyed
by the presence of the* ACTORS.) Go away will you! Leave
us alone! Mother there, with that son of hers — me with the
little girl — that poor little kid always on his own — and then
me with him (*Pointing to the* FATHER.) and then at last,
just me, on my own, all on my own, in the shadows. (*She
turns quickly as if she wants to cling on to the vision she has
of herself, in the shadows.*) Ah, what scenes, what scenes we
suggested to him! What a life I could have had! I tempted
him more than the others!

FATHER. Oh yes, you did! And it was probably all your fault
that he did nothing about it! You were so insistent, you made
too many demands.

STEPDAUGHTER. But he wanted me to be like that! (*She comes
closer to the* PRODUCER *to speak to him in confidence.*)
I think it's more likely that he felt discouraged about the
theatre and even despised it because the public only wants to
see . . .

PRODUCER. Let's get on, for God's sake, let's get on. Come to
the point will you?

STEPDAUGHTER. I'm sorry, but if you ask me, we've got too
much happening already, just with our entry into his house.
(*Pointing to the* FATHER.) You said that we couldn't put
up a notice or change the set every five minutes.

PRODUCER. Right! Of course we can't! We must combine things,
group them together in one continuous flowing action: not
the way you've been wanting, first of all seeing your little
brother come home from school and wander about the house
like a lost soul, hiding behind the doors and brooding on
some plan or other that would — what did you say it would
do?

STEPDAUGHTER. Wither him . . . shrivel him up completely.

PRODUCER. That's good! That's a good expression. And then
you 'can see it there in his eyes, getting stronger all the
time' — isn't that what you said?

STEPDAUGHTER. Yes, that's right. Look at him! (*Pointing to
him as he stands next to his* MOTHER.)

PRODUCER. Yes, great! And then, at the same time, you want to show the little girl playing in the garden, all innocence. One in the house and the other in the garden — we can't do it, don't you see that?

STEPDAUGHTER. Yes, playing in the sun, so happy! It's the only pleasure I have left, her happiness, her delight in playing in the garden: away from the misery, the squalor of that sordid flat where all four of us slept and where she slept with me — with me! Just think of it! My vile, contaminated body close to hers, with her little arms wrapped tightly round my neck, so lovingly, so innocently. In the garden, whenever she saw me, she would run and take my hand. She never wanted to show me the big flowers, she would run about looking for the 'little weeny' ones, so that she could show them to me; she was so happy, so thrilled! (*As she says this, tortured by the memory, she breaks out into a long desperate cry, dropping her head on her arms that rest on a little table. Everybody is very affected by her. The* PRODUCER *comes to her almost paternally and speaks to her in a soothing voice.*)

PRODUCER. We'll have the garden scene, we'll have it, don't worry: and you'll see, you'll be very pleased with what we do! We'll play all the scenes in the garden! (*He calls out to a* STAGE HAND *by name.*) Hey . . . . , let down a few bits of tree, will you? A couple of cypresses will do, in front of the fountain. (*Someone drops in the two cypresses and a* STAGE HAND *secures them with a couple of braces and weights.*)

PRODUCER (*to the* STEPDAUGHTER). That'll do for now, won't it? It'll just give us an idea. (*Calling out to a* STAGE HAND *by name again.*) Hey, ... give me something for the sky will you?

STAGE HAND. What's that?

PRODUCER. Something for the sky! A small cloth to come in behind the fountain. (*A white cloth is dropped from the flies.*) Not white! I asked for a sky! Never mind: leave it! I'll do something with it. (*Calling out.*) Hey lights! Kill everything will you? Give me a bit of moonlight — the blues in the batten and a blue spot on the cloth . . . (*They do.*) That's it!

That'll do! (*Now on the scene there is the light he asked for, a mysterious blue light that makes the* ACTORS *speak and move as if in the garden in the evening under a moon. To the* STEPDAUGHTER.) Look here now: the little boy can come out here in the garden and hide among the trees instead of hiding behind the doors in the house. But it's going to be difficult to find a little girl to play the scene with you where she shows you the flowers. (*Turning to the* LITTLE BOY.) Come on, come on, son, come across here. Let's see what it'll look like. (*But the* BOY *doesn't move.*) Come on will you, come on. (*Then he pulls him forward and tries to make him hold his head up, but every time it falls down again on his chest.*) There's something very odd about this lad . . . What's wrong with him? My God, he'll have to say something sometime! (*He comes over to him again, puts his hand on his shoulder and pushes him between the trees.*) Come a bit nearer: let's have a look. Can you hide a bit more? That's it. Now pop your head out and look round. (*He moves away to look at the effect and as the* BOY *does what he has been told to do, the* ACTORS *watch impressed and a little disturbed.*) Ahh, that's good, very good . . . (*He turns to the* STEPDAUGHTER.) How about having the little girl, surprised to see him there, run across. Wouldn't that make him say something?

STEPDAUGHTER (*getting up*). It's no use hoping he'll speak, not as long as that creature's there. (*Pointing to the* SON.) You'll have to get him out of the way first.

SON (*moving determinedly to one of the sets of steps leading off the stage*). With pleasure! I'll go now! Nothing will please me better!

PRODUCER (*stopping him immediately*). Hey, no! Where are you going? Hang on!

> The MOTHER *gets up, anxious at the idea that he is really going and instinctively raising her arms as if to hold him back, but without moving from where she is.*

SON (*at the footlights, to the* PRODUCER *who is restraining him there*). There's no reason why I should be here! Let me go will you? Let me go!

PRODUCER. What do you mean there's no reason for you to be here?

STEPDAUGHTER (*calmly, ironically*). Don't bother to stop him. He won't go!

FATHER. You have to play that terrible scene in the garden with your mother.

SON (*quickly, angry and determined*). I'm not going to play anything! I've said that all along! (*To the* PRODUCER.) Let me go will you?

STEPDAUGHTER (*crossing to the* PRODUCER). It's all right. Let him go. (*She moves the* PRODUCER's *hand from the* SON. *Then she turns to the* SON *and says.*) Well, go on then! Off you go!

> The SON *stays near the steps but as if pulled by some strange force he is quite unable to go down them: then to the astonishment and even the dismay of the* ACTORS, *he moves along the front of the stage towards the other set of steps down into the auditorium: but having got there, he again stays near and doesn't actually go down them. The* STEPDAUGHTER *who has watched him scornfully but very intently, bursts into laughter.*

STEPDAUGHTER. He can't, you see? He can't! He's got to stay here! He must. He's chained to us for ever! No, I'm the one who goes, when what must happen does happen, and I run away, because I hate him, because I can't bear the sight of him any longer. Do you think it's possible for him to run away? He has to stay here with that wonderful father of his and his mother there. She doesn't think she has any other son but him. (*She turns to the* MOTHER.) Come on, come on, Mummy, come on! (*Turning back to the* PRODUCER *to point her out to him.*) Look, she's going to try to stop him ... (*To the* MOTHER, *half compelling her, as if by some magic power.*) Come on, come on. (*Then to the* PRODUCER *again.*) Imagine how she must feel at showing her affection for him in front of your actors! But her longing to be near him is so strong that — look! She's going to go through that scene with him again! (*The* MOTHER *has now actually come close to the* SON *as the* STEPDAUGHTER *says the last line: she gestures to show that she agrees to go on.*)

SON (*quickly*). But I'm not! I'm not! If I can't get away then I suppose I shall have to stay here; but I repeat that I will not have any part in it.

FATHER (*to the* PRODUCER, *excitedly*). You must make him!

SON. Nobody's going to make me do anything!

FATHER. I'll make you!

STEPDAUGHTER. Wait! Just a minute! Before that, the little girl has to go to the fountain. (*She turns to take the* LITTLE GIRL, *drops on her knees in front of her and takes her face between her hands.*) My poor little darling, those beautiful eyes, they look so bewildered. You're wondering where you are, aren't you? Well, we're on a stage, my darling! What's a stage? Well, it's a place where you pretend to be serious. They put on plays here. And now we're going to put on a play. Seriously! Oh, yes! Even you ... (*She hugs her tightly and rocks her gently for a moment.*) Oh, my little one, my little darling, what a terrible play it is for you! What horrible things have been planned for you! The garden, the fountain ... Oh, yes, it's only a pretend fountain, that's right. That's part of the game, my pretty darling: everything is pretends here. Perhaps you'll like a pretends fountain better than a real one: you can play here then. But it's only a game for the others; not for you, I'm afraid, it's real for you, my darling, and your game is in a real fountain, a big beautiful green fountain with bamboos casting shadows, looking at your own reflection, with lots of baby ducks paddling about, shattering the reflections. You want to stroke one! (*With a scream that electrifies and terrifies everybody*.) No, Rosetta, no! Your mummy isn't watching you, she's over there with that selfish bastard! Oh, God, I feel as if all the devils in hell were tearing me apart inside ... And you ... (*Leaving the* LITTLE GIRL *and turning to the* LITTLE BOY *in the usual way*.) What are you doing here, hanging about like a beggar? It'll be your fault too, if that little girl drowns; you're always like this, as if I wasn't paying the price for getting all of you into this house. (*Shaking his arm to make him take his hand out of his pocket*.) What have you got there? What

are you hiding? Take it out, take your hand out! (*She drags
his hand out of his pocket and to everyone's horror he is
holding a revolver. She looks at him for a moment, almost
with satisfaction: then she says, grimly.*) Where on earth did
you get that? (*The* BOY, *looking frightened, with his eyes
wide and empty, doesn't answer.*) You idiot, if I'd been you,
instead of killing myself, I'd have killed one of those two:
either or both, the father and the son. (*She pushes him towards
the cypress trees where he then stands watching: then she takes
the* LITTLE GIRL *and helps her to climb in to the fountain,
making her lie so that she is hidden: after that she kneels
down and puts her head and arms on the rim of the fountain.*)
PRODUCER. That's good! It's good! (*Turning to the* STEP-
DAUGHTER.) And at the same time . . .
SON (*scornfully*). What do you mean, at the same time? There
was nothing at the same time! There wasn't any scene between
her and me. (*Pointing to the* MOTHER.) She'll tell you the same
thing herself, she'll tell you what happened.

> The SECOND ACTRESS *and the* JUVENILE LEAD *have
> left the group of* ACTORS *and have come to stand nearer
> the* MOTHER *and the* SON *as if to study them so as to play
> their parts.*

MOTHER. Yes, it's true. I'd gone to his room . . .
SON. Room, do you hear? Not the garden!
PRODUCER. It's not important! We've got to reorganise the
events anyway. I've told you that already.
SON (*glaring at the* JUVENILE LEAD *and the* SECOND
ACTRESS). What do you want?
JUVENILE LEAD. Nothing. I'm just watching.
SON (*turning to the* SECOND ACTRESS). You as well! Getting
ready to play her part are you? (*Pointing to the* MOTHER.)
PRODUCER. That's it. And I think you should be grateful —
they're paying you a lot of attention.
SON. Oh, yes, thank you! But haven't you realised yet that
you'll never be able to do this play? There's nothing of us
inside you and you actors are only looking at us from the
outside. Do you think we could go on living with a mirror
held up in front of us that didn't only freeze our reflection

for ever, but froze us in a reflection that laughed back at us with an expression that we didn't even recognise as our own?

FATHER. That's right! That's right!

PRODUCER (*to* JUVENILE LEAD *and* SECOND ACTRESS). Okay. Go back to the others.

SON. It's quite useless. I'm not prepared to do anything.

PRODUCER. Oh, shut up, will you, and let me listen to your mother. (*To the* MOTHER.) Well, you'd gone to his room, you said.

MOTHER. Yes, to his room. I couldn't bear it any longer. I wanted to empty my heart to him, tell him about all the agony that was crushing me. But as soon as he saw me come in . . .

SON. Nothing happened. I got away! I wasn't going to get involved. I never have been involved. Do you understand?

MOTHER. It's true! That's right!

PRODUCER. But we must make up the scene between you, then. It's vital!

MOTHER. I'm ready to do it! If only I had the chance to talk to him for a moment, to pour out all my troubles to him.

FATHER (*going to the* SON *and speaking violently*). You'll do it! For your Mother! For your Mother!

SON (*more than ever determined*). I'm doing nothing!

FATHER (*taking hold of his coat collar and shaking him*). For God's sake, do as I tell you! Do as I tell you! Do you hear what she's saying? Haven't you any feelings for her?

SON (*taking hold of his* FATHER). No I haven't! I haven't! Let that be the end of it!

> There is a general uproar. The MOTHER frightened out of her wits, tries to get between them and separate them.

MOTHER. Please stop it! Please!

FATHER (*hanging on*). Do as I tell you! Do as I tell you!

SON (*wrestling with him and finally throwing him to the ground near the steps. Everyone is horrified*). What's come over you? Why are you so frantic? Do you want to parade our disgrace in front of everybody? Well, I'm having nothing to do with it! Nothing! And I'm doing what our author wanted as well — he never wanted to put us on the stage.

PRODUCER. Then why the hell did you come here?

SON (*pointing to the* FATHER). He wanted to, I didn't.

PRODUCER. But you're here now, aren't you?

SON. He was the one who wanted to come and he dragged
all of us here with him and agreed with you in there about
what to put in the play: and that meant not only what had
really happened, as if that wasn't bad enough, but what hadn't
happened as well.

PRODUCER. All right, then, you tell me what happened. You
tell me! Did you rush out of your room without saying
anything?

SON (*after a moment's hesitation*). Without saying anything. I
didn't want to make a scene.

PRODUCER (*needling him*). What then? What did you do then?

SON (*he is now the centre of everyone's agonised attention and
he crosses the stage*). Nothing . . . I went across the garden . . .
(*He breaks off gloomy and absorbed.*)

PRODUCER (*urging him to say more, impressed by his reluctance
to speak*). Well? What then? You crossed the garden?

SON (*exasperated, putting his face into the crook of his arm*).
Why do you want me to talk about it? It's horrible! (*The*
MOTHER *is trembling with stifled sobs and looking towards
the fountain.*)

PRODUCER (*quietly, seeing where she is looking and turning
to the* SON *with growing apprehension*). The little girl?

SON (*looking straight in front, out to the audience*). There, in
the fountain . . .

FATHER (*on the floor still, pointing with pity at the* MOTHER).
She was trailing after him!

PRODUCER (*to the* SON, *anxiously*). What did you do then?

SON (*still looking out front and speaking slowly*). I dashed
across. I was going to jump in and pull her out . . . But
something else caught my eye: I saw something behind the
tree that made my blood run cold: the little boy, he was
standing there with a mad look in his eyes: he was standing
looking into the fountain at his little sister, floating there,
drowned.

> The STEPDAUGHTER *is still bent at the fountain hiding
> the* LITTLE GIRL, *and she sobs pathetically, her sobs*

sounding like an echo.
There is a pause.

SON (*continued*). I made a move towards him: but then . . .

From behind the trees where the LITTLE BOY *is*
standing there is the sound of a shot.

MOTHER (*with a terrible cry she runs along with the* SON *and*
all the ACTORS *in the midst of a great general confusion*).
My son! My son! (*And then from out of the confusion and*
crying her voice comes out.) Help! Help me!

PRODUCER (*amidst the shouting he tries to clear a space whilst*
the LITTLE BOY *is carried by his feet and shoulders behind*
the white skycloth.) Is he wounded? Really wounded?
(*Everybody except the* PRODUCER *and the* FATHER *who*
is still on the floor by the steps, has gone behind the skycloth
and stays there talking anxiously. Then independently the
ACTORS *start to come back into view.*

LEADING ACTRESS (*coming from the right, very upset*). He's
dead! The poor boy! He's dead! What a terrible thing!

LEADING ACTOR (*coming back from the left and smiling*).
What do you mean, dead? It's all make-believe. It's a sham! He's
not dead. Don't you believe it!

OTHER ACTORS FROM THE RIGHT. Make-believe? It's real!
Real! He's dead!

OTHER ACTORS FROM THE LEFT. No, he isn't He's
pretending! It's all make-believe.

FATHER (*running off and shouting at them as he goes*). What
do you mean, make-believe? It's real! It's real, ladies and
gentlemen! It's reality! (*And with desperation on his face he*
too goes behind the skycloth.)

PRODUCER (*not caring any more*). Make-believe?! Reality?! Oh,
go to hell the lot of you! Lights! Lights! Lights!

At once all the stage and auditorium is flooded with light.
The PRODUCER *heaves a sigh of relief as if he has been*
relieved of a terrible weight and they all look at each other
in distress and with uncertainty.

PRODUCER. God! I've never known anything like this! And

we've lost a whole day's work! (*He looks at the clock*.) Get
off with you, all of you! We can't do anything now! It's too
late to start a rehearsal. (*When the* ACTORS *have gone, he
calls out.*) Hey, lights! Kill everything! (*As soon as he has said
this, all the lights go out completely and leave him in the pitch
dark.*) For God's sake!! You might have left the workers! I
can't see where I'm going!

> *Suddenly, behind the skycloth, as if because of a bad
> connection, a green light comes up to throw on the cloth
> a huge sharp shadow of the* CHARACTERS, *but without
> the* LITTLE BOY *and the* LITTLE GIRL. *The*
> PRODUCER, *seeing this, jumps off the stage, terrified. At
> the same time the flood of light on them is switched off
> and the stage is again bathed in the same blue light as
> before. Slowly the* SON *comes on from the right,
> followed by the* MOTHER *with her arms raised towards
> him. Then from the left, the* FATHER *enters.*
>
> They *come together in the middle of the stage and stand
> there os if transfixed. Finally from the left the*
> STEPDAUGHTER *comes on and moves towards the steps
> at the front: on the top step she pauses for a moment to
> look back at the other three and then bursts out in a
> raucous laugh, dashes down the steps and turns to look
> at the three figures still on the stage. Then she runs out of
> the auditorium and we can still hear her manic laughter
> out into the foyer and beyond.*
>
> *After a pause the curtain falls slowly.*

HENRY IV

Translated by Julian Mitchell

Characters

. . . . (HENRY IV)
MARCHESA MATILDA SPINA
FRIDA, her daughter
CARLO DI NOLLI, a young Marchese
BARON TITO BELCREDI
DOCTOR DIONISIO GENONI
LANDOLFO (LOLO) ⎫
ARIALDO (FRANCO) ⎪
                     ⎬ four pretended Privy Councillors
ORDULFO (MOMO) ⎪
BERTOLDO (FINO) ⎭
GIOVANNI, an old retainer
TWO SERVANTS, in costume

Scene: a lonely villa in the Umbrian countryside
Time: the early 1920s

Act One

A large room in the villa, furnished to represent as accurately as possible the throne-room of Henry IV in the imperial palace at Goslar. But among the antique furnishings are two life-size modern portraits in oils, standing out from the back wall. They are slightly off the ground, on a wide projecting ledge of carved wood, like a long bench for sitting on, which runs the whole length of the wall. Between them is the throne, set in the middle of the wall, and breaking the line of the ledge. It has an imperial seat and a low canopy. The two portraits represent a man and a woman, both young and dressed in carnival costume, the man as 'Henry IV', the woman as 'Matilda of Tuscany'. There are exits to right and left.

As the curtain rises, the two SERVANTS, *caught by surprise, leap down from the ledge on which they've been sprawling, and take up positions like statues on either side of the throne. They carry halberds. A moment later, from the second entrance on the right, enter* ARIALDO, LANDOLFO, ORDULFO *and* BERTOLDO. *They are young men employed by the Marchese* CARLO DI NOLLI *to play the parts of 'Privy Councillors', royal vassals from the low aristocracy at the court of Henry IV. They are dressed, therefore, as eleventh-century German knights. The last of them,* BERTOLDO, *whose real name is* FINO, *is taking up his duties for the first time. The three old hands are briefing him, and taking the opportunity to enjoy themselves in the process. The whole scene should be acted with animation and vivacity.*

LANDOLFO (*to* BERTOLDO, *as if continuing an explanation*).
     And this is the throne room!
ARIALDO. At Goslar!
ORDULFO. Schloss Hartzburg, if you prefer it!
ARIALDO. Or Worms!

LANDOLFO. It depends what scene we're playing. Like us, it leaps about from here to there.

ORDULFO. Saxony!

ARIALDO. Lombardy!

LANDOLFO. On the Rhine!

FIRST SERVANT (*without altering his position and scarcely moving his lips*). Hey! Psst!

ARIALDO (*turning at the sound*). Yes?

FIRST SERVANT (*still statuesque, in a whisper*). Is he coming or not? (*He means* HENRY IV.)

ORDULFO. Not. He's asleep. You can take it easy.

SECOND SERVANT (*relaxing along with his mate, breathing easily again, and going back to stretch out on the ledge*). My God, you might have said!

FIRST SERVANT (*going up to* ARIALDO). Got a light, please?

LANDOLFO. Hey! No pipes in here!

FIRST SERVANT (*while* ARIALDO *offers him a lighted match*). It's only a fag. (*Lights up and goes to lie smoking on the ledge.*)

BERTOLDO (*who has been looking round in wonder and bewilderment, first at the room, then at his costume and the costumes of his companions*). Excuse me, but . . . this room . . . these clothes . . . Which Henry the Fourth are we . . . I don't understand. Isn't it Henry the Fourth of France?

LANDOLFO, ARIALDO and ORDULFO *burst into loud laughter at the question.*

LANDOLFO (*still laughing, and pointing at* BERTOLDO *inviting his companions, who are also still laughing, to make even more fun of him*). Henry the Fourth of *France!*

ORDULFO (*same*). He thought it was Henry the Fourth of France!

ARIALDO. Henry the Fourth of Germany, old boy! The Salian dynasty!

ORDULFO. The great and tragic Holy Roman Emperor!

LANDOLFO. Henry the Fourth of Canossa! We're engaged here, day in, day out, in the most frightful war between Church and State! Tantara!

ORDULFO. The Empire versus the Papacy! Tantara!

ARIALDO. Popes versus anti-popes!

LANDOLFO. Kings versus anti-kings!

ORDULFO. *Plus* war against the Saxons!

ARIALDO. *And* all the rebel princes!

LANDOLFO. Against the Emperor's very own sons!

BERTOLDO (*protecting his head with his hands against this avalanche of information*). I see, I see! *That's* why I couldn't understand . . . dressed up like this, and coming in here . . . I thought so! This isn't a sixteenth-century costume!

ARIALDO. Sixteenth!

ORDULFO. This is the middle of the eleventh!

LANDOLFO. Work it out for yourself. If we're outside Canossa on January the twenty-fifth 1071 . . .

BERTOLDO (*more dismayed than ever*). Oh, my God, but this is absolute disaster!

ORDULFO. It certainly is, if you thought you were coming to the French court!

BERTOLDO. All the preparation I've done, the history!

LANDOLFO. We're four hundred years ahead of you, old boy! You're a mere toddler to us!

BERTOLDO (*getting angry*). Well, for God's sake, someone might have told me it was Henry the Fourth of Germany, not France! You don't know how many books I've been through this last fortnight, mugging it all up!

ARIALDO. But didn't you know poor old Tito played Adalbert of Bremen here?

BERTOLDO. Adalbert of where? I knew damn all!

LANDOLFO. No, don't you see? When Tito died, the young Marchese di Nolli . . .

BERTOLDO. Yes, him! The young Marchese! Why couldn't he have told me?

ARIALDO. He must have thought you knew already!

LANDOLFO. He didn't want to take on a replacement at all. He thought the three of us remaining would be enough. But *he* started yelling 'They've driven Adalbert away' . . . because he didn't realise poor old Tito was dead, you see, he thought Bishop Adalbert had been driven from court by his rival bishops of Cologne and Mainz.

BERTOLDO (*burying his head in his hands*). But I don't know the first thing about all this!

ORDULFO. Then you really are in rather a mess, old boy.

ARIALDO. And the trouble is, *we* don't know who you are, either.

BERTOLDO. You don't? You don't know who I'm supposed to be playing?

ORDULFO. Hm! 'Bertoldo'.

BERTOLDO. But Bertoldo who? And why Bertoldo?

LANDOLFO. 'All right — if they've driven Adalbert away . . . I'll have Bertoldo! I want Bertoldo!' . . . that's what he started shouting.

ARIALDO. We all looked at each other. We didn't know who Bertoldo was.

ORDULFO. And now here you are, old boy . . . Bertoldo!

LANDOLFO. And a very fine fellow you'll be!

BERTOLDO (*protesting and making as if to go*). Oh, no! Thanks very much, but I'm going! I'm off!

ARIALDO (*laughing and restraining him with* ORDULFO). Now, now . . . calm down, calm down!

LANDOLFO. If it's any comfort, we don't know who we are, either. He's Arialdo, he's Ordulfo, I'm Landolfo . . . that's what he calls us. We're used to it now. But who we actually are . . . Just names from the period! You'll just be a name from the period, too . . . 'Bertoldo'. Poor old Tito was the only one who had a decent role, something you could read about in history . . . he was Bishop of Bremen. He really looked like a bishop, too. He was terrific, old Tito!

ARIALDO. So he should have been, with all those books to get it up from!

LANDOLFO. He even gave His Majesty orders . . . he took command, gave him advice like a guardian and councillor, almost. We're 'Privy Councillors' ourselves, for what it's worth . . . but it's only to make up numbers, because it says in history that Henry IV was hated by the high nobility for surrounding himself at court with young men from the low.

ORDULFO. I.e., us.

LANDOLFO. Exactly. Little royal vassals . . . devoted, slightly dissolute, cheerful company . . .

BERTOLDO. Do I have to be cheerful company too?

ARIALDO. Rather! Just like us!

ORDULFO. It's not always so easy, you know.

LANDOLFO. It's a shame . . . really it is. Because, look . . . here's
the set. And these costumes would look tremendous in a
history play . . . history plays are all the rage these days. And
as for material . . . we've got enough for half a dozen tragedies,
not just one. The history of Henry IV certainly offers that.
But the four of us, and those two clowns there (*Indicating the
two* SERVANTS.) . . . *when* they're standing stiffly to
attention at the foot of the throne . . . we're all . . . we're all
just *here,* with no one to direct us, no one to give us a scene
to *act.* I don't know . . . we've got the form, but where's the
content? We're not even so well off as Henry IV's real privy
councillors. Because . . . all right, no one had given them parts
to play, either . . . but at least they didn't know they were
supposed to be acting. They were acting because they were
acting. It wasn't a part, I mean, it was their life. They were
looking after their own affairs, and the hell with everyone
else. They were selling investitures and I don't know what
besides. We, though, we're just stuck here in this marvellous
court for no purpose at all. We're like six puppets hanging on
the wall, waiting for someone to take us down and move us
about and give us something to *say.*

ARIALDO. Steady on, old chap . . . steady on! You do have to
answer correctly! You do have to know how to answer
correctly! If he speaks to you and you're not ready with the
right answer . . . watch out!

LANDOLFO. Well, yes, that's perfectly true.

BERTOLDO. Oh, that's terrific! And how am I going to give
the right answer when I've mugged up Henry IV of France,
and now I have some Henry IV of Germany suddenly sprung
on me?

> LANDOLFO, ARIALDO, *and* ORDULFO *start laughing
> again.*

ARIALDO. Well, you'd better do something about it double
quick!

ORDULFO. Get on through there . . . we'll help you.

ARIALDO. You'd better begin with a quick whip through the
books. There's a mass of them in there.

ORDULFO. You'll soon get a rough grasp of it . . .

ARIALDO. Look there! (*He turns him round and shows him the
portrait of the Marchesa of Tuscany on the back wall*.) Who's
that, for instance?

BERTOLDO. That lady there? (*Looking.*) Well, to start with,
she looks completely out of place, if I may say so. Two modern
pictures in the middle of all these genuine antiques!

ARIALDO. Perfectly true. As a matter of fact, they used not to
be here. There are two niches behind there, meant for statues
done in the style of the period. But they were never filled, so
they've been covered over by these two paintings.

LANDOLFO (*interrupting and continuing*). Which certainly
would be out of place, if they actually were paintings.

BERTOLDO. Well, what are they? Aren't they paintings?

LANDOLFO. Oh, if you go up to them and touch them, yes,
they're paintings. But he doesn't touch them, and for him . . .

BERTOLDO. Well, what are they for him?

LANDOLFO. Well, it's only my interpretation, mind! But I think
I'm right, fundamentally. They're images. Images like . . .
well, like reflections in a mirror, if you see what I mean. That
one (*Indicating the portrait of Henry IV.*) represents him just
as he is . . . the living man, here in this throne-room, which is
in the style of the period, just as it should be. What's so
surprising about that? If someone put a mirror in front of
you, wouldn't you see yourself just as you are, here and now,
dressed in ancient costume? Well, then, it's as if there were
two mirrors there, giving back living images to us here in the
middle of a world which . . . Don't worry! You'll see! Living
with us, it'll all come to life . . . you'll see.

BERTOLDO. No, thanks! I'm not going bonkers with you lot!

ARIALDO. Why not? You'll enjoy it!

BERTOLDO. I say, but . . . how did you all get to know so much?

LANDOLFO. My dear chap, one doesn't go back eight hundred
years into history without taking a little experience with one!

ARIALDO. Come on, let's go. You'll see, we'll have you genned up in no time at all.

ORDULFO. You, too, shall be a scholar!

BERTOLDO. Well, you'll have to help me, for heaven's sake, and fast! Explain the first principles, at least.

ARIALDO. We'll manage! I'll tell you one thing, he'll tell you another . . .

LANDOLFO. We'll connect your strings and get you into shape, till you're a most accomplished and qualified puppet. Let's go, come on. (*Taking him by the arm to lead him off.*)

BERTOLDO. Wait a minute! You haven't told me who the lady is. Is she the Emperor's wife? (*Stopping and looking at the portrait on the wall.*)

ARIALDO. No, the Emperor's wife is Bertha of Susa, sister of Amadeus the Second of Savoy.

ORDULFO. And the Emperor, who'd like to be a young blood like us, can't stick her and wants to divorce her.

LANDOLFO. This lady is his great enemy . . . Matilda, Marchesa of Tuscany.

BERTOLDO. Oh, I know . . . the one who played host to the Pope.

LANDOLFO. Exactly. At Canossa.

ORDULFO. To Pope Gregory the Seventh.

ARIALDO. Our bogeyman! Come on, let's go.

All four go towards the right-hand exit through which they entered, when the old manservant GIOVANNI enters left in a tailcoat.

GIOVANNI (*hurried and anxious*). Hey . . . psst! Franco! Lolo!

ARIALDO (*stopping and turning*). What do you want?

BERTOLDO (*astonished to see him enter the throne-room in a tailcoat*). Hey, what's this? What's he doing in here?

LANDOLFO. A man from the twentieth century! Be off with you!

With the other two he pretends to threaten him and chase him away.

ORDULFO. He's a messenger from Gregory the Seventh . . . begone!

ARIALDO. Out! Out!

GIOVANNI (*warding them off, not amused*). That'll do!

ORDULFO. You can't set foot in here!

ARIALDO. Away! Away!

LANDOLFO (*to* BERTOLDO). It's all sorcery, you know! He's a devil summoned by the Wizard of Rome! Unsheath your sword, unsheath!

GIOVANNI (*shouting*). I said, that'll do! Don't play the fool with me! The young Marchese's arrived, and a lot of people with him.

LANDOLFO (*rubbing his hands together*). Ah, excellent! Any women?

ORDULFO (*the same*). Old ones? Young ones?

GIOVANNI. There are two gentlemen.

ARIALDO. But the women . . . what about the women?

GIOVANNI. The Marchesa and her daughter.

LANDOLFO (*astonished*). What!

ORDULFO (*the same*). Did you say, the Marchesa?

GIOVANNI. Yes, yes! The Marchesa!

ARIALDO. And the gentlemen?

GIOVANNI. I don't know.

ARIALDO (*to* BERTOLDO). They're coming to give us our content, you'll see!

ORDULFO. All of them messengers from Gregory the Seventh! This should be fun!

GIOVANNI. Are you going to let me tell you or not?

ARIALDO. Well, come on, then . . . tell!

GIOVANNI. It seems that one of the gentlemen is a doctor.

LANDOLFO. Oh, we know . . . one of the usual doctors!

ARIALDO. Well done, Bertoldo . . . you've brought us luck.

LANDOLFO. Watch how we set to work on this gentleman doctor!

BERTOLDO. I've got an awful feeling I'm going to be dropped straight in the soup!

GIOVANNI. Will you listen to me! They want to come in here.

LANDOLFO (*amazed and dismayed*). What? Her? The Marchesa in here?

ARIALDO. More content than we bargained for in that case!

LANDOLFO. The tragedy really will begin!

BERTOLDO (*curious*). But why? Why?

ORDULFO (*indicating the portrait*). That's her there . . . don't you see?

LANDOLFO. Her daughter's engaged to the young Marchese di Nolli.

ARIALDO. But what are they doing here? May we know?

ORDULFO. If he sees her . . . watch out!

LANDOLFO. Perhaps he won't recognise her any more!

GIOVANNI. If he wakes up, you're to keep him amused in there.

ORDULFO. Oh, yes? Are you kidding? How?

ARIALDO. You know what he's like!

GIOVANNI. Good God, use force, if you have to! Those are my orders. Go on, go on!

ARIALDO. Yes, yes . . . he may be awake already!

ORDULFO. Come on . . . let's go!

LANDOLFO (*going with the others, to* GIOVANNI). You'll explain later?

GIOVANNI (*shouting after them*). Lock that door and hide the key! And that door, too. (*Indicating the other door on the right.*)

> LANDOLFO, ARIALDO, *and* ORDULFO *leave by the second door on the right, with* BERTOLDO.

GIOVANNI (*to two* SERVANTS). You can get out, too! That way! (*Indicating first exit on right.*) Lock the door and hide the key!

> *The two* SERVANTS *leave by the first exit on right.* GIOVANNI *goes to left entrance and opens it to allow the* MARCHESE DI NOLLI *to enter.*

DI NOLLI. You've given the orders?

GIOVANNI. Yes, my lord. Everything under control.

> DI NOLLI *goes out a moment to invite the others to come in. Enter first* BARON TITO BELCREDI *and* DOCTOR DIONISIO GENONI, *then* MATILDA SPINA *and her daughter* FRIDA. GIOVANNI *bows and leaves.*

MATILDA SPINA *is about forty-five, still shapely and
beautiful, though she repairs the inevitable ravages of time
too blatantly, and her violent but skilful use of make-up
gives her the proud look of a valkyrie. This paintwork
makes a sharp and highly disturbing contrast with her
mouth, which is very lovely and sorrowful. A widow of
long standing, her friend is* BARON TITO BELCREDI, *a
man who has never been taken seriously by her or anyone
else, or so it seems. What* TITO BELCREDI *is for her,
deep down, only he really knows, so he can afford to laugh
when his lady pretends she's not sure; and always to smile
at the laughter provoked in others by the Marchesa's jokes
against him. Slim, prematurely grey, a little younger than
her, he has a curious, bird-like head. He would be very
lively, if his litheness and agility (which make him a
formidable swordsman) were not cloaked in a sleepy, almost
oriental idleness, revealed in a rather nasal and drawling
voice.* FRIDA, *the Marchesa's daughter, is nineteen.
Languishing in the shade of her formidable and striking
mother, she is outraged at the easy gossip the Marchesa
provokes, no longer so much at her own expense as at her
daughter's. Fortunately, however, she is now engaged to the
Marchese* CARLO DI NOLLI; *a stiff young man, very
indulgent to others, but reserved and critical about himself.
He considers himself to be worth little in the world; and
deep down, perhaps, is not even sure how much that little is.
Anyway, he is dismayed by the numerous responsibilities he
feels are weighing him down; it's all very well for others,
they can talk and enjoy themselves, lucky devils, but he . . .
he can't; not because he doesn't want to, he just can't. He is
in deepest mourning for the recent death of his mother.*
DOCTOR DIONISIO GENONI *has a fine, impudent,
rubicund satyr's face, with protruding eyes, short, pointed
beard, small and shiny as silver, fine manners; he is almost
bald.
They enter nervously, almost fearfully, looking curiously
round the room (apart from* DI NOLLI), *and at first they
keep their voices down.*

BELCREDI. Ah, magnificent! Magnificent!

DOCTOR. Most interesting! Madness is so precise, even in details! Magnificent . . . yes, indeed . . . magnificent.

MATILDA (*looking round for her portrait, finding it and going to it*). There it is! Yes . . . yes . . . Oh, my God, look! Frida . . . Frida, look! (*Looking at it from a suitable distance, mixed feelings rising in her, then calling her daughter.*)

FRIDA. Ah . . . your portrait?

MATILDA. But no . . . look! It's not me, it's you!

DI NOLLI. But isn't it! I told you.

MATILDA. I'd never have believed it! God, what a peculiar feeling. (*She gives a little shake, as though a shiver was running down her spine. Then she looks at her daughter.*) Frida? (*She puts an arm round her waist and draws her to her.*) Look! Can't you see yourself in me up there?

FRIDA. Well, to tell the truth . . .

MATILDA. You don't see it? But how can you not? (*Turning to* BELCREDI.) Tito, you look! Tell her!

BELCREDI (*not looking*). Oh, no! I'm not looking on principle!

MATILDA. Idiot! He thinks he's paying me a compliment! (*Turning to* DOCTOR GENONI.) Doctor, you tell her!

DOCTOR *makes to approach the portrait.*

BELCREDI (*with his back turned, pretending to call him back surreptitiously*). Psst! No, doctor! For heaven's sake, don't get involved!

DOCTOR (*puzzled, smiling*). But why not?

MATILDA. Pay no attention to him! Come here! He's insufferable!

FRIDA. He makes a profession of it, didn't you know?

BELCREDI (*to* DOCTOR, *watching him go*). Watch your feet, doctor, watch your feet! Your feet!

DOCTOR (*as before*). My feet? Why?

BELCREDI. You've got hobnailed boots on.

DOCTOR. Have I?

BELCREDI. Yes sir! And you're just about to trample all over four tiny glass feet!

DOCTOR (*laughing loudly*). Nonsense! There's nothing very astonishing, after all, about a daughter looking like her mother.

BELCREDI. Scrunch! He's done it!

MATILDA (*exaggerating her anger, coming to* BELCREDI).
Scrunch? What's that supposed to mean? What do you think
you're talking about?

DOCTOR (*candidly*). Well, is there?

BELCREDI (*answering the* MARCHESA). He said there's nothing
very astonishing about it, when you were staggered. May I ask
why, if it now seems so natural to you?

MATILDA (*still angrier*). Fool! Idiot! Just because it *is* so
natural! Because it's not my daughter there at all. (*Indicating
picture*.) It's a portrait of *me*. And it *did* astonish me to find
her there instead of me. And my astonishment was genuine,
and I forbid you to doubt it!

> *After this violent outburst, there is a moment of general
> embarrassed silence.*

FRIDA (*quietly, bored*). Oh, God, it's always the same. Bickering
over every little thing.

BELCREDI (*also quiet, his tail between his legs, apologetic*). I'm
not doubting anything. I've just noticed that from the start
you've not shared your mother's astonishment. If anything
does surprise you, it's that she finds such a strong likeness
between you and the portrait.

MATILDA. But of course! She can't recognise herself in me as
I was at her age, while I can easily recognise myself in her as
she is now.

DOCTOR. Exactly! Because a portrait is always fixed in one
particular moment of time — long ago in this case, and with
no meaning for the young lady. Whereas everything in it
can remind the Marchesa of so many things which aren't
there . . . gestures, movements, glances, smiles . . .

MATILDA. Precisely!

DOCTOR (*continuing, turning to her*). And naturally you can
see those now living again in your daughter.

MATILDA. But he always has to spoil the smallest indulgence in
genuine feeling, just for the pleasure of making me angry.

DOCTOR (*dazzled by the light he has thrown on the matter,
turning to* BELCREDI *and addressing him in a professorial*

voice). The cause of any resemblance, my dear baron, is often not to be guessed at. Which is how, as a matter of fact, we explain . . .

BELCREDI (*interrupting the lesson*). How someone could even find some resemblance between you and me, my dear professor.

DI NOLLI. May we now leave it, please? (*He gestures towards the two exits on the right to warn them that people may be listening.*) We wasted too much time on the way here . . .

FRIDA. Well, of course! When *he* was — (*Indicating* BELCREDI.)

MATILDA (*immediately*). That's why I didn't want him to come at all!

BELCREDI. Oh, what ingratitude! When you've had so many laughs at my expense!

DI NOLLI. That'll do . . . please, Tito! The doctor's here and we've come for a very serious purpose, one to which I attach great importance, as you know.

DOCTOR. Yes, indeed. Let's first try to clear up one or two points. May I ask, madam, why this portrait of you is here? Did you give it as a present?

MATILDA. No, no. What right did I have to give him presents? I was Frida's age, and not even engaged. I handed it over three or four years after the accident, at his mother's special request. (*Indicating* DI NOLLI.)

DOCTOR. And she was his sister? (*Gestures towards the left exit, meaning* HENRY IV.)

DI NOLLI. That's right, doctor. She passed away last month. We've come here today out of respect for her. Instead of being here, she and I (*Indicating* FRIDA.) should have been on our honeymoon.

DOCTOR. And taken up with very different matters . . . yes, indeed!

DI NOLLI. Well . . . My mother died in the firm belief that the recovery of her much loved brother was imminent.

DOCTOR. And what made her suppose that, may I ask?

DI NOLLI. It seems she had an odd conversation with him, shortly before she died.

DOCTOR. A conversation? Hm . . . hm . . . by Jove, it'd be very useful to know what he said!

DI NOLLI. Ah, that I don't know. All I do know is, my mother
came back from that last visit in great distress. It seems he
showed her an unusual tenderness, as though he had some
presentiment of her dying. And on her deathbed she made me
promise that I would never neglect him . . . that I would have
him examined and visited . . .

DOCTOR. I see. Good. Well now, let's see . . . Very often the
smallest thing . . . This portrait, then . . .

MATILDA. Oh, heavens, I don't think we should give it too
much importance, doctor. It only struck me so much because
I hadn't seen it for so many years.

DOCTOR. Please . . . please . . . one moment . . .

DI NOLLI. It's quite true. It's hung there fifteen years or so.

MATILDA. More! More than eighteen now.

DOCTOR. Please . . . excuse me . . . you don't yet know what
it is I want to ask you! I attach very great importance to these
two portraits, painted, I take it, before the celebrated . . . and
most unhappy . . . cavalcade took place. Is that so?

MATILDA. Yes, of course.

DOCTOR. While he was still in full possession of his senses,
then . . . that's what I mean to say! Was it his idea they should
be done?

MATILDA. No, doctor. Lots of us who were taking part in the
cavalcade had them done. For a memento.

BELCREDI. I had mine done, too. I was Charles of Anjou.

MATILDA. The moment we had our costumes.

BELCREDI. Because, you see, someone had the idea of collecting
them all together as a souvenir in the hall of the villa where
the cavalcade was being held . . . like in a picture gallery. But
then everyone wanted to keep his own.

MATILDA. And I handed mine over, as I say . . . without too
much regret . . . because his mother . . . (*Indicating* DI NOLLI.)

DOCTOR. You don't know whether or not he asked for it?

MATILDA. No, I don't. Perhaps. Or else his sister wanted to help,
and because she was so fond of him —

DOCTOR. Another thing . . . another thing . . . Was the cavalcade
his idea?

BELCREDI (*at once*). Oh, no! It was mine . . . mine.

DOCTOR. Please . . .

MATILDA. Ignore him. It was poor Belassi's.

BELCREDI. Belassi's!

MATILDA (*to* DOCTOR). Count Belassi. He died, poor man, two
   or three months later.

BELCREDI. But Belassi wasn't even there when . . .

DI NOLLI (*bored by the threat of another argument*). Surely,
   doctor, it's not really necessary to establish whose idea it was?

DOCTOR. Well, it might be useful . . .

BELCREDI. But it was mine! Oh, this is wonderful! Not that
   it's much to be proud of, of course, considering the result.
   Listen, doctor, what happened was this . . . I remember it
   perfectly . . . I was in the club one evening early in November,
   looking through a German illustrated magazine — only glancing
   at the pictures, you understand . . . I don't know German.
   And in one of them was the Emperor, in I don't know which
   university city, where he'd been a student.

DOCTOR. Bonn, Bonn.

BELCREDI. All right, Bonn. He was on horseback, and dressed
   up in one of the peculiar costumes they wear in those old
   German student societies, and he had a retinue of noble
   students, also mounted and in traditional costume. It was
   that picture which gave me the idea. You see, we at the club
   were thinking of putting on a grand masquerade for the next
   carnival. So I suggested a historical cavalcade . . . historical in
   a manner of speaking only . . . it was chaos. Each of us had
   to choose someone from one century or another; king or
   emperor, or prince, with his lady beside him, queen or empress,
   all on horseback. The horses, of course in period trappings.
   And my proposal was accepted.

MATILDA. I got my invitation from Belassi.

BELCREDI. If he claimed the idea was his, he filched it without
   acknowledgement. I tell you, he wasn't even at the club the
   evening I suggested it. Just as *he* wasn't there, either! (*Meaning*
   HENRY IV.)

DOCTOR. And he then chose the role of Henry IV?

MATILDA. Yes, because I . . . it was because of my name . . .
   it was just like that, I hardly gave it a thought . . . I said I
   wanted to be the Marchesa Matilda of Tuscany.

DOCTOR. I . . . I'm not altogether clear as to the relationship . . .

MATILDA. Oh, well, nor was I at first. He said, in that case he
would be at my feet, like Henry IV at Canossa, you see. Well,
I knew about Canossa, but to tell you the truth I didn't
remember the story very well, and in fact it gave me a peculiar
feeling, looking it all up for my part, and finding myself the
most faithful and zealous friend of Pope Gregory the Seventh
in a fierce struggle with the German Empire. But I understood
soon enough why he wanted to be beside me in the cavalcade
as Henry IV! I'd chosen to play his deadly enemy.

DOCTOR. Ah! Because, perhaps . . .

BELCREDI. Good God, doctor, because he was paying her
relentless court, and she (*Indicating the* MARCHESA.)
naturally . . .

MATILDA (*stung to the quick*). Of course naturally! Absolutely
naturally! And especially naturally in those days!

BELCREDI (*gesturing towards her*). There you are. She couldn't
stick him.

MATILDA. That's not true! I didn't dislike him at all. On the
contrary. But for me, as soon as someone starts wanting to
be taken seriously . . .

BELCREDI (*completing the sentence*). . . . that's dazzling proof
to her of his stupidity!

MATILDA. No, my dear! Not in this case. He wasn't nearly such
a fool as you.

BELCREDI. I've never asked to be taken seriously!

MATILDA. And don't I know it! But with him there was no
question of joking. (*In another tone, turning to the* DOCTOR.)
It is one of the many misfortunes of us women, my dear
doctor, every so often to see before us two eyes gazing with
the intense unspoken promise of eternal love. (*Bursts into
shrill laughter.*) There's nothing so ridiculous. If men could
only see themselves with eternal love in their eyes! I've always
just laughed. Those days, specially. But I must confess . . .
and I can do so now, after twenty years and more . . . when
I laughed at him, it was partly out of fear. Because one could
believe the promise in those eyes, perhaps. Though it would
be very dangerous to do so.

DOCTOR (*very interested, concentrating*). Ah, ha! It . . . it
     would interest me very much to know . . . why so very
     dangerous?

MATILDA (*lightly*). Because he wasn't like the others. And
     because . . . well, why not? . . . because I am a little . . . more
     than a little, to tell the truth . . . (*Searching for a modest
     word.*) . . . *impatient* . . . yes, that's the word . . . impatient
     of everything formal and stuffy. But I was too young then,
     you understand, and a woman . . . I had to champ the bit. It
     would have needed more courage than I felt I had. So I
     laughed at him, too. With regret, indeed with real anger at
     myself later on, because I realised my laughter sounded like
     everyone else's . . . like all the idiots' who made fun of him.

BELCREDI. Almost as they do with me.

MATILDA. My dear, you usually make people laugh by
     pretending to be humble, but not him. On the contrary.
     There's a great difference. And then, people laugh at you to
     your face!

BELCREDI. Well, better than behind my back, that's what I say.

DOCTOR. May we get back to the subject, the matter in hand?
     So . . . if I have understood you correctly . . . he was already
     rather excited.

BELCREDI. Yes, but in a very curious way, doctor.

DOCTOR. How was that, then?

BELCREDI. Well, I would say . . . coldly.

MATILDA. What do you mean, coldly? It was like this, doctor
     . . . he was a little odd, certainly . . . but only because he was
     so full of life . . . he was inspired!

BELCREDI. I'm not saying he was pretending to be excited. On
     the contrary, as a matter of fact. The truth is, he was often
     over-excited. But I would have sworn, doctor, that he would
     suddenly catch himself *being* excited, in the very act of it. And
     I think that must have happened even at his most spontaneous
     moments. I'd go further. I'm sure it made him unhappy. He
     used to have the funniest outbursts of temper against himself
     sometimes!

MATILDA. That's right!

BELCREDI (*to* MATILDA). Yes, but why? (*To* DOCTOR.) As I

see it, because the sudden sense that he was playing a role cut him off at once from all contact with his feelings, which he felt were . . . not bogus, because they were genuine . . . but something he must somehow . . . I don't know . . . give an immediate intellectual value to, to make up for the real heartfelt warmth he felt he lacked. And he spoke without thinking, exaggerated, let himself go, to try and confuse himself, so he wouldn't catch himself out any more. Which made him seem erratic, frivolous and sometimes, frankly, even ridiculous.

DOCTOR. And would you say . . . unsocial?

BELCREDI. Not in the least! He was in everything! He was famous for organising tableaux vivants and dances and charity do's . . . just for fun, of course. And he was a very good actor, you know.

DI NOLLI. And since his madness, he's become a brilliant and terrifying one!

BELCREDI. Oh, but he always was! Imagine, when the accident happened, after he'd fallen off the horse . . .

DOCTOR. He banged the back of his head, I take it?

MATILDA. It was awful. He was right beside me! I saw him lying between the hoofs of his horse, and it was reared right up . . .

BELCREDI. No one had the slightest idea at first that he was badly hurt. I mean, the cavalcade came to a halt, there was confusion . . . everyone wanted to see what had happened. But he'd already been taken up and carried into the house.

MATILDA. There was nothing! Not the tiniest scratch! Not a single drop of blood!

BELCREDI. We all thought he'd just fainted . . .

MATILDA. And when, about two hours later . . .

BELCREDI. Exactly, he turned up again in the hall of the villa . . . but what I was going to say was . . .

MATILDA. He looked so extraordinary! I saw it at once!

BELCREDI. That's not so! You mustn't say that! No one realised anything, you see, doctor!

MATILDA. Of course not! You were *all* acting like madmen!

BELCREDI. We were acting out our parts for fun! It was complete chaos!

MATILDA. Imagine the horror, doctor, when we realised he was acting his part for real.

DOCTOR. Ah, because by then he . . .

BELCREDI. Yes, yes! He came and joined in! We thought he'd recovered and was acting like the rest of us . . . only better than us, because, as I say, he was always extremely good. We thought he was just fooling around.

MATILDA. People started hitting him . . .

BELCREDI. And then . . . he was armed, you see, like a king . . . he suddenly drew his sword and flung himself at two or three of them. We were absolutely terrified!

MATILDA. I shall never get that scene out of my mind . . . all our masquerade faces gaping in utter confusion at *his* terrible face, which wasn't disguised any longer, but was madness itself.

BELCREDI. It was Henry IV . . . the real Henry IV in a moment of fury!

MATILDA. I'm sure his obsession with that masquerade must have had an influence, doctor. He'd thought of nothing else for more than a month. It came into everything he did, all the time.

BELCREDI. The research he did in preparation! Right down to the smallest details . . . absolute minutiae . . .

DOCTOR. Well, it's simple enough, then. What had been a temporary obsession became established with the fall and the blow on the back of the head which did the cerebral damage. Established and self-perpetuating. Sometimes people become half-witted, sometimes they go mad.

BELCREDI (*to* FRIDA *and* DI NOLLI). Can you imagine the fun it all was, my dears? (*To* DI NOLLI.) You were four or five. (*To* FRIDA.) Your mother thinks you've taken her place in that portrait . . . but it was done before she'd given the smallest thought to bringing you into the world. I've got grey hair. And as for him . . . look at him! (*Indicating the portrait.*) A blow on the back of the head and . . . bang . . . he's never altered. Henry IV.

DOCTOR (*who has been absorbed in his thoughts, spreading his hands before his face as if to concentrate the attention of the others, and about to start his scientific explanation).* Yes, yes . . . well, ladies and gentlemen, it seems to me like this . . .

> *But suddenly the downstage right door bursts open and a a very angry* BERTOLDO *appears.*

BERTOLDO (*bursting in like someone who can stand it no longer*). May I come in? I'm sorry, but . . .

> *But he stops short, seeing the confusion his appearance immediately causes among the others.*

FRIDA (*with yelp of terror, taking shelter*). Oh, God! Here he is!

MATILDA (*recoiling in alarm, an arm raised to prevent herself seeing him*). Is it him? Is it him?

DI NOLLI (*at once*). No, no! Keep calm!

DOCTOR (*astounded*). Then who is it?

BELCREDI. A fugitive from our masquerade!

DI NOLLI. He's one of the four young men we keep here to humour his madness.

BERTOLDO. I beg your pardon, my lord . . .

DI NOLLI. Beg my pardon! I gave orders that the doors were to be locked and no one was to enter!

BERTOLDO. Yes, my lord. But I can't stand it. I want permission to leave!

DI NOLLI. Oh, are you the one who was starting work this morning?

BERTOLDO. Yes, my lord, and I'm telling you . . . I can't stand it.

MATILDA (*to* DI NOLLI, *in great consternation*). You mean he's not quiet like you said?

BERTOLDO. It's not him, madam, no. It's my three colleagues. You said we're here to 'humour' him, my lord, but what does that mean? Those three don't 'humour' him . . . *they're* the ones who are barmy! I arrive here for the first time, and instead of helping me, my lord . . .

> LANDOLFO *and* ARIALDO *appear in the same doorway on the right in a great hurry. They are anxious, but stay by the door before coming forward.*

LANDOLFO. Excuse me, my lord . . .

ARIALDO. My lord . . .

DI NOLLI. Come in! What is all this? What are you doing?

FRIDA. Oh God, I'm getting out of here, I'm going! It's scary!
(*She makes as if to exit left.*)

DI NOLLI. No, Frida!

LANDOLFO. My lord, this idiot . . . (*Indicating* BERTOLDO.)

BERTOLDO (*protesting*). Oh, thanks very much, old chap! I'm
not carrying on like that . . . I won't do it!

LANDOLFO. What do you mean, you won't do it?

ARIALDO. My lord, he's ruined everything, running in here.

LANDOLFO. He's put him in one of his rages! We can't handle
him in there any more. He's ordered his arrest, and wants
to sentence him immediately from his 'throne'! What do you
want us to do?

DI NOLLI. Shut that door . . . and lock it! Go and lock that
door!

LANDOLFO *goes and locks the door.*

ARIALDO. Ordulfo'll never be able to manage him on his own.

LANDOLFO. Couldn't we suddenly announce your arrival, my
lord? It might distract him at least. If these ladies and gentlemen
have decided how they want to be presented . . .

DI NOLLI. Yes, yes, it's all arranged. (*To* DOCTOR.) Doctor, if
you think you can examine him at once . . .

FRIDA. Not me, Carlo, not me! I'm going. You too, Mama . . .
come with me, for heaven's sake!

DOCTOR. I say, he's not still armed at all, is he?

DI NOLLI. Of course not! How could he be? Really, doctor!
(*To* FRIDA.) I'm sorry, Frida, but you're being absolutely
childish. You wanted to come . . .

FRIDA. I beg your pardon, I did *not*! It was Mama!

MATILDA (*with resolution*). Well, I'm ready. So . . . what do you
want us to do?

BELCREDI. I say, do we really have to dress up like that?

LANDOLFO. It's absolutely essential, sir. Unfortunately! I
mean, look at us . . . (*Shows costume.*) But there'd be terrible
trouble if he saw you dressed in modern clothes like that!

ARIALDO. He'd think you were the devil in disguise.

DI NOLLI. Just as they seem dressed up to you, so we'd seem dressed up to him in these clothes.

LANDOLFO. It might not matter so much, my lord, except he'd think it was the work of his mortal enemy.

BELCREDI. Pope Gregory the Seventh?

LANDOLFO. Exactly. He says he was a 'pagan'!

BELCREDI. The Pope? That's not bad!

LANDOLFO. Yes, sir. He thinks he can call up the dead! He accuses him of every trick in the devil's bag. He's scared stiff of him.

DOCTOR. Persecution mania!

ARIALDO. He'd be furious!

DI NOLLI (to BELCREDI). It won't be necessary for you to be here, if you don't mind. We'll go out there. It'll be quite sufficient for the doctor to see him.

DOCTOR. Do you mean . . . me on my own?

DI NOLLI. You've got these three! (Indicating the three young men.)

DOCTOR. I didn't mean that, I meant . . . doesn't the Marchesa . . . ?

MATILDA. Of course. I certainly mean to be here! I want to very much! I want to see him again!

FRIDA. But why, Mama? Please come with us!

MATILDA (imperiously). Leave me alone! It's what I'm here for! I'll be his mother-in-law, Adelaide. (To LANDOLFO.)

LANDOLFO. Very good. The Empress Bertha's mother . . . excellent. It'll be enough if madam will wear the ducal coronet and a cloak to cover everything else. (To ARIALDO.) Fetch them, Arialdo!

ARIALDO. Just a moment. What about the gentleman? (Indicating DOCTOR.)

DOCTOR. Ah, yes . . . we said, I think, a bishop . . . Bishop Hugo of Cluny.

ARIALDO. You mean the Abbot, sir? Very well . . . Hugo of Cluny.

LANDOLFO. But he's always coming here.

DOCTOR (astonished). What?

LANDOLFO. It's all right. I only meant, as it's a quick disguise . . .

ARIALDO. We've often used it before.

DOCTOR. But . . .

LANDOLFO. There's no danger he'll remember. He pays more attention to the costume than who's in it.

MATILDA. That's fortunate for me, too, then.

DI NOLLI. Shall we go, Frida? Come on, Tito.

BELCREDI. Oh, no. If she's staying, so am I. (*Indicating the* MARCHESA.)

MATILDA. I don't need you, not in the least.

BELCREDI. I didn't say you did. I want to see him again, too. Can't I?

LANDOLFO. Well, it might be better if there were three of you.

ARIALDO. What shall we do for him?

BELCREDI. You can find something quick for me, too, can't you?

LANDOLFO. Of course. A Cluniac monk. (*To* ARIALDO.)

BELCREDI. A Cluniac monk? What would that mean?

LANDOLFO. A Benedictine habit in the style of the Abbey of Cluny. You can be one of Monsignor's attendants. (*To* ARIALDO.) Off you go! (*To* BERTOLDO.) You, too! And don't show your face again today! (*But, as soon as they start to go.*) No, wait. (*To* BERTOLDO.) You bring the clothes he gives you. (*To* ARIALDO.) And you go and announce the visit of the Duchess Adelaide and Monsignor Hugo of Cluny. At once. All right?

> ARIALDO *and* BERTOLDO *leave via first door on right.*

DI NOLLI. We'll disappear, then.

> *He and* FRIDA *go out left.*

DOCTOR (*to* LANDOLFO). He should be very pleased to see me as Hugo of Cluny, I imagine.

LANDOLFO. Very. You have nothing to worry about. The Monsignor has always been received here with great respect. And you needn't worry, either, madam. He never forgets he owes it to the intercession of the two of you that when he was almost frozen stiff, after two days waiting in the snow, he

was admitted to the castle of Canossa and the presence of
Gregory the Seventh who didn't at all want to see him.

BELCREDI. What about me, please?

LANDOLFO. You should stay respectfully to one side.

MATILDA (*irritated and on edge*). You'd do best to go away!

BELCREDI (*softly, angry*). You're very agitated . . .

MATILDA (*proud*). I am what I am! Leave me alone!

>BERTOLDO *re-enters with their clothes.*

LANDOLFO (*seeing him come in*). Ah, here are your costumes.
The cloak for you, madam.

MATILDA. Wait, let me get my hat off! (*She does so, and hands
it to* BERTOLDO.)

LANDOLFO. You can take it through there. (*Then to the*
MARCHESA, *placing the ducal coronet on her head.*) Allow
me, madam.

MATILDA. My God, isn't there a mirror here?

LANDOLFO. Through there. (*Indicating exit left.*) If you'd
rather do it yourself, madam . . .

MATILDA. I think it'd be better. Give it here. I'll only be a
moment.

>*She takes the hat back and goes out with* BERTOLDO,
>*who carries the cloak and coronet. Meanwhile the* DOCTOR
>*and* BELCREDI *are dressing themselves, as best they can,
>in their Benedictine habits.*

BELCREDI. I certainly never expected all this business of
dressing up as monks. I say! This madness of his must cost a
fortune!

DOCTOR. Well, most madness does really . . .

BELCREDI. If you've a fortune to back it up . . .

LANDOLFO. Yes, sir. We've a whole wardrobe through there,
all authentic costumes, perfectly made to period designs. It's
my special responsibility. I go to proper theatrical costumiers.
Oh, yes, we spend a good deal.

>MATILDA *re-enters wearing the cloak and coronet.*

BELCREDI (*at once, admiring her*). Oh, magnificent! Truly
regal!

MATILDA (*seeing* BELCREDI *and bursting out laughing*). Oh,
　　my God, no! Take him away! You're impossible! You look
　　like an ostrich got up as a monk!

BELCREDI. Well, look at the doctor!

DOCTOR. Never mind! Never mind!

MATILDA. The doctor's not so bad. But you're ridiculous!

DOCTOR (*to* LANDOLFO). Do you have many visitors here, then?

LANDOLFO. It depends. Sometimes he orders someone or other
　　to be brought before him. And then we have to find someone
　　to do it. Ladies, too.

MATILDA (*hurt, and wishing to conceal the fact*). Oh? Ladies?

LANDOLFO. At first, yes. Lots of them.

BELCREDI (*laughing*). Wonderful! In costume? Like her?
　　(*Indicating the* MARCHESA.)

LANDOLFO. Well, ladies, you know, of a certain sort . . .

BELCREDI. Ready for anything! Yes, I know. (*Wickedly, to the*
　　MARCHESA.) You'd better watch out! It could be dangerous!

　　　The second door on the right opens and ARIALDO *enters.*
　　　He first makes a stealthy sign for talking to stop in the
　　　room, then solemnly announces:

ARIALDO. His majesty the Emperor!

　　　Enter first the two SERVANTS *who go and take their*
　　　places at the foot of the throne. Then, between ORDULFO
　　　and ARIALDO, *who keep a respectful slight distance*
　　　behind him, HENRY IV. *He is close to fifty, extremely*
　　　pale, and already grey at the back of his head, though at the
　　　temples and forehead he seems fair, the result of an almost
　　　childishly obvious use of dye. He wears equally very
　　　obvious doll-like make-up on his cheekbones, over his
　　　tragic pallor. He wears penitential sackcloth over his royal
　　　clothes, as at Canossa. His eyes are fixed in a frightening
　　　agonised stare. This is in contrast with his bearing, which is
　　　that of a man who wants to show humble repentance,
　　　and all the more ostentatiously because he feels the
　　　humiliation is undeserved. ORDULFO *bears the imperial*
　　　crown in both hands, ARIALDO *the sceptre with the*
　　　eagle, and the orb with the cross.

HENRY IV (*bowing first to* MATILDA, *then to the* DOCTOR).
My lady . . . Monsignor . . . (*Then he sees* BELCREDI *and is
about to bow to him too; but he turns to* LANDOLFO, *who
has remained close beside him, and asks softly and suspiciously.*)
Is that Peter Damian?

LANDOLFO. No, your majesty. He's a monk from Cluny, one of
the Abbot's retinue.

HENRY IV (*turning and looking at* BELCREDI *with growing
suspicion, and, seeing him turn irresolutely and with
embarrassment to* MATILDA *and the* DOCTOR *as if to
consult them with his eyes, he straightens up and shouts*). It's
Peter Damian! It's no use you looking to the Duchess, Father!
(*Turning suddenly to* MATILDA *as if to ward off some danger.*)
I swear to you, my lady, I swear my heart has changed
towards your daughter! I admit that if *he* (*Indicating*
BELCREDI.) had not come to prevent it in the name of Pope
Alexander, I should have repudiated her. Oh, yes, and there
was someone willing to countenance the divorce . . . the
Bishop of Mainz, for a hundred and twenty manors. (*He
looks sideways at* LANDOLFO *as if lost, then says suddenly.*)
But this is not the time to speak ill of the bishops. (*He goes
back humbly to* BELCREDI.) I am grateful, believe me,
Peter Damian, I am grateful to you now that you prevented
it! My life has been nothing but humiliations: . . . my mother,
Adalbert, Tribur, Goslar . . . and now this sackcloth you see
me in. (*He changes his tone unexpectedly and speaks like
someone going over his part in a lucid interval.*) No matter!
Clearness of mind, perspicacity, firmness of bearing, and
patience in adversity! (*After which he turns to everyone and
says with demureness and gravity.*) I know how to put right
what I've done wrong. I humble myself before you, too,
Peter Damian! (*He bows profoundly, and stays bowed before
him, as though weighed down by a sudden new suspicion
which makes him add, almost in spite of himself, and in a
menacing tone.*) So long as it wasn't you who started the
obscene slander that my sainted mother Agnes committed
adultery with Bishop Henry of Augsburg!

BELCREDI (*since* HENRY IV *remains bowed, with a finger*

pointing at him threateningly, he places his hands on his chest and denies it). No, no . . . not me . . .

HENRY IV (*straightening up*). No? Truly? It's an infamous libel! (*He looks him up and down then says.*) No. I don't think you're capable of that. (*He goes over to the DOCTOR and pulls at his sleeve, winking slyly.*) It was 'them'! It's always 'them', Monsignor!

ARIALDO (*soft and sighing to prompt the DOCTOR*). Yes, yes . . . those rapacious bishops!

DOCTOR (*keeping his part up, turning to ARIALDO*). Them . . . oh, yes, it was them . . .

HENRY IV. Nothing has ever been enough for them! Monsignor, a poor boy spends his time playing . . . even when without knowing it he's King. I was six when they kidnapped me from my mother, and used me against her . . . I didn't know . . . used me against the authority of the Dynasty itself, profaning everything, pillaging, plundering . . . one greedier than another. Anno greedier than Stefano, Stefano greedier than Anno!

LANDOLFO (*softly, persuasively, bringing him back to business*). Your majesty . . .

HENRY IV (*turning at once*). Yes, yes. This is not the time to speak ill of the bishops. But, Monsignor, this libel on my mother goes beyond all bounds! (*Looks at MATILDA and grows calmer.*) And I can't even weep for her, my lady. I appeal to you, you must have a mother's heart. She came from her convent to visit me here, about a month ago. Now I hear she's dead. (*Long pause, full of emotion. Then he smiles very sadly.*) I can't weep for her, because if you're here and I'm dressed like this (*Indicating the sackcloth.*), that means I'm twenty-six.

ARIALDO (*quiet, gentle, comforting*). And therefore she's still living, your majesty.

ORDULFO (*the same*). Still in her convent.

HENRY IV (*turning and looking at them*). Yes. And so I can put off mourning to some other time. (*Showing the MARCHESA the dye in his hair, almost coquettishly.*) Look! Still fair! (*Then softly, confidentially.*) For you! I don't need it. But some external sign is useful. Of one's temporal limits, if you follow me, Monsignor? (*Returning to the* MARCHESA *and looking at her hair.*) Oh, but I see you, too, Duchess . . . (*Winks and gestures expressively.*) Ah, Italian women! (*Meaning 'How false they are!', but not disdainfully, rather with malicious admiration.*) Not that I'm disgusted or surprised . . . Heavens, no! It's only a little foolishness! No one wants to recognise that obscure but inescapable force of destiny which sets the boundaries to human will. Yet of course we're all born, we all die! Did you ask to be born, Monsignor? I didn't. And between birth and death, neither of which have anything to do with our desiring them, so many things happen we'd all so much rather didn't! But we have to resign ourselves to them, no matter how unwillingly.

DOCTOR (*just to say something while he watches him closely*). I'm afraid so!

HENRY IV. And when we can't resign ourselves, then out come the silly fantasies. A woman wants to be a man . . . an old man wants to be a boy . . . And no one's lying, no one's pretending! There's really not much one can say. All of us, in good faith, have a firmly established notion of who we are. Yet, Monsignor, while you're holding fast to yours, gripping your holy habit with both hands, look! Out of your sleeve comes sliding, sliding, slithering like a snake, something you've not noticed. Life, Monsignor! You're astonished to see it suddenly escaping you like that, in front of your very eyes . . . you're furious, angry with yourself. Or full of remorse . . . yes, remorse. If you could only know how much of that I've felt! Seeing a face which was my face, but so horrible I couldn't look at it . . . (*Returning to the* MARCHESA.) Has that never happened to you, my lady? Do you remember yourself as having always been the same? Oh, God, but once . . . how could you do such a thing? (*He looks at her so keenly she turns pale.*) Yes, exactly! *That* thing! We understand each other! But don't be afraid, I shan't tell a soul! And how you, Peter Damian, could be a friend of a man like that . . .

LANDOLFO (*as before*). Your majesty . . .

HENRY IV (*at once*). All right, all right! I won't mention his name, I know how it annoys him! (*Turning briefly to*

BELCREDI.) What did you think, eh? What did you think of
him? . . . Yet we all go on holding fast, nonetheless, to our
idea of ourselves, just as some people, growing old, touch up
their hair. What does it matter that to you this tint can't be
the real colour of my hair? You surely don't use dye to
deceive anyone, my lady, least of all yourself. But to deceive
a little . . . just a little little . . . your image in the glass. I do
it as a joke. You do it seriously. But however serious you
are, you too are wearing a disguise, my lady, I assure you.
And I don't mean the venerable crown on your forehead, to
which I bow, or your ducal cloak. I simply mean the memory
of the fair hair which once gave you so much pleasure, and
which you'd like to make permanent by artificial means. Or
of the brown hair, if your hair was brown. The fading image
of your youth. For you, on the other hand, Peter Damian, the
memories of who you were and what you did now seem like
reminders of a life long over, which only exists for you now
as a dream. Isn't that so? It's the same for me . . . like a dream
. . . and so much of it inexplicable when I think about it
now . . . Well, it's not so astonishing, Peter Damian. Our life
today will seem like that tomorrow! (*Suddenly angry, pulling
at his sackcloth.*) This sackcloth here! (*Alarmed by the fierce
joy with which he seems about to rip it off,* ARIALDO *and*
ORDULFO *go quickly to him to restrain him.*) By God!
(*Backing away from them, removing the sackcloth and
shouting.*) Tomorrow, at Bressanone, twenty-seven German
and Lombard bishops will sign with me the deposition of
Pope Gregory the Seventh! He's no Pope, he's a lying monk!

ORDULFO (*with the other two begging him to be silent*). Your
majesty, your majesty, for heaven's sake!

ARIALDO (*urging him to put the sackcloth on again*). Be
careful what you're saying!

LANDOLFO. The Monsignor and the Duchess are here to
intercede on your behalf! (*He makes unobtrusive but urgent
signs to the* DOCTOR *to say something at once.*)

DOCTOR (*confused*). Ah, yes, indeed . . . to intercede . . .

HENRY IV (*repentant at once, almost frightened, letting the
three dress him in the sackcloth again, and clasping it to him*

in agitation). Pardon . . . yes, pardon, pardon, Monsignor.
Pardon, my lady. I feel, I promise you, the full weight of my
excommunication! (*He cowers down, head in hands, as though
expecting something to crush him. He stays like that a
moment, then, in another tone of voice, whispers confidentially
to* LANDOLFO, ARIALDO *and* ORDULFO.) I don't know
why, but I cannot bear to humble myself before that man
there today. (*Stealthily indicating* BELCREDI.)

LANDOLFO (*whispering*). That's because your majesty will
insist on thinking it's Peter Damian when it's not.

HENRY IV (*looking at him sideways, as though frightened*).
No?

ARIALDO. No, your majesty, he's a poor monk, that's all!

HENRY IV (*sadly, sighing, exasperated*). Ah, we none of us
know what we're doing when we act instinctively . . . Perhaps
my lady understands me better than the rest, because she is
a woman.* Consider your daughter Bertha, my lady, towards
whom, as I said, my heart is altered . . . (*Turning suddenly
on* BELCREDI *and shouting in his face as though he's said
'No'.*) . . . altered, altered, because of the love and devotion
she's shown me at this dreadful time! (*Stops, shaking from
his burst of rage, and groaning with exasperation makes an
effort to contain himself. Then he turns again to the*
MARCHESA, *gently, sadly and humbly.*) She's come with me,
my lady. She's down there in the courtyard. She's insisted
on following me like a beggarwoman, and she's cold, frozen,
from two nights in the open . . . in the snow! You're her
mother! It should move the bowels of your compassion to
plead with him (*Indicating the* DOCTOR.) for my pardon
from the Pope! If he would only give me audience!

MATILDA (*trembling, in a low voice*). Yes, yes . . . at once . . .

DOCTOR. We'll plead with him, we'll plead with him!

HENRY IV. And another thing! There is one other thing!
(*Calling them close and speaking softly and secretly.*) An
audience is not enough. You know he can do anything . . .
anything, I tell you . . . he can even call up spirits from the

---

* See Appendix for passage omitted.

dead! (*He beats his breast.*) Here I am! A witness to it! . . .
There's not a magic trick he doesn't know. Well, Monsignor,
my lady . . . my true punishment is this . . . or rather *that* . . .
look! (*He points to his portrait, as if afraid.*) I can never be
free of this magical picture! I'm repentant now, and shall
remain so . . . I swear to you I shall remain penitent till he
receives me. But then, once the Pope has lifted my excommunication, you two must beg him . . . he's the only man who
can do it . . . to set me free from *that* . . . (*He points again
to the picture.*) . . . and let me live my poor life properly,
which now I can't. I can't be twenty-six for ever, my lady!
I ask you for your daughter's sake as well . . . so I can give her
the love she deserves, now I am well-disposed towards her,
moved as I am by her compassion. There. That's it. I'm in
your hands . . . (*He bows.*) My lady! Monsignor!

> *He starts to withdraw, bowing, by the door through which
> he entered. But seeing BELCREDI has drawn near to
> overhear, and observing him glance towards the rear of the
> stage, and imagining that he means to steal the imperial
> crown, which is lying on the throne, he runs over to get it,
> amid general amazement and dismay. He conceals it under
> his sackcloth, and with a very sly smile on his lips and in
> his eyes, he disappears, bowing continually. The
> MARCHESA is so deeply moved she collapses into a chair,
> almost fainting.*

Curtain

Act Two

Another room in the villa, next to the throne-room, austerely furnished with antique furniture. On the right, about two hands-breadths from the ground there is a sort of platform with a wooden rail round it on little pillars. It is interrupted at the side and front by two lots of steps leading up to it. On the platform are a table, and five period chairs, one at the head, two to each side. The main entrance is at the back. On the left, two windows look on to the garden. On the right a door leads to the throne-room.

It is late afternoon of the same day. MATILDA, the DOCTOR and TITO BELCREDI are on stage, in mid-conversation, MATILDA standing gloomily to one side, clearly annoyed by what the other two are saying. However she cannot stop herself listening, because in spite of herself everything interests her in her restless state, and distracts her from concentrating on and developing a very tempting, indeed irresistible, idea which has just crossed her mind. She is paying attention to the others' words because she instinctively feels the need for restraint at this moment.

BELCREDI. Well, it may be as you say, my dear doctor, it may be. But that's my impression.

DOCTOR. I don't say you're wrong. But believe me . . . it is only that; an impression.

BELCREDI. I'm sorry, but he said it perfectly clearly! (*Turning to the* MARCHESA.) Didn't he, Marchesa?

MATILDA (*turning, distracted*). Said what? (*Then disagreeing.*) Oh . . . yes. But not for the reason you think.

DOCTOR. He meant our clothes . . . your cloak (*Indicating the* MARCHESA.), our Benedictine habits. It's all infantile.

MATILDA (*suddenly turning again, indignantly*). Infantile? What do you mean, doctor?

DOCTOR. In one sense. Please let me explain, my lady. In another

sense, of course, it's all much more complex than you can
imagine.

MATILDA. It's all perfectly clear to me.

DOCTOR (*with the tolerant smile of the man who knows for
the one who doesn't*). No doubt! But you need to understand
the special psychology of the mad, whereby ... Look, yes, one
may be absolutely certain that a madman recognises, and
recognises clearly, that the person before him is disguised; and
takes him for what he is. And yet believes in the disguise as
well. Which is just like children, for whom fact and fiction
are one. Which is why I said infantile. But it is also very
complex in this sense; that he is, he must be, perfectly well
aware of himself being an image in front of himself ... that
image in there! (*Meaning the portrait in the throne-room, and
gesturing therefore to his left.*)

BELCREDI. That's what he said!

DOCTOR. Exactly! An image in front of which other images
have appeared ... ours, if you follow me. Now he, in his
sharp and extremely clear-headed madness, recognised at
once a difference between his image and ours; that is, that
in us, in our images, there was a deception. And he was
distrustful. All madmen are always continually and
vigilantly suspicious. But that's all. Naturally he couldn't
understand that we were playing a game ... his game ...
for his sake. And the game seemed all the more tragic to us
because, goaded by his suspicion, if you follow me, he wanted
to expose it as a game as a sort of challenge. And then his
coming before us, too, with the little bit of make-up at his
temples and on his cheeks, and telling us he'd done it on
purpose, for a joke!

MATILDA (*bursting in again*). No! It wasn't like that, doctor!
It wasn't like that at all ... not at all!

DOCTOR. Wasn't it?

MATILDA (*decisive, vibrant*). I am absolutely certain that he
knew who I was.

DOCTOR. Impossible, impossible.

BELCREDI (*at the same time*). Oh, come on!

MATILDA (*still more decisive, almost trembling*). He recognised

me, I tell you. When he came close to speak to me, and looked
me in the eyes, right in the eyes . . . he recognised me!

BELCREDI. But he was talking about your daughter . . .

MATILDA. No, me! He was talking about me!

BELCREDI. Well, perhaps, when he was saying . . .

MATILDA (*at once, without waiting for him*). About the dye in
my hair! Didn't you notice how he quickly added 'Or of the
brown hair if your hair was brown'? He'd remembered
perfectly well that in those days my hair was brown.

BELCREDI. Come on! Come on!

MATILDA (*ignoring him and turning to the* DOCTOR). In fact
my hair *is* brown, doctor, like my daughter's. That's why he
started talking about her!

BELCREDI. But he doesn't know her . . . he's never seen her!

MATILDA. But exactly! Don't you understand anything? By my
daughter he meant me, as I was then!

BELCREDI. Oh, this madness is like measles . . . it's catching!

MATILDA (*quietly, scornfully*). What do you mean? Idiot!

BELCREDI. Wait a minute . . . were you ever his wife? In his
lunatic world your daughter's his wife . . . Bertha of Susa.

MATILDA. Precisely! Because I'm no longer brunette as he
remembered me but blonde, like this, and I presented myself
as Adelaide, Bertha's mother. He's no idea of Frida's existence
. . . he's never seen her, as you say yourself. So how could he
know whether she's dark or fair?

BELCREDI. Oh, my God, but he was talking in general, when he
said 'brown' like that! He was talking about people wanting
to fix the memory of their youth through the colour of their
hair, blonde, brunette or anything else! You've started
fantasising, as usual! She says I shouldn't have come, doctor,
but she's the one who should have stayed away!

MATILDA (*momentarily cast down by* BELCREDI's *remarks,
she remains thoughtful, then recovers herself, but rather
desperately, because still doubtful*). No . . . No . . . he was
talking about *me*. All the time he was talking *to* me, and
with me and *about* me . . .

BELCREDI. God in heaven, you say he was talking to you the
whole time, when he never gave me a moment to catch my

breath! I suppose you think he meant you when he was
talking about Peter Damian!

MATILDA (*challengingly, almost breaking the rules of propriety*).
Who knows? Can you tell me why he took against you, and
only you, from the very first moment?

> *From the tone of her question, the implied answer must be
> clear: 'Because he understood that you're my lover'.*
> BELCREDI *understands this perfectly, and at once becomes
> lost in a vain smile.*

DOCTOR. It could have been . . . If I may? . . . that only the
Duchess Adelaide and the Abbot of Cluny were announced.
Finding a third person there unannounced, he at once became
suspicious . . .

BELCREDI. Exactly, and his suspicion led him to see me as an
enemy, Peter Damian. But she's quite determined that he knew
who she was . . .

MATILDA. There's no doubt about it. I could see it in his eyes,
doctor. You know how it is when someone looks at you in a
certain way . . . so you just can't doubt it! It may only have
been for a split second, but . . . what more can I say?

DOCTOR. We shouldn't rule it out . . . a moment of lucidity . . .

MATILDA. Perhaps! But then everything he said seemed to me so
full of regret for his and my youth . . . for the horrible thing
that happened and left him stuck in that mask which he can't
get out of, and which he longs and longs to escape from!

BELCREDI. Right! So he can love your daughter. Or you, as you'd
have it . . . he's so touched by your feeling for him.

MATILDA. Which is very real, believe me.

BELCREDI. So we see, Marchesa! So real a magician would
undoubtedly claim it as a miracle!

DOCTOR. Would you be so good as to let *me* speak now? I don't
work miracles, I'm not a magician, I'm a doctor. I listened
very carefully to everything he said, and I say again, it's
obvious that a certain analogical elasticity, absolutely
characteristic of systematised madness, is already . . . how
shall I put it? . . . slackened in him. That is, the elements of
his madness no longer keep themselves mutually rigid. It's

clear to me that he can hardly keep the balance within his superimposed personality any longer. I deduce this from the sharp reproofs he gives himself and which are a very encouraging sign. They raise him . . . not from a state of incipient apathy, but rather from one of morbid decline into one of reflective melancholy, which demonstrates, I think, a really remarkable degree of cerebral activity. Very encouraging, I say. Now, if by the violent stratagem that we've agreed . . .

MATILDA (*turning to the window, speaking like a sick woman complaining*). Why isn't the car back yet? Three and a half hours . . .

DOCTOR (*taken aback*). I beg your pardon?

MATILDA. The car, doctor! It's been more than three and a half hours!

DOCTOR (*taking out his watch and looking at it*). More than four hours by my watch!

MATILDA. It should have been here half an hour ago at least. But, as usual . . .

BELCREDI. Perhaps they can't find the dress.

MATILDA. But I told them exactly where it was! (*Very impatient.*) Frida, rather. Where is Frida?

BELCREDI (*leaning out of the window a little*). Perhaps she and Carlo are in the garden.

DOCTOR. He'll persuade her not to be afraid.

BELCREDI. Oh, she's not afraid . . . don't you believe it. She just thinks it's a bore.

MATILDA. I'd rather you didn't even ask her. I know her!

DOCTOR. We must just wait in patience. After all, it'll all be over very quickly, and it must be in the evening. If we succeed in giving him a shock, as I was saying, in snapping with one blow, with this single violent jerk, the already weakened threads which still bind him to his fantasy, giving him back what he himself asks for . . . he said 'I can't be twenty-six for ever, my lady' — giving him freedom from that punishment which he himself recognises as a punishment; if, in sum, we achieve a sudden recovery of his sense of the passage of time . . .

BELCREDI (*at once*). He'll be cured! (*Then spelling it out ironically*.) We'll have set him free!

DOCTOR. We can hope to restore him to his senses, like a watch which has stopped at a certain time. Yes, indeed, with our watch in our hand, we wait till that hour comes round again, and then . . . a shake . . . and we hope it will start to tell the right time again, even after being stopped so long.

At this moment DI NOLLI *enters from the main door.*

MATILDA. Oh, Carlo . . . where's Frida? Where's she got to?

DI NOLLI. She's on her way. She'll be here in a moment.

DOCTOR. Is the car back?

DI NOLLI. Yes.

MATILDA. It is? And they've brought the dress?

DI NOLLI. It's been here some time.

DOCTOR. Excellent, excellent!

MATILDA. But where is it, where is it? (*Trembling*.)

DI NOLLI (*shrugging his shoulders, and smiling sadly like someone who has unwillingly got himself involved in a bad-taste joke*). Well . . . Now you can see . . . (*Points to the entrance*.) Here you are . . .

BERTOLDO *appears on the threshold of the main entrance and solemnly announces.*

BERTOLDO. Her Highness the Marchesa Matilda of Canossa!

And at once FRIDA *enters, magnificent and very beautiful, dressed in her mother's costume as 'Marchesa Matilda of Tuscany' so that she appears the living image of the portrait in the throne-room.*

FRIDA (*passing the bowing* BERTOLDO, *she says with scorn and condescension*). Of Tuscany, if you don't mind . . . Tuscany. Canossa is just one of my castles.

BELCREDI (*in admiration*). Oh, but look at her . . . just look! She's a different person!

MATILDA. It's me! Oh, my God, do you see? Stop, Frida! You see? She really is my portrait come to life!

DOCTOR. Yes . . . yes . . . perfect, perfect . . . the portrait!

BELCREDI. No two ways about it! It's it! Look, look . . . what style!

FRIDA. Don't make me laugh, I'll burst! God, what a tiny waist you had, Mama. I had to suck myself in like mad to get into it!

MATILDA (*agitated, fiddling with the dress*). Wait . . . stop . . . these pleats . . . Is it really so tight for you?

FRIDA. I'm gasping for breath! Do be quick, for God's sake . . .

DOCTOR. Oh, but we have to wait until evening . . .

FRIDA. Oh, no! I can't last, not till this evening!

MATILDA. What made you suddenly put it on now?

FRIDA. Oh, the moment I saw it . . . the temptation was irresistible!

MATILDA. You might at least have sent for me . . . to help you. And, oh my God, it's all so creased . . .

FRIDA. I know, Mama. But these old folds . . . they'll be very difficult to get out.

DOCTOR. It doesn't matter, my lady. The illusion is perfect. (*He goes over to her and invites her to stand a little in front of her daughter, without, however, hiding her.*) Allow me. If you stand here . . . there . . . a little farther . . . a little bit forward . . .

BELCREDI. To give a sense of the passage of time!

MATILDA (*turning a little towards him*). Twenty years after! It's too appalling, isn't it?

BELCREDI. Oh, let's not exaggerate!

DOCTOR (*embarrassed, trying to put things right*). No, no! I only meant . . . I only mean for the dress . . . to see the dress . . .

BELCREDI (*laughing*). But for the dress, doctor, it's not twenty years, it's eight hundred! An abyss! You really want to make him leap over it with a single violent shove? (*Gesturing at* FRIDA *then the* MARCHESA.) From here to there? I hope you've a basket for picking up the pieces! Look here, do let's all consider what we're doing. I mean, seriously. For us, it's twenty years, two costumes and a disguise. But for him, as the doctor says, time has stood still. If he's living there, with her, (*Indicating* FRIDA.) eight hundred years ago . . .

well, he'll get such vertigo, jumping and landing in the middle
of us . . . (*The* DOCTOR *shakes his head.*) You think not?

DOCTOR. No. Because, my dear baron, life will resume its
course! Our life here will suddenly become real for him,
too. And he'll be able to cope with it at once, the illusion
will be broken at a single stroke, and he'll see that the eight
hundred years you speak of are scarcely twenty. Look, it's
only like similar tricks . . . the masonic initiation, for instance,
with its leap into space. It seems like God knows what, but it
turns out you've only gone down one step.

BELCREDI. Oh, look . . . a revelation! Look, everyone! Look
at Frida and the Marchesa! Which is the more advanced? We
old people, doctor! The young think they're ahead of us, but
it isn't so. We're ahead of them, because we've been alive
longer.

DOCTOR. Ah, if only the past didn't set us further apart!

BELCREDI. But no! Why should it? (*Indicating* FRIDA *and*
DI NOLLI.) If they've still got to go through what we've been
through already, doctor . . . growing old, doing over and over
again the same more or less stupid things . . . This is the
illusion: that we leave life by a door ahead of the one we came
in by. But it's not true. If we start dying the moment we're
born, those born first are ahead of everyone else. And the
youngest of all is old Adam! (*Indicating* FRIDA.) Look at the
Marchesa Matilda of Tuscany there, eight hundred years
younger than the lot of us. (*He bows profoundly.*)

DI NOLLI. Please, Tito . . . please don't play the fool.

BELCREDI. You think I'm fooling?

DI NOLLI. My God, yes. From the moment you arrived . . .

BELCREDI. What! When I've even dressed up as a monk!

DI NOLLI. Yes. We've come here for a serious purpose . . .

BELCREDI. Well, I mean . . . if it were serious for the others . . .
for Frida, now, for example . . . (*Turning to the* DOCTOR.)
I swear, doctor, I still haven't the faintest idea what it is you
want to do.

DOCTOR (*cross*). You'll see. Just let me get on with it . . .
Of course if you see the Marchesa still dressed like this . . .

BELCREDI. Ah, you mean she too has to . . .

DOCTOR. Of course! Of course! In another dress from the
wardrobe, for when he thinks he's with the Marchesa Matilda
of Canossa.

FRIDA (*talking quietly to* DI NOLLI, *she notices the* DOCTOR's
mistake). Tuscany! Tuscany!

DOCTOR (*as before*). Oh, it's all the same!

BELCREDI. Ah, I understand! If he finds himself in front of
two of them . . .

DOCTOR. Precisely. Two of them. And then . . .

FRIDA (*calling him aside*). Doctor, come here . . . listen . . .

DOCTOR. Yes? (*Goes over to the two young people and makes
as if to explain something to them.*)

BELCREDI (*quietly, to* MATILDA). Oh, my God, but then . . .

MATILDA (*turning to him with resolution*). Then what?

BELCREDI. Does it really mean so much to you? You're
prepared to lend yourself to all this? It's an extraordinary
thing for a woman to do!

MATILDA. For an ordinary woman, perhaps!

BELCREDI. For any woman, my dear, come to that. It's a great
sacrifice . . .

MATILDA. I owe it to him!

BELCREDI. Oh, come on, tell the truth. You know that doing
this isn't going to hurt your reputation.

MATILDA. Then why did you say 'sacrifice'?

BELCREDI. Because though you may not be lowering yourself
in the eyes of other people, you are offending me.

MATILDA. And who gives a damn about you?

DI NOLLI (*coming forward*). All right, then, yes. This is what
we'll do. (*Turning to* BERTOLDO.) You . . . go and fetch one
of those three through there!

BERTOLDO. Yes, sir! (*Goes out through main entrance.*)

MATILDA. But first, surely, we have to pretend to take our
leave!

DI NOLLI. Right! I've sent for one of the men to prepare him
for precisely that. (*To* BELCREDI.) You needn't bother . . .
you can stay here.

BELCREDI (*shaking his head ironically*). Oh yes, I needn't
bother, I needn't bother!

DI NOLLI. Just so long as he doesn't get suspicious again . . . all
   right?

BELCREDI. Of course! Ignore me altogether!

DOCTOR. He must be absolutely and utterly certain that we've
   gone.

   LANDOLFO *and* BERTOLDO *enter from the right.*

LANDOLFO. My lord?

DI NOLLI. Come in, come in! Now, you're called Lolo, aren't
   you?

LANDOLFO. Lolo or Landolfo, whichever you wish!

DI NOLLI. Good . . . listen. The Doctor and the Marchesa will
   now take their formal leave . . .

LANDOLFO. Very good, sir. It'll be quite sufficient to say
   they've gained the favour of an audience with the Pope. He's
   in his rooms there, groaning repentence for everything he
   said, and in despair that no pardon will be granted. If you
   want to encourage him . . . If you'll be good enough to put
   your costumes on again . . .

DOCTOR. Yes, yes . . . let's go, come on.

LANDOLFO. One moment. May I make a suggestion? That you
   add that the Marchesa Matilda of Tuscany pleaded with you
   to persuade the Pope to be merciful enough to grant him an
   audience.

MATILDA. There! You see! He did recognise me!

LANDOLFO. No, madam, excuse me. It's just that he's so
   afraid of this Marchesa's hostility, because she gave the Pope
   hospitality in her castle. It's rather odd. As far as I know, in
   history . . . and I'm sure you know far better than I . . .
   it's not said anywhere, is it, that Henry IV was secretly in love
   with the Marchesa of Tuscany?

MATILDA (*at once*). No. Nowhere. It's *not* said! On the contrary!

LANDOLFO. That's what I thought. But he says he was in love
   with her . . . he keeps saying it. And now he's afraid that her
   scorn for this secret love of his must act to his disadvantage
   with the Pope.

BELCREDI. Then you must make him understand that the
   hostility no longer exists.

LANDOLFO. Excellent! I shall.

MATILDA (*to* LANDOLFO). Excellent indeed! (*Then to* BELCREDI.) Because in case you didn't know, history relates that the Pope gave in precisely because of pleas from the Marchesa and the Abbot of Cluny. And I can tell you, my dear Belcredi, that when the cavalcade took place, I had every intention of taking advantage of just that fact to show him that my heart was no longer as unfriendly to him as he imagined.

BELCREDI. You're doing splendidly, my dear Marchesa! More history . . . more, more!

LANDOLFO. Well, in that case, madam could save herself a double change, and be presented with the gentleman (*Indicating the* DOCTOR.) as the Marchesa.

DOCTOR (*at once, vehemently*). No, no! For God's sake, not that! It'd ruin everything. The shock of confrontation must be sudden . . . instantaneous. No, no. Let's go, Marchesa . . . you'll be the Duchess Adelaide again, mother of the Empress. And we'll take our leave. It's absolutely essential that he knows we've gone. Come on, let's not waste any more time, there's still so much to do.

> The DOCTOR, MATILDA, *and* LANDOLFO *leave by the right exit.*

FRIDA. I'm beginning to feel scared again.

DI NOLLI. Not again, Frida.

FRIDA. It'd feel better if I'd seen him first . . .

DI NOLLI. There's really nothing to be frightened of . . . honestly.

FRIDA. He's not violent?

DI NOLLI. No, no. Quiet as a lamb.

BELCREDI (*ironically, with sentimental affection*). He's melancholy! Didn't you hear? He's in love with you!

FRIDA. Thanks very much . . . that's just the trouble!

BELCREDI. Oh, he won't do you any harm . . .

DI NOLLI. It'll all be over in a moment . . .

FRIDA. Yes, but to be in the dark . . . with him!

DI NOLLI. Only for a moment. And I'll be very near, and all the

others'll be waiting behind the door, ready to rush in. As
soon as he sees your mother, it'll be all over as far as you're
concerned. All right?

BELCREDI. I'm much more frightened the whole thing will be
a waste of time.

DI NOLLI. Now don't you start! It seems like a very effective
cure to me!

FRIDA. Me, too, me, too! I can feel it already . . . I'm all trembly!

BELCREDI. Ah, but madmen, my dears . . . though they, alas,
don't know it . . . are happy in a way we don't realise . . .

DI NOLLI (*interrupting, cross*). What do you mean, happy, for
heaven's sake?

BELCREDI (*vehemently*). They don't have to perform feats of
reason!

DI NOLLI. What's reason got to do with it?

BELCREDI. It's a feat of reason we want him to perform, isn't
it, when he sees her (*Indicating* FRIDA.) and her mother? But
we've set it all up ourselves!

DI NOLLI. Not at all. Where does reasoning come into it? We
show him a double image of his own fantasy, as the doctor said.

BELCREDI (*sudden outburst*). Listen, I've never understood
why those people take medical degrees.

DI NOLLI (*taken aback*). Who?

BELCREDI. Psychiatrists.

DI NOLLI. Well, good heavens, what do you expect them to take
degrees in?

FRIDA. If they're going to be psychiatrists!

BELCREDI. Law, my dear! Of course! It's all gobbledygook!
And the more they drivel, the better they are! 'Analogical
elasticity'! 'The sense of the passage of time'! And then
the first thing they say is they can't perform miracles, when
a miracle's precisely what's required! But they know the more
they say they're not magicians, the more the rest of us will
take them seriously. Oh, no, they don't work miracles, but
they certainly always land on their feet!

BERTOLDO (*who has been looking through the keyhole of the
door on the right to see what's going on*). Here they are . . .
they're coming! And I think they're coming in here!

DI NOLLI. Here?

BERTOLDO. I think he's coming with them . . . Yes, yes, he is!
He's coming!

DI NOLLI. Then we must get out . . . quick! (*Turning to*
BERTOLDO *at the threshold of the door.*) You stay here!

BERTOLDO. Must I?

> *Without replying,* DI NOLLI, FRIDA *and* BELCREDI
> *hurry through the main exit, leaving* BERTOLDO *in*
> *bewildered suspense. The door on the right opens, and*
> LANDOLFO *enters first. He bows at once. Then* MATILDA
> *enters, wearing the ducal cloak and coronet as in Act One,*
> *with the* DOCTOR *dressed as the Abbot of Cluny. Between*
> *them, in royal costume, is* HENRY IV. *Last come*
> ORDULFO *and* ARIALDO.

HENRY IV (*continuing a speech begun in the throne-room*). And
I ask you, how can I be so cunning, if they think me obstinate?

DOCTOR. Oh, no, not obstinate . . . heavens, no!

HENRY IV (*smiling, pleased*). So you think I really am cunning?

DOCTOR. No, no, not obstinate, and not cunning, either!

HENRY IV (*stopping and exclaiming like someone who wishes*
to point out with irony but also benevolence that something
cannot be so). Monsignor! If obstinacy isn't a vice which can
rub along with cunning, I had hoped that in denying me the
one you would at least be willing to concede me a little of
the other. I need it badly, I promise you! But if you want to
keep it all for yourself . . .

DOCTOR. What? Me? You think me cunning?

HENRY IV. Oh, no Monsignor! What are you saying? You don't
strike me as cunning in the least! (*Breaking off to talk to*
MATILDA.) Will you excuse me? I'd like a final private word
with the Duchess. (*Takes her aside, and asks her anxiously*
and very secretly.) You do really love your daughter?

MATILDA (*confused*). Of course . . .

HENRY IV. And you want me to make up to her with my whole
heart and soul for the grave wrongs I've done her . . . though
you mustn't believe my enemies' stories about my dissoluteness.

MATILDA. I don't. I don't believe them . . . I never have.

HENRY IV. Then that's what you'd like me to do?

MATILDA (*confused again*). What?

HENRY IV. Love your daughter again? (*He looks at her, and adds suddenly and mysteriously, warning and discouraging her.*) Don't make friends, whatever you do, don't make friends with the Marchesa of Tuscany!

MATILDA. But I've told you, she's begged and beseeched for your pardon as much as we have . . .

HENRY IV (*at once, quietly, trembling*). Don't tell me, don't tell me! Good God, my lady, don't you see how it upsets me?

MATILDA (*looking at him, very soft and confidential*). Do you still love her?

HENRY IV (*taken aback*). Still? What do you mean, still? How can you know? No . . . no one knows! No one must ever know!

MATILDA. Unless perhaps she knows . . . if she's pleaded so strongly for you.

HENRY IV (*looking at her a moment before speaking*). You do love your daughter, then? (*Short pause. Then he turns laughing to the* DOCTOR.) Ah, Monsignor, it's all too true, I only knew I had this wife of mine too late . . . too late . . . And now . . . well, I must have her . . . indeed, I do have her . . . and yet I'd swear I hardly ever think of her. It may be a sin, but I don't feel anything for her. Not in my heart. And lo and behold, nor does her mother, either! Admit it, my lady, she means nothing very much to you! (*Turning to the* DOCTOR *with exasperation.*) She will talk to me about that other woman! (*Getting more excited.*) And on and on . . . so insistently I don't know what to make of it!

LANDOLFO (*humbly*). Perhaps, your majesty, she wishes to change the unfavourable opinion you hold of the Marchesa of Tuscany. (*Embarrassed by his own comment he quickly adds.*) Hold at the moment, that is . . .

HENRY IV. And do you, too, consider she's acted like a friend to me?

LANDOLFO. She's acting like one now, your majesty.

MATILDA. Exactly, which is why . . .

HENRY. I see. You mean you don't think that I love her. I see,

I see. No one ever has believed it; no one's ever suspected. So much the better! Enough of this! (*He breaks off and addresses the* DOCTOR *with a completely different tone and expression.*) Have you heard, Monsignor? The Pope's conditions for withdrawing my excommunication have nothing . . . but absolutely nothing . . . to do with his reasons for imposing it in the first place! Tell Pope Gregory we'll meet again at Bressanone. And you, my lady, should you have the good fortune to encounter your daughter in the courtyard of the castle of your friend the Marchesa . . . well, what do you want me to say? Tell her to come on up, and we'll see if I can't succeed in keeping her with me, wife and empress. Many women have turned up here, assuring me, swearing blind that they were she . . . and I, knowing I had a wife . . . well, I've looked for her from time to time . . . and no shame attached, after all, she was my wife! But . . . I don't know why . . . all of the women who said they were Bertha and claimed that they came from Susa . . . none of them could help laughing! (*Confidentially.*) You know what I mean? In bed . . . me out of my costume, she out of hers . . . yes, my lord, naked . . . a man and a woman . . . it's only natural . . . We don't bother about who we are any more, with our clothes abandoned on their hangers like dreams! (*In another tone, confidentially to the* DOCTOR.) And I think, Monsignor, that in general dreams are fundamentally nothing more than little stirrings of the soul; fantasies which can't be kept within the realm of sleep; they even appear as daydreams, when we're awake; and they scare us. I'm often so afraid at night, when I see in front of me so many jumbled figures, laughing, jumped down from their horses . . . Sometimes I'm even afraid of my own blood pulsing in my veins in the silence of the night, like the dull thud of footsteps in far rooms . . . But I've kept you standing here far too long. I wait upon your ladyship. My respects, Monsignor.

> *He accompanies them to the threshold of the main entrance, saying goodbye, and receiving their bows.* MATILDA *and the* DOCTOR *go. He closes the door, then turns suddenly round, a changed man.*

HENRY IV. Idiots! Clowns! Buffoons! It's like playing a piano
with colours instead of notes! Plunk, plunk, plunk, plunk . . .
white, red, yellow, green! And as for that other one, that
Peter Damian! Oh, it was perfect . . . a hit, a palpable hit!
He was far too scared to show his face again! (*He says this in
a joyful explosion of frenzy, moving about, his eyes moving,
too, till he suddenly sees* BERTOLDO, *not just dumbfounded,
terrified by the sudden change. He stops in front of him and
points him out to his three companions, who are equally
astounded.*) Oh, dear, but look at this imbecile here, now,
gaping in wonder. (*Shakes him by the shoulders.*) Don't you
see? Don't you understand how I make the terrified idiots
dress and doll themselves up, then solemnly appear before me?
And they're only scared I'll rip their stupid masks off and
reveal their disguises for what they are! As though *I* hadn't
made them dress up in the first place, so they could play the
fool for me!

LANDOLFO ⎫
ARIALDO ⎬ (*confused, shocked, looking at each other*).
ORDULFO ⎭ What? What's he saying? What's this?

HENRY IV (*turning suddenly at their exclamations and shouting
imperiously*). It's all over! Finished! I'm bored with it! (*Then
immediately, as if he can't leave it, or believe it.*) My God,
what cheek, coming here to see me now, with her lover in
tow . . . And pretending to be so compassionate, careful not
to put the poor man in a temper, a man already lost to the
world, lost to time, lost to life! And then *him*! Imagine him
submitting to such persecution! And every moment of the
day, them wanting everyone to be as *they* want . . . *that's*
not persecution, of course . . . oh, no! That's just their way
of thinking, feeling, seeing . . . well, to each his own! You've
got yours, no doubt, though God knows what it is. You're
just a flock of sheep . . . paltry, ephemeral, hesitant sheep.
And they take advantage of that, they make you submit and
accept *their* way, so you'll feel and see like them! At least
they delude themselves they do! But what do they actually
succeed in imposing on you? Words! Which they all interpret
and use in their own ways. Which is precisely how so-called

current opinion gets formed! And it's just too bad if someone wakes up one morning and finds himself labelled with one of these fashionable words! 'Mad', for instance. Or . . . I don't know . . . 'imbecile'. Tell me, can you stand quietly by, knowing there's someone doing his damnedest to persuade people you're what he says you are, trying to fix his opinion of you in their heads? 'Mad'! 'Mad'! I'm not telling you now I'm doing it for a joke! Before . . . before I banged my head falling off that horse . . . (*He stops suddenly, seeing the four men are agitated, more and more confused and astounded.*) Why are you looking at each other like that? (*He grimaces, mimicking their amazement.*) Oh, I see! Well, what a revelation! Am I or aren't I? Oh, have it any way you want . . . all right, I'm mad! (*Becomes awesome.*) In that case on your knees, by God! On your knees! (*He makes them kneel one by one.*) I order you to kneel before me! Like that! And touch the floor three times with your forehead! Down you go! Everyone must bow before madmen! (*At the sight of the four men kneeling his fierce gaiety evaporates, he feels scornful.*) Come on, sheep! Up! Why did you obey me? You could have put me in a strait-jacket . . . To crush someone with a single word is nothing . . . it's swatting flies! The whole of life is crushed to death like that, with words! Dead-weights . . . Well, here I am. Do you seriously believe that Henry IV is still alive? But then . . . I'm speaking to you, I'm giving you orders, and you're alive. Which is how I want you! Do you think this too, is a practical joke, that the dead go on making life? Yes, it is a joke, in here. But go outside, into the living world. Day is breaking. Time lies before you. Dawn. This day before us, you say . . . let's really live it! You do that, don't you? Well, say hello to all the old traditions for me! Say hello to all the old customs! Start talking . . . use all the words that have ever been said! You think you're living? You're just chewing over the life of the dead! (*Stops in front of* BERTOLDO, *by now utterly amazed.*) You don't understand a thing, do you? What's your name?

BERTOLDO. Me? Er . . . Bertoldo . . .

HENRY IV. What do you mean, 'Bertoldo', idiot! Just between

ourselves now . . . what's your name?

BERTOLDO. Well, really . . . my real name is Fino.

HENRY IV (*turning suddenly to the other three, who are giving warning signs, to shut them up*). Fino?

BERTOLDO. Fino Pagliuca, yes, sir.

HENRY IV. I've heard you call each other by your real names among yourselves so often. (*To* LANDOLFO.) You're called Lolo?

LANDOLFO. Yes, sir. (*Then in a burst of joy*.) But then . . . oh, God!

HENRY IV (*brusque at once*). What?

LANDOLFO (*turning pale at once*). Nothing . . . I mean . . .

HENRY IV. I'm not mad any more? Oh, no. Can't you see me? We laugh behind the backs of those who think I am. (*To* ARIALDO.) You're called Franco, I know. (*To* ORDULFO.) And you . . . wait a minute . . .

ORDULFO. Momo!

HENRY IV. That's right! Momo! Well, how splendid it all is, eh?

LANDOLFO (*as before*). But then . . . Oh, God . . .

HENRY IV (*as before*). Then nothing! We three can have a good, long, enormous laugh . . . (*Laughs.*) Ha, ha, ha, ha, ha, ha!

LANDOLFO ⎱ (*looking at each other, uncertain and confused*
ARIALDO ⎰ *between joy and dismay*). Is he cured? Is it true?
ORDULFO ⎰ What *is* going on?

HENRY IV. Hush! Hush! (*To* BERTOLDO.) You're not laughing? You're still feeling offended? Oh, surely not! I wasn't talking about you. It suits everyone, you see, it suits the whole world to consider certain people mad, and have an excuse to lock them up. You know why? They can't bear to hear them talking. What do I think of those who've just left? One's a whore, one's a revolting libertine, one's an impostor . . . Oh, but it's not true! No one would believe that! . . . But they stand there listening to me, scared to death. Well, I'd like to know why, if what I say's not true. . . . You can't believe a word of what these madmen say! . . . And yet, they stand and they listen, their eyes popping out with fright. Now why? Tell me, tell me, why? I'm quite calm, look.

BERTOLDO. Because . . . perhaps they think that . . .

HENRY IV. No, no, my dear boy . . . Look me carefully in the eye . . . I'm not saying it's true, don't worry! Nothing is true! But look me in the eye!

BERTOLDO. All right. Well, then?

HENRY IV. You see it? You see yourself? There's fear in your eyes now, too! Because I'm acting like a madman! That's the proof! That's the proof! (*Laughs.*)

LANDOLFO (*on behalf of the others, plucking up courage, exasperated*). What proof?

HENRY IV. Your dismay when you think I'm mad again! And yet, good God, you know I'm mad! You believe it . . . you've believed it right up to this very moment. Yes or no? (*Looks at them a moment and sees they are frightened.*) Do you see? Do you feel your dismay turn to terror, like something making the earth give way beneath your feet, taking away the very air you breathe? Of course, gentlemen! You know what it means to be with a madman? To be with someone who shakes the foundations, the logic of the whole structure of everything you've built in and around yourselves. So . . . what do you expect? Madmen, and good for them, do build without logic! Or with their own feather-brained logic! They're unstable, they're inconstant! Today one way, tomorrow God knows how! You stick to things, they don't. Instability! Inconstancy! You say 'This can't be so' . . . but for them anything can be. But that's not true, you say. Why? Because it's not true for you, and you, and you, (*Indicating the three of them.*) . . . and a hundred thousand others. Oh, my dear fellows! Then we'd better see what sort of thing does seem true to these hundred thousand who aren't called mad, and what sort of a show they can put on with their unanimous agreement and exquisite logic! When I was a child, I thought the moon in a puddle was the real thing. So many things seemed true! I believed everything they told me, and was happy! Because . . . look out, look out . . . you must cling fiercely to what seems true to you today, and to what will seem true to you tomorrow, even if it's the opposite of what seemed true yesterday! Watch out that you don't sink without trace like me, trying to grasp

this awful fact, which really does drive one mad . . . that you
can be beside someone, looking them in the eyes . . . as I was
looking a certain person in the eyes one day . . . and you can
see you're a beggar at a gate through which you'll never enter;
whoever does go in, it won't be you, ever, you with your
world inside your head, the world you see and touch; but
someone you don't even know, seeing and touching you in
his own impenetrable world . . .

> *Long pause. The shadows in the room grow deeper,
> increasing the sense of bewilderment and ever deeper
> consternation in which the four costumed youths are caught
> up, distanced further and further from the great
> MASQUERADER, who is lost in the contemplation of
> a terrible sadness, not just his personally, but that of all
> mankind. Then he shakes himself out of it, looks round at
> the other four, feeling them distant from him and says:*

HENRY IV. It's got dark in here.

ORDULFO (*stepping forward at once*). Would you like me to go
and get the lamp?

HENRY IV (*ironical*). The lamp? Do you think I don't know
you turn on the electric light the moment I turn my back and
take my oil lamp to bed? Here, and in the throne-room. Of
course, I pretend not to see it . . .

ORDULFO. Ah. Then would you like me . . .

HENRY IV. No. It would dazzle me. I'd rather have my lamp.

ORDULFO. It's here, ready behind the door.

> *He exits through main door, opening it, and returning at
> once with an antique lamp, the sort with a ring on the top
> for carrying.*

HENRY IV (*taking the lamp, then indicating the table on the
platform*). There. A little light. Sit yourselves down, round
the table. Not like that! Nice relaxed attitudes. (*To
ARIALDO.*) You like this . . . (*Arranging him, then to
BERTOLDO.*) And you like this . . . (*Arranging him.*) Like
that, that's it . . . (*Goes and sits himself.*) And me here . . .
(*Turning his head towards one of the windows.*) We should

be able to order a nice decorative ray of moonlight. It's useful, the moon. Myself, I feel a great need of it. I often lose myself, looking at it from my window. When you look at it up there, who could believe that it knows eight hundred years have passed, and that I, seated at my window, can't be the real Henry IV looking at the moon, like any poor man. But look, what a wonderful nocturnal picture . . . the Emperor, with his trusty consellors . . . don't you like it?

LANDOLFO (*quietly to* ARIALDO, *as if not to break the spell*). Do you realise, if we'd known it wasn't true . . .

HENRY IV. What wasn't true?

LANDOLFO (*hesitating, to excuse himself*). Well . . . you see . . . (*Indicates* BERTOLDO.) . . . because he was new to the job . . . I was saying only this morning . . . What a pity, dressed up like this . . . and with such beautiful costumes in the wardrobe . . . and with a room like that . . . (*Gesturing towards the throne-room.*)

HENRY IV. Well? What a pity what?

LANDOLFO. Well, that we didn't know . . .

HENRY IV. That you weren't acting this play out for real?

LANDOLFO. Well, we thought . . .

ARIALDO (*coming to his aid*). We thought it *was* for real!

HENRY IV. Well? And don't you think it is for real?

LANDOLFO. Oh, but if you say that . . .

HENRY IV. I say you're idiots! You should have played the whole thing for your own sakes . . . not just acted it out in front of me and anyone who happened to drop in; but like this, as you are now, naturally, day in, day out, for no one . . . (*To* BERTOLDO, *taking him by the arm.*) . . . for yourself, do you see? . . . so that in this imaginary world of yours you could eat, sleep, scratch your back if you felt an itch . . . (*Addressing the others as well.*) . . . feeling yourselves alive and truly living in the history of the eleventh century, here at the court of your Emperor Henry IV! You should have imagined from here, from this remote, colourful, sepulchral period, you should have imagined that at a distance of eight hundred years, far, far away, men of the twentieth century were meanwhile quarrelling and striving in ceaseless anxiety

to know how their affairs would turn out, to see how the
things which kept them in such anguish and agitation would
be resolved. While you, on the other hand, were here with me
in history! However sad my lot, horrible my deeds, bitter the
struggles and grievous the vicissitudes . . . they're all history,
they can't alter, and they can't be altered . . . do you see?
They're fixed for ever. So you can settle gently into them,
gazing in wonder at the way every effect obediently follows
from its cause, with perfect logic, and every event unrolls
itself as it should, coherent in every detail. The satisfaction . . .
oh, the satisfaction of history is really something!

LANDOLFO. Marvellous! Marvellous!

HENRY IV. Yes, marvellous; but done with. Now that you know,
I couldn't go on. (*Takes the lamp to go to bed with*.) Nor
could you, for that matter, if you haven't understood why
till now. I'm sick of it now. (*Almost to himself, with
contained but violent anger*.) By God, I'll make her sorry she
ever came here! Dressing herself up as my mother-in-law! And
that man as an abbot . . . bringing a doctor to have me
examined . . . God knows, they probably hope to cure me
. . . Clowns! I'll have the pleasure of slapping one of them in
the face, at least . . . *him*! Famous swordsman, is he? He'll
run me through . . . Well, we'll see, we'll see . . .

    Knock at the door.

Who is it?

GIOVANNI (*off*). Deo Gratias!

ARIALDO (*delighted at the thought of the joke they can play*).
It's Giovanni, coming to play the poor monk, like every
evening!

ORDULFO (*the same, rubbing his hands*). Oh, let's make him
do it, do let's!

HENRY IV (*severe at once*). Idiot! Don't you understand? Why?
Why play a joke behind the back of a poor man who comes
here out of love for me?

LANDOLFO (*to* ORDULFO). It must be for real, don't you see?

HENRY IV. Exactly! For real! Because that's the only way
reality is not a joke! (*He goes to the door and lets in*

GIOVANNI *who is dressed as a humble friar, with a roll of parchment under his arm.*) Come in, father . . . come in! (*Then putting on a voice of tragic gravity and sombre resentment.*) All the evidence of my life and reign that was at all favourable to me has been deliberately destroyed by my enemies. The only thing to survive the destruction is this history of my life written by a humble and devoted monk . . . and you'd make a joke of it? (*Turns lovingly to* GIOVANNI *and invites him to be seated at the table.*) Sit down, father . . . sit here. With the lamp beside you. (*He sets the lamp he's carrying next to* GIOVANNI.) There. Now write. Write this.

GIOVANNI (*unrolling the parchment scroll and preparing to write from dictation*). At your majesty's service.

HENRY IV (*dictating*). The peace decree promulgated at Mainz gave succour to the poor and worthy, just as it frustrated the wicked and powerful.

   Curtain begins to fall.

It brought wealth to the former, hunger and misery to the latter . . .

Curtain

Act Three

The throne-room, dark. In the gloom the rear wall can only just be made out. The canvasses with the two portraits have been removed, and in their place, within the frames which remain surrounding the hollows of the niches, placed in the exact poses of the portraits, are FRIDA, *dressed as the 'Marchioness of Tuscany', as in Act Two, and* CARLO DI NOLLI *as 'Henry IV'.*

As the curtain rises, the stage seems for a moment empty. The door on the left opens, and HENRY IV *enters, carrying his lamp by the ring on the top, and turning to talk off-stage to the four young men who we suppose are in there with* GIOVANNI, *as at the end of Act Two.*

HENRY IV. No, no. Stay there. I'll manage. Good night.

> *He closes the door and moves very sadly and wearily across the room, aiming for the second door on the right, which leads to his apartments.*

FRIDA (*as soon as she sees he is just beyond the throne, whispering from the niche like someone almost fainting with fear*). Henry . . .
HENRY IV (*stopping at the sound of the voice, as though stabbed treacherously in the back. He turns his terrified face towards the rear wall, half-raising his arms instinctively to protect himself*). Who's there? (*It is not so much a question as an exclamation shot out in a shudder of terror, not expecting any reply from the darkness and dreadful silence of the room, which has suddenly become full, for him, of the suspicion that he really is mad.*)
FRIDA (*in response to his fear, and no less frightened by what she has agreed to do, repeating a little louder*). Henry . . . (*She sticks her head out of the niche a little and looks towards the other niche, though still trying to keep up the role she's been allotted.*)

HENRY IV *shrieks, and lets the lamp fall from his hands in order to hide his head in them. He is about to flee.*

FRIDA (*jumping from the niche to the ledge, yelling like a madwoman*). Henry . . . Henry . . . Oh, I'm scared, I'm scared!

And while DI NOLLI *also jumps down to the ledge, and from there to the ground, to run to* FRIDA, *who continues to scream convulsively and is on the point of fainting away, enter* OMNES *from the door on the left: the* DOCTOR, MATILDA, *also dressed as the 'Marchioness of Tuscany',* TITO BELCREDI, LANDOLFO, ARIALDO, ORDULFO, BERTOLDO, GIOVANNI. *One of them at once switches on the light . . . an unusual light, coming from bulbs concealed in the ceiling, so that the scene is only well-lit high up. Without worrying about* HENRY IV, *who stands looking astounded at this unexpected invasion, after the moment of terror which has left his whole body still shaking, the others go solicitously to support and comfort* FRIDA, *who is still trembling and moaning and raving in her fiancé's arms. Everyone talks confusedly.*

DI NOLLI. It's all right, I'm here, I'm with you!

DOCTOR (*arriving with the others*). All right! That's it! All over!

MATILDA. He's cured, Frida! Look, he's cured . . . do you see?

DI NOLLI (*astonished*). Cured?

BELCREDI. It was all just a joke! Nothing to worry about!

FRIDA (*as before*). I'm scared! I'm scared!

MATILDA. But there's nothing to be scared of! Look at him! It wasn't true, it's not true!

DI NOLLI (*as before*). What's not true? What are you talking about? Did you say he was cured?

DOCTOR. So it seems. Though in my opinion . . .

BELCREDI. Yes, yes! They've told us all about it! (*Indicating the four young men.*)

MATILDA. He's been cured for ages! He confessed to them!

DI NOLLI (*now more angry than amazed*). What? But a moment ago . . .

BELCREDI. It's true! He was acting up to laugh at you behind your back . . . and at us, who came here in good faith to . . .

DI NOLLI. It's not possible! Even at his sister, right up to her death?

> HENRY IV *has been watching first one then another,*
> *hunched against their accusations and the scorn they all*
> *feel for a cruel joke now revealed. He shows by the flashing*
> *of his eyes that he is contemplating revenge, though what*
> *form it will take he cannot yet see because of the contempt*
> *bubbling inside him. He now rises, feeling injured, and with*
> *the firm idea of acting as if the fiction they have so*
> *underhandedly prepared for him were true. He shouts at*
> *his nephew.*

HENRY IV. Go on . . . go on!

DI NOLLI (*taken aback by his shout*). What?

HENRY IV. It won't only be 'your' sister who's dead!

DI NOLLI (*as before*). My sister! I mean your sister! Whom you made come here as your mother Agnes, right to the end!

HENRY IV. And wasn't she 'your' mother?

DI NOLLI. My mother! Of course she was my mother!

HENRY IV. For me, your mother died 'far away and long ago'! You jump down now from there, all fresh and new! (*Pointing to the niche from which he jumped.*) How do you know I haven't spent hours and hours weeping for her in secret . . . even if I was dressed up like this?

MATILDA (*in consternation, looking at the others*). What's he talking about?

DOCTOR (*very struck, observing him*). Sh, sh, for pity's sake!

HENRY IV. What am I talking about? I'm asking you all if Agnes wasn't the mother of Henry IV? (*Turning to* FRIDA *as if she really were the Marchesa of Tuscany.*) I think the lady Marchioness should know!

FRIDA (*still terrified, clinging still more to* DI NOLLI). Not me, no! Not me!

DOCTOR. The madness is coming back. Sh, everyone.

BELCREDI (*scornful*). It's not madness, doctor! He's just starting to playact again!

HENRY IV (*at once*). Am I? *You* emptied those two niches. *He's* standing there pretending to be Henry IV . . .

BELCREDI. Come on, enough of this fooling!

HENRY IV. Who says it's fooling?

DOCTOR (*vehemently to* BELCREDI). Don't provoke him, for
God's sake!

BELCREDI (*paying him no attention, more forcefully*). They do!
(*Again indicating the four young men.*) They say it is!

HENRY IV (*turning and looking at them*). You? You called it
fooling?

LANDOLFO (*timid and embarrassed*). No. We said . . . honestly
. . . we said you were cured.

BELCREDI. And there's an end of it! (*To* MATILDA.) Don't
you think the sight of you and him (*Indicating* DI NOLLI.)
dressed up like that has become insufferably 'infantile'?

MATILDA. Oh, be quiet! Who cares what we're wearing, if he's
really cured?

HENRY IV. Cured! Oh, yes, I'm cured! (*To* BELCREDI.) But not
so it can all be ended as quickly as that! (*Attacking him.*) Do
you realise, in twenty years, no one has ever dared to appear
before me dressed like you and that man there? (*Indicating
the* DOCTOR.)

BELCREDI. Oh, I know! And as a matter of fact I dressed up
myself to appear before you this morning . . .

HENRY IV. As a monk!

BELCREDI. And you thought I was Peter Damian! And I didn't
laugh at all, I thought . . .

HENRY IV. That I was mad! And now that I'm cured and you
see her like that, you do want to laugh? And yet you should
realise that in my eyes, the way she looks now . . . (*Interrupting
himself with a scornful outburst.*) Ah! (*He turns suddenly on
the* DOCTOR.) You're a doctor?

DOCTOR. I am, yes.

HENRY IV. And it was your idea to dress her up as the Marchesa
of Tuscany? Doctor, do you realise for a moment you risked
bringing back the blackness in my head? My God, making
pictures talk and jump down living from their frames . . .
(*He looks at* FRIDA *and* DI NOLLI, *then* MATILDA, *and
finally at the costume he's wearing himself.*) Well, it's a very
lovely combination . . . Two married couples . . . Very good,

doctor, very good . . . for a madman. (*A slight gesture towards*
BELCREDI.) And all this strikes you as an out-of-season
carnival, does it? (*Turning and looking at him*.) All right, then
. . . away with my disguise too! If I'm to come away with
you.

BELCREDI. With me! With us!

HENRY IV. Where shall we go? The club? In white tie and tails?
Or to the Marchesa's house, the two of us arm-in-arm?

BELCREDI. Wherever you like! You surely don't want to stay
here, all by yourself, going on with an unhappy carnival joke?
It's incredible, really incredible, you could have gone on with
it at all, once your illness was over!

HENRY IV. Yes. But you must realise, falling off my horse and
banging my head, I really did go mad, for I don't know how
long . . .

DOCTOR. I see, I see! But it was a long time?

HENRY IV (*very rapidly, to* DOCTOR). Yes, doctor, a long time.
About twelve years. (*Turning at once to speak to* BELCREDI.)
And I knew nothing whatever, my dear fellow, of what
happened after the day of the carnival. It happened to you,
but not to me. How things changed . . . my friends betrayed
me . . . how others took my place, for instance, in . . . I don't
know! But let's say . . . in the heart of the woman I loved.
And how some were dead, and others went away . . . All of
that, you know? It wasn't such a joke for me as you seem to
imagine!

BELCREDI. I didn't mean that . . . I meant later!

HENRY IV. Oh, yes? Later? One day . . . (*He stops and turns to
the* DOCTOR.) It's a very interesting case, doctor! You must
study me, study me closely! (*He shudders all over as he speaks*.)
I don't know how, but one day, of its own accord, the damage
here . . . (*Touching his forehead*.) . . . I don't know . . . it got
better. Little by little I opened my eyes again. At first I
couldn't be sure whether I was asleep or awake. But then . . .
yes! I was awake. I touched this, then that. Yes, I could see
clearly! Ah, as he says . . . (*He gestures at* BELCREDI.) . . .
Let's drop the disguise! The nightmare! Let's open the
windows and breathe life again! Come on, let's go, let's run

outside! (*Enthusiasm suddenly failing.*) But where to? And to
do what? To have everyone secretly point me out as Henry IV,
no longer like this, but arm-in-arm with you, among my
dearest friends?

BELCREDI. Of course not! What are you saying? Why?

MATILDA. Who could possibly . . . No one's ever dreamed of
such a thing! It was an accident!

HENRY IV. But everyone was already saying I was mad before!
(*To* BELCREDI.) You know they were! You said it more
than anyone . . . you blew up whenever anyone tried to
defend me!

BELCREDI. Oh, come on . . . only for a joke!

HENRY IV. And look at my hair! (*Showing the hair at his neck.*)

BELCREDI. Well, I'm grey, too!

HENRY IV. Yes, but with this difference. I went grey here, as
Henry IV . . . do you understand? And I hadn't the faintest
idea! I just suddenly noticed it one day, when I opened my
eyes again. And it was a great shock, because I realised at once
that it wasn't only my hair, but everything else must have
gone grey, everything had crumbled, it was all finished. And
I would arrive at the feast as hungry as a wolf, only to find
everything already cleared away.

BELCREDI. Oh, but other people, after all . . .

HENRY IV (*at once*). I know. They couldn't hang about waiting
for me to be cured, not even those behind me who jabbed my
caparisoned horse until it bled . . .

DI NOLLI (*stunned*). What? What's that?

HENRY IV. Oh, yes. Treachery. Making the horse rear and me
fall off.

MATILDA (*at once, horrified*). It's the first I've ever heard of
such a thing!

HENRY IV. Oh, that was done for a joke, too, I'm sure!

MATILDA. But who was it? Who was behind us?

HENRY IV. It doesn't matter! The people who went on feasting,
and would now let me pick up the crumbs, Marchesa, of their
lean and flabby charity, or the odd fishbone of remorse stuck
to their dirty plate. Thank you very much! (*Turning suddenly
on the* DOCTOR.) Yes, doctor, you see if this case really

isn't entirely new in the annals of lunacy! I preferred to stay mad . . . everything was here to hand for this new kind of pleasure. To live my madness out, fully aware of what I was doing, and so revenge myself on the inhumanity of the stone which bruised my head! To clothe this solitude again . . . however squalid and empty it seemed when I opened my eyes again . . . suddenly to clothe it again and better, in all the colour and splendour of that long lost carnival day when you . . . (*Looking at the* MARCHESA, *and indicating* FRIDA *to her.*) . . . yes, you, Marchesa, had your triumph! And to make everyone who came to see me continue . . . but, by God, with me in charge this time . . . that famous old masquerade which . . . for you, but not for me . . . was a day for fancy dress. To make it no longer fancy dress, but a permanent reality, the reality of true madness: here: with everyone in costume, and the throne-room, and these four privy councillors of mine . . . traitors, naturally! (*Turning suddenly towards them.*) I'd like to know how it helps you, letting on that I'm cured! If I'm cured, you're not needed! You can go! Telling someone secrets . . . that really is the act of a madman! Yes, it's my turn to accuse you now! Do you know, they imagined they could go on playing the joke with me behind your backs?

He burst out laughing. The others laugh too, uncertainly. Except MATILDA.

BELCREDI (*to* DI NOLLI). Look, it's not so bad . . .

DI NOLLI (*to four youths*). Is this true?

HENRY IV. Oh, but you must forgive them! (*Grasping his clothes.*) This . . . for me this is an obvious, deliberate caricature of that other masquerade which goes on all the time, in which we're all involuntary clowns without knowing it . . . (*Indicating* BELCREDI.) . . . when we dress up as who we think we are. You have to forgive them, because they still don't see that clothes . . . habits . . . are the same as personality itself. (*Turning to* BELCREDI *again.*) You soon get used to it, you know. And it's very easy to stroll about like this . . . (*Demonstrating.*) . . . being some tragic character

in a splendid room! Look, doctor, I remember a priest . . . an
Irishman, I'm sure . . . a handsome man . . . sleeping one day
in the November sun, resting his arm on the back of his chair
in the park; lost in the golden enjoyment of that pleasant
warmth . . . he must have imagined it was summer. I'm certain
he didn't know he was a priest at that moment, he didn't
know where he was. He was dreaming! Of God knows what!
And a cheeky little boy went by, who'd torn up a flower by
its roots. And as he went by, he tickled him, here, on the neck
And I saw his eyes laughing as he opened them, his whole
mouth laughing with the blissful laughter of his dream . . .
quite unaware of it. But suddenly he sat up straight in his
priest's habit, and into his eyes there came back the same
seriousness you've seen in mine. Because Irish priests defend
the seriousness of their Catholic faith with the same zeal I
defend the inviolable edicts of hereditary monarchy. I am
cured, gentlemen, because I'm perfectly aware I play at
being mad here, and I do it quite calmly. Your trouble is, you
live your madness out in a fearful panic, without realising
it or seeing it for what it is.

BELCREDI. Oh, I see, so we've come to the conclusion that
we're the madmen now!

HENRY IV (*bursting out, making an effort to control himself*).
Would you have come to see me, either of you . . . (*Indicating
the* MARCHESA.) . . . if you weren't both mad?

BELCREDI. Quite frankly, I came here thinking you were the
madman.

HENRY IV (*suddenly loud, gesturing at the* MARCHESA). And
her?

BELCREDI. Oh, her, I don't know . . . She seems struck dumb
by what you say . . . spellbound by your 'conscious' madness!
(*Turning to her.*) You could stay and live it too, Marchesa,
dressed like that . . .

MATILDA. Don't be insolent!

HENRY IV (*at once, placating her*). Pay no attention . . . ignore
him. He's always stirring up trouble. Though the doctor did
warn him not to, not to provoke me. (*Turning to* BELCREDI.)
Don't think I'm still angry at what happened between us, at

the part you played with her in the accident. (*Indicating*
MATILDA *and then addressing her and pointing to*
BELCREDI.) The same part he plays for you now! My life is
here. It's not your life! I haven't lived the one you've grown
old in! Is that what you wanted to tell me and show me,
making your sacrifice, and dressing up like this on doctor's
advice? Oh, very well done, doctor, like I said. 'Who were we
then, eh? And how are we now?' But I'm not your kind of
madman! I know very well that he . . . (*Indicating* DI NOLLI.)
. . . can't be me, because *I* am Henry IV . . . I've been him
here for twenty years . . . don't you understand? Stuck in
this eternity of fancy dress! (*Indicating* MATILDA.) She's
lived through these last twenty years . . . and I hope she's
enjoyed them . . . to become . . . look at her . . . someone
I can't recognise. Because I know her like this . . . (*Indicating*
FRIDA.) . . . for me, she is always like this . . . (*To* FRIDA.)
You seem to me like so many children I can scare away. And
you really were scared, little girl, by the joke they persuaded
you to play without realising that for me it couldn't be the
joke they thought. What a terrible miracle! The dream that has
come to life in you, more vividly than ever! Up there you
were an image . . . they've made you flesh and blood . . .
you're mine . . . mine! You're mine by right!

*He puts his arms round her, laughing like a madman, while
the others all shriek in terror; but when they rush up to
pull* FRIDA *from him, he becomes menacing and shouts
to his four young men:*

HENRY IV. Keep them back! Keep them back! I order you to
keep them back!

*The four youths, stunned, but acting as though under a
spell, automatically try to restrain* DI NOLLI, *the* DOCTOR
and BELCREDI.

BELCREDI (*freeing himself at once and throwing himself on*
HENRY IV). Let her go! Let her go! You're not mad!
HENRY IV (*quick as lightning, drawing the sword from*

LANDOLFO's *side, who is standing beside him*). Not mad?
Take that, then!

> *And he wounds him in the stomach. There is a shriek of
> horror. Everyone rushes to prop up* BELCREDI, *shouting
> in confusion.*

DI NOLLI. Are you hurt?
BERTOLDO. He's wounded him! He's wounded him!
DOCTOR. I said so!
FRIDA. Oh, God!
DI NOLLI. Frida . . . here!
MATILDA. He's mad! He is mad!
DI NOLLI. Hold him!
BELCREDI (*as they carry him out through the left exit,
   protesting furiously*). No! You're not mad! He's not mad! Not
   mad at all!

> *They go through the door on the left, shouting, and the
> shouting continues offstage until we hear a shrill scream
> from* MATILDA *over the other voices. After which there is
> silence.*

HENRY IV (*with* LANDOLFO, ARIALDO, *and* ORDULFO,
   *he has remained on stage, eyes wide, appalled at the force of
   his own acting, which has so suddenly made him commit a
   crime*). Yes . . . no choice now . . . (*He calls them round him,
   as if for protection.*) Here together . . . here together . . . and
   for always!

Curtain

Appendix

This passage from Act One, p. 30, is recommended for omission in performance by Pirandello.

This is a solemn and decisive moment. I could, you realise, here and now, even as I'm speaking, accept the assistance of the Lombard bishops and seize the Pope, besieging him here in the castle; then speed to Rome and elect an anti-pope for you; and sign the alliance with Robert Guiscard. Gregory the Seventh would be lost! But I resist the temptation, and I'm wise, believe me. I can sense the spirit of the age, and the majesty of a man who behaves as he should . . . a Pope! Seeing me like this, you want to laugh at me? You'd be foolish to do so. You'd fail to see that I wear this penitential costume for good political reasons. Tomorrow, I tell you, the roles could be reversed! Then what would you do? Laugh at the Pope in prison clothes? No. We'd be equals then. Me disguised as a penitent today, him as a prisoner tomorrow. And woe to him who doesn't know how to wear his disguise, be he King or Pope. Perhaps he's being a little too cruel now; yes, indeed.